The Democratic Revolution in the Philippines

FERDINAND E. MARCOS

Prentice/Hall International

Englewood Cliffs, N.J. U.S.A.

Library of Congress Cataloging in Publication Data

Marcos, Ferdinand Edralin, Pres. Philippines.
    The democratic revolution in the Philippines.

    Comprises the author's Today's revolution:
democracy and his Notes on the new society of the
Philippines.
      1. Philippine Islands—Politics and government—
1946–   2. Democracy. I. Title.
J663.N3M3 1974   320.9′59   74–9948
ISBN 0–13–198010–6

THE DEMOCRATIC REVOLUTION IN THE PHILIPPINES
By Ferdinand E. Marcos

Printed in the United States of America

Prentice-Hall International Inc., London
Prentice-Hall of Australia Pty. Ltd., Sydney
Prentice-Hall of Canada Ltd., Toronto
Prentice-Hall of India Private Ltd., New Delhi
Prentice-Hall of Japan Inc., Tokyo

TO THE
PHILIPPINE PEOPLE

CONTENTS

v

Part Two
The New Society

Appendix A

Appendix B

PREFACE

Philippine martial law was proclaimed on September 21, 1972.

Martial law, of course, has dark connotations to the contemporary Western mind. For good reason: that mind still retains memories of absolutism, military or otherwise, from the age of the Caesars to the present age of the military-industrial complex. This is only one side of the picture, however.

The other side is that martial law has been an instrument for the preservation of the *status quo* in former colonized territories.

Thus, for the Western or Westernized mind, for nationalists and liberals, martial law by definition is a scandal, although for some reason, they do not seem overly outraged by successful and efficient totalitarian dictatorships.

This book, however, argues the particularity of Philippine martial law. Its thesis is that martial law became a moral and political necessity under the peculiar circumstances my country found itself in on the eve of September 21, 1972. More than a mere justification of the proclamation of martial law in the Philippines, it offers the philosophy and ideology of those who now seek to restructure Philippine society. It relates the background of the rightist and leftist rebellion, Muslim secessionism, private armies, political overlords, economic oligarchs, criminal syndicates, and the feudalistic economic system.

I endeavor to explain what I believe is the novel idea of a new society under a "crisis government." Actually this is a reform government under martial law. The purpose is not only the ancient initial function of reestablishing civil order but, more extensively, the legal mechanism the democracies, especially in developing countries, may utilize to bring about urgently needed radical or revolutionary reforms and changes in their societies.

In developing or developed societies of the Americas, the Middle East, Europe, or Asia, democracy must now confront the problem of how to change or replace institutions and practices which have ossified through the years, rendering both government and the people in general impotent to meet any grave crisis, especially a crisis of the internal or domestic type. This work must be done swiftly and radically.

The problem is acute because, through the long years of aspiring for the best form of government, man in the Americas and Europe has always had to use the mechanism of revolution, the bloody, traumatic, and costly kind, to attain any radical change in his institutions.

Because of the diffusion of power among the people, democracy is supposed to provide a better alternative. But all of man's swift and decisive steps towards modernization have always been through bloodshed. Is this democracy's only solution? Is bloodshed mankind's answer to the search? Must man finally admit his lack of ingenuity to provide for a mechanism through constitutional means when all other democratic alternatives have failed—freedom of speech and criticism, elections, legislatures, and constitutional conventions? When all these democratic processes have failed, what can the citizen do to bring about radical change? Bloody revolution, the right to which is inherent in every society? But at what price in human lives, pain, and reversion of progress!

Assuming that revolution is a necessity in our times, what kind of revolution should it be? If we can cast off our superstitions and prejudices, if we adhere to the spirit and not the dry letter of the law, martial law as authorized by our Constitution, with certain safeguards including referendum, can be utilized to reestablish civil order and to create a New Society—without bloodshed and without crippling, much less eliminating, civil government.

I cannot overemphasize the fact that this can be accomplished with the consent of the governed.

This may not have been done before. But we are doing it in the Philippines now.

What the classical constitutionalist may reject as incredible is not the bloodless nature of the revolution, but that a bloodless and constitutional revolution actually achieves radical reforms. All these are contradictions in terms, for how can a government revolt against itself?

For indeed as I have said in this book:

> Martial law was never conceived nor has it ever been utilized to attain revolutionary or radical reforms. On the contrary it was the ultimate weapon for stability—in short, the final power to freeze the *status quo*. Injustices there may be in the *status quo;* it was not for martial law to redress them.
>
> For the Philippines, history dictated this persuasion. The constitutional provision on martial law had been lifted *verbatim* from organic laws adopted by the American Congress for the Philippines (similar provisions were found in the organic laws of the U.S. territorial possessions, Puerto Rico and Hawaii as well as Alaska). These were the Philippine Bill of 1902 and the Jones Law of 1916.
>
> They were meant to consolidate the power of the American Governor-General over a colony.
>
> The legalist and historian were outraged that martial law, the

weapon *against* Revolution, should be converted into a revolution for reform!

The purpose of this book, then, is to offer to mankind the Philippine experience as a less costly and time-consuming means, a more graceful and more effective, because constitutional, method of recreating a society that recognizes freedom and values—the individual.

This work comprises two books I have written on the subject. The first, *Today's Revolution: Democracy,* is a candid exposition of the ills of our society before martial law and a study of the general types of revolution. It is now part one, retitled *Democracy and Revolution.* The second book, *Notes on the New Society of the Philippines,* is an exposition of the reasons that made martial law a necessity in my country and the events that have occurred since its proclamation. It is now part two, retitled *The New Society,* of the present edition.

Today's Revolution: Democracy was a warning that if the Jacobin revolutionists did not desist from their violent design the president would be compelled to impose martial law not only to neutralize them but also to restructure the society that created them.

The book was also a diagnosis of the ills of our society and the plan for meeting the crisis produced by those ills.

The second was the implementation of the plan.

Except for some slight alterations, fusing or transferring some material for the sake of unity, I have retained the form and content of the original two books.

F. E. M.

FOREWORD

by Carlos P. Romulo

The Philippine student rebellion of the 1970s brought to us the world mood of discontent and disenchantment—a rebellion that escalated into an assault on the established order. This was true of the developed and developing societies, the violence dependent upon the virulence of current and ancient causes of grievance.

For us in the Philippines, however, the student rebellion was just another, if new, manifestation of deep-rooted historical discontent with society over issues which had been long ignored and glossed over by ceremonial paeans to the blessings under the "show-window" of democracy in Asia.

Twenty-five years of independence hardly gave the Philippines the full measure of political freedom. In spite of the "prerequisites" of growth, the Philippines had a slow-moving economy, abetted principally by a sophisticated political machinery designed to maintain the *status quo*. As a result, the ruling

5

classes enjoyed the full benefits of freedom while the masses enjoyed civil rights irrelevant to their social conditions.

The result was a lopsided society, in which the rich grew richer and the poor poorer, with the attendant ills of rampant crime and anarchy.

Foreign observers watched the conditions of the times with critical pessimism. They more or less agreed with the observations of *Time* Magazine (October 21, 1966):

> . . . Behind broad Roxas Boulevard, where young hotrodders zigzag furiously, is one of Manila's commercial centers: boutiques, which attract American wives all the way from Hong Kong, stand side by side with gun shops that sell everything from matchbox-size pistols to automatic rifles. The Philippines' private citizenry owns more weapons (365,000) than the entire military and police forces. Nightclubs, bars, even the Supreme Court mount signs reading: "Check Your Firearms Before Entering." No self-respecting, lawless Filipino would think of complying.
>
> All that firepower is bound to lead to trouble, as the Philippines crime rate proves. According to the National Bureau of Investigation, crimes in the Philippines jumped ten percent in 1965. There were 8750 murders (many times more than in New York), 5000 rapes and 6519 robberies. In Manila's Tondo slums is a combination of the worst in American and Asian street gangs: the "Canto Boys," with their distinctive *madre* tattoos, who would as soon knife a stranger as zip-gun a passing police car.

What made criminal conditions worse, however, was the connivance of the police and many politicians with criminal elements. For a variety of reasons, policemen, who were otherwise sworn to uphold and enforce the law, were largely no better than the criminals. Politicians, on the other hand, maintained private armies ostensibly for "personal security," but during elections, these private armies were employed against opponents and the peaceful population as well.

The Philippine press, the "liveliest and freest in the world," denounced this state of affairs, but the press itself, owned by the so-called "oligarchs," was used to defend the social order which spawned and encouraged these very conditions. The oligarchy, just as much as individual newspapermen, traded favorable comment with favors extracted from the government. But the press was indeed powerful: when a former president said, from firsthand knowledge, that certain columnists were "on the take," he was quickly and ruthlessly pilloried, so that he had to eat his words.

As a former newspaperman myself, I agree with Thomas Jefferson's preference for newspapers without government to a government without newspapers. But the other side of the picture is that when newspapers are generally corrupt, there is not much help for society at large. The few journalists who maintained their integrity in the face of cajolings and threats from their publishers were themselves the first to denounce the state of the Philippine press. The old established standards of accuracy and fairness, which distinguish a free press at all times and all places, were blithely ignored for a downright manipulation of government for personal ends.

Thus the abuse in the public press of prominent persons took the place of social and political criticism, corrupting and beclouding the sanity of public forums.

All these conditions existed amidst the undiscussed grievances of the Filipino masses—undiscussed, that is, except by the revolutionary elements which had then appealed to the young men of the country. The appeal of communism spread from the peasantry to the studentry, although it must be noted that communism in the Philippines had always recruited its leadership from the intellectuals.

There was a revolutionary situation in the wake of public anarchy and social greed.

A century ago, the Philippines' foremost hero coined the famous phrase, "social cancer." In more than two decades of Philippine independence, this "cancer" gnawed at the vitals of the political and social life of the Filipinos. It was Watergate at its worst. Nothing much was done about it, so that the task of every government, it seemed, was to postpone the inevitable by panaceas and unfulfilled promises to the people.

By 1971, crime, rebellion, terrorism and hard times cast a black veil over the "happy land." Even the few who were rich and secure in their guarded homes began to feel a nameless threat to their lives, their properties, and their progeny. The result was a mass exodus abroad, not only of men but also of capital, mainly to the United States and Canada. The "brain drain" was not just the result of lack of economic opportunity; it was also caused by despair over corruption and lawlessness, a lack of faith in the future of the country.

It became quite clear that the old order was no longer workable. Seventy-five years of experiment in the classical Western democratic forms, it was sadly admitted, had failed and threatened disastrous consequences for the country unless a way could be found to restore its dynamism and vitality.

It is tempting to recall the *Filipino* democratic tradition but this is not the occasion for it. Suffice to say that the American democratic concept was accepted by Filipinos, not because it adhered to their practice, but because it was a condition imposed by the United States for the eventual grant of independence. No one will dispute the virtues of American democracy, or even the strong advantages gained by Filipinos in their practice of it for three-quarters of a century. But in the specific Philippine context after the country regained its independence, the seams began to fall apart. It failed disastrously to foster the overriding need for national unity and cohesion in a nation which, like all developing countries, suffered from the contrary pulls of centripetal forces.

Many reasons can be given for the inadequacies, in the Philippine situation, of the American concept of democracy. A highly sophisticated political system was engrafted on a society still feudal in many respects; an egalitarian base, the necessary foundation of any democratic system, was lacking; real participation in the political and economic life of the country was limited to the small upper classes; the required minimum of affluence in a broad segment of the population still had to be attained; and, perhaps the most telling argument of all, it did not accord with Filipino political traditions and was therefore abused and misused.

But the alternative as President Marcos saw it was not to abolish democracy and substitute autocracy. On the contrary, he seeks to create the conditions which will enable democracy to flourish in a truly healthy fashion. This is the meaning of the New Society, the massive reform program dedicated, among other objectives, to the restructuring of Philippine society, to the creation of new political, economic, and social institutions more closely reflective of Filipino tradition and aspiration.

Virtually alone in his concern, one man attempted to understand the times we live in and offered his endeavor to his people. The man is Ferdinand E. Marcos, President of the Philippines; the attempt is this book, actually the synthesis of two books, *Today's Revolution: Democracy* and *Notes on the New Society.* Under the present title of *The Democratic Revolution in the Philippines,* it is being offered for foreign readers who are interested in knowing the facts and the thinking behind democracy and revolution in my country.

This essay on democracy and revolution was written at the height of crisis, "at the barricades" so to speak, when President Ferdinand E. Marcos had to make quick, and as it turned out, far-reaching decisions.

He was clearly the man on the spot. The crisis was all the more problematical since he had just won an unprecedented second term as President of the Philippines. This overwhelming victory (by 2 million votes in an electoral turnout of 8 million) was based on achievements conceded by every knowledgeable Filipino. I shall enumerate them.

For the first time in history the barrios, or rural villages, were given a share of the resources, limited though they were, of the national government. There were 80,000 schoolhouses constructed, 6,000 kilometers of roads and hundreds of irrigation systems built. By actual count these improvements exceeded all the roads and irrigation systems built from the time of the discovery of the Philippines in 1521 to the assumption to office of President Marcos in 1966. Cooperatives were formed for all kinds of agricultural produce, and a complete system of warehousing and marketing known as "terminal markets" was organized to serve the farmers. And it was in the Philippines that the "Green Revolution" in Asia was launched.

Business had much reason to support President Marcos for his government rehabilitated 2,000 small and large industries, which otherwise would have gone into bankruptcy, and put thousands of Filipinos out of work.

The new land reform program, deficient though it was as Congress had drafted its final version, was vigorously implemented in spite of considerable opposition, sometimes violent, from vested interests.

The country was on the verge of an intellectual and cultural renascence, symbolized by the Cultural Center of the Philippines, which was built amid the protestations of the philistines.

Above all, the Marcos government offered to the Congress a whole program of legislation which would transfer the burden of taxation from the poor to the rich, reform the electoral system, and equalize opportunities in education, housing, and land ownership.

But the "golden age of contentment" was not to come. In President Marcos's own words, "the poignant wish for a tranquil life will find no sanctuary in today's world. We live in a revolutionary era. It is an era of swift, violent, often disruptive change, and rather than lament this vainly, we must decide whether we should be the master or victims of change. . . . Our recent experience teaches us that change merely whets the appetite for more change, that reform in one sphere calls for reform in others, and that finally, performance raises its own standards."

President Marcos was conversant enough with history not to

be misled by achievement in a traditional society. He knew that the slightest social change would unleash two kinds of forces: the accelerative and the obstructive. For all the radical rhetoric reverberating in the political forums, he knew that the noisiest voices were those who were actually *against* social change: radical rhetoric was employed merely to catapult the power-seekers to power. This sort of thing could, perhaps, be tolerated in a stable, developed society. But in Philippine society this rhetoric could only foster a revolution that was bloody and catastrophic—in Marcos's words, a *Jacobin* not a liberal revolution.

In the entire book, President Marcos stresses the dangers of a Communist rebellion, simply because the Communists are organized, possessed of an ideology, and are "programmed for revolution." But he is keenly aware of more dangerous threats at work, principally the rightists who would use the Communist menace as an occasion for *coup d'état,* and the Muslim separatist movement. In any case, his estimate of the magnitude of the threats to the life of the young republic has been proved by events.

There is hardly any Filipino today (if we discount those who are themselves power-seekers) who does not generally approve of the present political dispensation. This book will tell the foreign reader why. In lean, lucid prose, President Marcos expresses what many Filipinos have felt in their hearts about the society they lived in before their president launched his movement to save the Republic and build a New Society.

Who is this man who dared so much for his country? I have served all the presidents of the Philippines, with the obvious exceptions of General Emilio Aguinaldo and Dr. Jose P. Laurel. I can offer my own personal opinion that no president before Marcos has had as keen an insight into the people that he is now privileged to lead as he has.

Among the more notable qualities of his leadership is the confidence he reposes in his subordinates. In the six years that I have served as secretary of foreign affairs in his cabinet, I have had complete access to him, and he has been scrupulous about the niceties of that relationship. Although he is surrounded by numerous advisers, many of them brilliant people of accomplishment, he prefers to deal directly with me on matters of foreign policy, without the intervention of third parties, no matter how well-intentioned.

This close working relationship, a rare one as many who work in a bureaucracy can testify, has resulted in a complete understanding between us on the objectives and the implementation of Philippine foreign policy, an aspect of national policy which he, perhaps more than any Filipino president before him, has done so much to change. The fact that President Marcos came to the presidency with a wide background in international affairs, as well as a sharp insight into the requirements of Philippine foreign policy, has made it easier, and even a pleasure, for me to collaborate with him in the far-reaching innovations he has introduced in foreign policy-making.

Conscious of the country's historical traditions yet immersed in the currents of international change, he has fashioned a foreign policy both wise and flexible, a shrewd mixture of the needs of national independence and the requirements of worldwide interdependence.

I think he will be remembered as the man who anticipated the current detente and as the man who broke the mesmeric spell of the cold war on his country's foreign policy. In a strongly Catholic country, with a bitter experience of near-civil war with domestic Communists, this decision required more than ordinary courage and firmness of conviction. As will be evident in this book, domestic communism remains one of the great threats to national stability. But he has not allowed it to becloud his thinking on international affairs as these impinge on his country.

Having said that President Marcos will occupy a place in history for his decision to establish relations with socialist-communist states, I hasten to add that his greater accomplishment in Philippine foreign relations is to establish firmly the cardinal principle that foreign policy is an extension of domestic policy, and should therefore reflect the latter as closely as possible. This is axiomatic but to appreciate it in the Philippine context, it has to be said that this was not always the case in the past. The return to the first principles, so to speak, accounts for the marked nationalistic tone of Philippine foreign policy today.

To return to President Marcos's qualities as leader, he is a man to whom crisis is a comrade and ally. He is such a whole man that his enemies call him every name in the book. I will state these facts baldly.

He is, first of all, a man in whom clashing passions play. As a law student at the University of the Philippines, he was scholarly, a visionary, nearly a pacifist. The title of his prize-winning oration in 1935 was "We Renounce War," and yet he was the most decorated Filipino soldier (twenty-eight medals) of World War II. He earned a recommendation for the Congressional Medal of Honor from the U.S. Armed Forces during the fighting in Bataan, but refused to pursue its documentation as a protest against the shabby treatment of his comrades-in-arms after the war. A guerrilla leader, he was almost court-martialled by the U.S. Armed Forces for refusing to blow up the motorcade of Jose P. Laurel, the president of the Japanese puppet government, who was withdrawing from the cities of Manila and Baguio to the sanctuaries of Northern Luzon and ultimately Japan in 1945 passing through Marcos guerrilla territory, Marcos stoutly maintaining that his mission was limited to military objectives which he had accomplished. "Filipino civilians have suffered enough," he is reported to have told Gen. Kreuger of the U.S. Sixth Army when asked to explain his action.

In 1945, when the Japanese highest commander in the Philippines, Gen. Tomoyuki Yamashita (the "Tiger of Malaya") surrendered to his guerrilla unit, Marcos was said to have located the fabulous Yamashita treasure and reportedly gave this to his destitute comrades with whom he had lived in slums and in the mountains, as well as to the hill tribes who protected him during his guerrilla days. Sentimental about his guerrilla comrades, he nonetheless filed grave charges of smuggling and corruption against one of them, who was then the secretary of national defense.

From early youth Marcos was a popular hero. At age twelve he was a noted pistol and rifle shot, at sixteen the national small-bore rifle champion. As a law student he topped the bar examinations—a great honor in the Philippines—with the highest score ever achieved. At twenty-three he was named "Lawyer of the Year" for arguing personally and winning before the Philippine Supreme Court a reversal of his conviction on a charge of murdering his father's political adversary. He was first elected to Congress from his native Ilocos Norte (where he was born in the town of Sarrat on September 11, 1917) with 70 percent of the vote, whereas the country's president, also a Liberal party member, won by only 50.93 percent. Marcos was the youngest Liberal party congressman ever elected. In succession he became the youngest minority leader in the history of the House of Representatives, the youngest minority leader of the Senate, the youngest Senate president, and youngest president of his political party.

Soon after the war, in 1946, he had wanted to enroll at Harvard University to earn a doctorate degree in law and from there take up teaching, which he describes to this day as his "first love." But like most of the young men who had lived violent and nomadic lives as soldiers and guerrillas, he could not settle down. In the meantime, because it offered the opportunity to travel around the Philippines, he had accepted the offer of then President Manuel Roxas for a position as technical assistant to aid him in mapping out an economic development program. While waiting in the United States for a chance to apply for admission to Harvard, orders were issued by Roxas for him to put on his military uniform and proceed to Washington as the youngest member of the Philippine Veterans Mission. The mission obtained passage by the U.S. Congress of two bills, which granted $160 million in arrears-in-pay to veterans, and set up a Veterans Administration headquarters in Manila to process veterans claims.

His job with Roxas prepared him for the major responsibilities of the presidency in his own time, nearly twenty years later. At Roxas's bidding, he helped prepare a survey of the nation's resources, thus informing himself thoroughly of the problems and potentials of the Philippines. It is to confront these problems and fulfill these potentials that he has taken a firm grip on the nation's affairs, and is succeeding as no president before him ever has.

As a politician he was obsessed with the small man, and, in a society where his friends were known as big landowners, authored the first land reform bill in the 1950s, the agricultural rural credit bill, rural health bill, rural bank bill, the Social Security System, the Government Service Insurance System, and many more social laws designed to improve the level of living of the poor.

He loves being with and talking to the small man, but has a strong aversion to any kind of demagoguery. In a political culture that requires constant exposure on the part of political leaders, he has a marked preference for solitary meditation.

His enemies have called him "the richest man in Asia," and yet all his worldly goods are assigned to the Marcos Foundation created for the benefit of his people.

The most powerful man in the Philippines today, he is rather circumspect about using his powers extensively, preferring to persuade and appeal in spite of the command society that he leads. As practicing lawyer and member of Congress, he has been the staunchest legal defender of civil libertarians who found themselves afoul of the law. And yet his has been the task of suspending civil rights upon the proclamation of marital law. He is a humanist, deeply contemplative, charged by history to make difficult decisions and to live in the arena of conflict.

The philosopher and politician, the soldier and statesman,

largely account for the uniqueness of "Philippine-style" martial
law, which some foreign correspondents call "smiling martial
law." The explanation for this lies in this book, clearly the
work of a lucid mind, versed in history and committed to the
highest tradition of humanism.

As a young man, he refused to accept appointment in 1945
for the government solicitor general's office. He was disdainful
of politics because of the half-hearted measures that the government took in favor of the poor. This provoked a former ~~persident~~ president
to challenge him with, "Why don't you become president so you
can change the Philippines?" The words burned in his brain.
And he did just that.

Perhaps President Marcos is just a lucky man. Crisis is the
dominant theme of his personal and public life: he has been on
the brink of death and oblivion many times in the past, and
when he became president in 1965, it was simply to liberate his
people out of grave national crisis. But I chose to believe that the
man was produced by the times, in one of those rare occurrences
in which the man and the hour coincide.

This book, therefore, reveals the man behind the martial-law
situation in the Philippines. This situation has been called by
friends a "smiling martial law," for it is led and managed by a
man who insists on the subordination of the military to the
civilian power. Only Marcos in the entire spectrum of Philippine
leadership could have done this.

It is not that the Filipino people passively tolerate the situation. This would be an insult to the courage and love of freedom
that our people have indelibly demonstrated during the Philippine
revolution of 1896, and, most importantly, during World War II.
The Filipino people accept the constraints of martial law not
only because there is peace and order, principally through the
collection of more than half a million of loose firearms but more
so because of the New Society it offers—the transitional society
that will lead to greater freedom and grants true dignity and
equal opportunity to every man of whatever station in life. They

accept it for the new integrity and efficiency in government. They accept it because their own desires for this moment in history reflect the egalitarian measures undertaken during the first year of martial law.

Finally, this book reveals the man and his times. It was written by a leader who knew how it felt to be "'sitting, along with his people, on the top of a social volcano." It was written as a cautionary essay; to explain the demands of the times and to warn the people of the dangers ahead of them. The country, in 1971, was on an inexorable march towards destruction.

Ferdinand E. Marcos was destined to stop it.

Part One

DEMOCRACY AND REVOLUTION

MY FIGHTING FAITH

I believe that revolution is inevitable in our time.

We live in an era that has long needed—and often seen—swift and on occasion disruptive change. Like those of many other countries around the globe in this time of pain, hope, and revolution, Philippine society must test itself by means of a drastic transformation. The process will test the courage and honesty of the Filipino, his capacity for sacrifice, above all his self-respect and sense of purpose. For I believe that revolutionary change is a test of the validity of man's claim to humanity.

For the Filipino, especially, revolution is self-examination. In his heart he knows that in the democratic setting where he has lived all his life, he has come to a point of crisis where the institutions conceived to protect his freedoms, fulfill his hopes, and redress the injustices he may suffer have failed. The institutions of free speech, universal suffrage, association, and assembly; and some agencies for a just and responsive government, like the legislature and, now, the recently convened constitutional convention: these have fallen far short of their aims. The institutions have been abused, the agencies have become self-serving instruments of many of their members. Faced by these failures of *his* democracy, frustrated to the point of despair by the callousness of the powerful, but filled nevertheless with a longing for a better life, what can the Filipino do?

I believe that while the institutions of democracy have failed to safeguard and promote the citizen's welfare, the concept of democracy continues to hold the key to his survival and growth. Democracy provides the only means to redeem the country from democracy's own failures, right wrongs in the name of democracy, and restore to the citizen the dignity that was taken from him. All this democracy can do without violence and bloody strife.

Each one of the ills of our society today represents a loss of human values. To remove these ills by bloodshed is to add to this already enormous, dehumanizing loss. The task of responsible leadership is to regain for each citizen the human values lost through the abuses of oligarchs, the opportunism of the media of communication, the prevalence of corruption in the public and private sectors, the existence of private armies, and the avarice and ambition of politicians. This cannot be done by a process of transformation that would further dehumanize society through vengeance, anarchy, and bloodshed.

The process we need—and want—is thus a revolution by democratic means, the only method of cleansing society and rescuing it from its ills which at the same time preserves, indeed enriches, the values that had given life to the social contract. By proving its ability to undergo revolutionary change without a further loss of the traditional values, a society reasserts its humanity. Such a society will not provide for its own extinction because it is a respecter of goodwill, neighborliness, compassion, and therefore of life itself.

Unfortunately, the desire for revolutionary change has not always been moved by the peaceable spirit.

This fact was dramatically and shockingly expressed on January 26, 1970, in a riot that caused the deaths of at least five persons and inflicted injuries on many. I regret to say that the news media played up the violence that was due to two factors: the inexperience in riot and mob control of the police and military authorities and the designs of Communists and nihilist radicals in the demonstration. There was no attempt to understand the issues and sentiments behind the militancy of the student demonstrators and the ideologues in their midst. It was sufficient to dismiss the incident as a sign of "disenchantment" with my administration rather than as the inevitable outcome of the modernizing process.

Modernization can be a constant danger to the Republic when manipulated by those who seek to establish an alternative regime.

On January 30, 1970, demonstrators numbering about 10,000 students and laborers stormed Malacañang Palace, the President's residence, burned part of the medical building, crashed through gate 4 with a fire truck that had been forcibly commandeered by some laborers and students amid shouts of "Mabuhay Dante!" and slogans from Mao Tse-tung, the new Communist party of the Philippines, and the New People's Army. The rioters sought to enter Malacañang but the Metropolitan Command (METROCOM) of the Philippine Constabulary and the Presidential Guards repulsed them, pushing them towards Mendiola Bridge, where, in an exchange of gunfire, four persons were killed and scores from both sides injured. The crowd was finally dispersed by tear gas grenades.

The nonparticipants of that tragic night could easily accuse the military and the police of "fascist" and "repressive" methods. But what was apparent to the participants was the beginnings of a "revolutionary confrontation" *stage-managed* by a determined minority. The cries of "revolution" in these and subsequent demonstrations, culminating in the brief "communization" of the University of the Philippines in 1971, indicated that these were experiments in destroying the will of and in overthrowing a duly constituted regime. There was no doubt that some sectors of the media were abetting an undemocratic design, until the full dimension of their "sympathy" dawned on them and made them appeal for sobriety and calm before the opening of the Congress in 1971. A great many of the student activists could indeed have been merely "playing at revolution," but they were playing according to the wishes of those who knew that revolution was a serious business.

From the beginning the liberality and permissiveness of my leadership has been a matter of faith in the strength of democratic government. Before I assumed the presidency in 1965, militant nationalists were branded as "subversives" and "Communists." They were disgraced in the society they wished to reform. Now these nationalists are in my government, in a position to accept responsibility for their ideals. Because of this policy, we have tolerated every abuse hurled at the government and its administrators, at political authority and its leaders and representatives.

Every unfortunate confrontation between militants and public authorities was due, not to the invectives and abuse hurled by protesters and demonstrators, but to physical acts, to the actual infliction of bodily harm and vandalism.

In a democracy, the war of ideas is conducted through free and open debate—in polemics, if you will, on the platform and in the media. The violence of political language and the rhetoric of radicalism achieved their peak under the permissive atmosphere of this administration.

The toleration of all expression is fundamental in our democratic society, but the use of terror and violence is frowned upon. Those who provoke and employ violence, even in the name of the loftiest principles, are announcing in advance that they reject the democratic dialogue. They merely reveal that their objective is to impose their will rather than to win the people to their ideas.

Only a legitimate government in a constitutional polity is empowered to employ violence, and *only* for the sake of public order and the preservation of the state. This monopoly in the use of violence is crucial in the concept of the rule of law. All must obey the law, no one should employ violence illegally. When the government itself uses its monopoly on violence for illegal ends, that government is exposed to overthrow by the people.

For this reason oppressive regimes are destroyed by democratic revolutions.

The strategy of the nihilist radicals and Communists should, therefore, be clear. By provoking the military and police authorities into acts of violence, they hope to show before society— before all the people—that the government is "fascistic" and undemocratic. This is the reason behind the repetitious charges of "fascism" against the duly constituted authority: to deprive it of its legitimacy conferred by the people in a free election.

It is necessary to ask whether these radicals and Communists could still be carrying their revolution in the streets, openly and with "sympathetic" encouragement, if the government were truly fascistic and oppressive. This is the basic dishonesty, and naked contradiction, of the so-called "Maoist" appeal.

This appeal has a long history; Maoism is only its most recent expression. The Communists were from the very beginning dedicated to the armed overthrow of all existing non-Communist governments.

Communists are programmed for revolution. Everything else about them—their indoctrination, their training—is subordinated to this supreme end. This was clearly shown by their behavior in all countries right after World War II, when from partisans fighting the common foe, they quickly became subversives. In the Philippines, the Hukbong Bayang Laban sa Hapon (The People's Army against the Japanese), or Hukbalahap, for short —later known as the Hukbong Magpapalaya ng Bayan (HMB), or the People's Liberation Army—led by Supremo Luis Taruc in the field and by Jose Lava in the local politburo, sought to overthrow the government of the newly established Republic.

The high point came in 1950, when with 14,000 fully armed men, the Huks launched an attack on the environs of Manila, but were repulsed. In time, without the aid of foreign troops, the government overcame this rebellion.

The remnants of the subversive army then broke up into two main bands operating in the two Central Luzon provinces of Tarlac and Pampanga. One was led by Faustino del Mundo (Commander Sumulong), and the other by Cesario Manarang (Commander Alibasbas). Upon my assumption of the presidency in 1965, I reversed the policy of tolerance of the rebel groups and Commander Alibasbas and his entire staff and security units were liquidated in Tarlac.

The Communists by then had been reduced to small squads of seven men each, dispersed in a large area and engaging principally in "Mafia-type" extortion against businessmen in Angeles City near Clark Air Base (the headquarters of the Thirteenth U.S. Air Force) and the landlords and peasants in the provinces of Pampanga and Southern Tarlac. By 1968, however, a new group of young Communists under the leadership of Jose Ma. Sison (alias Amado Guerrero), founder of the Kabataang Makabayan and former secretary general of the Movement for the Advancement of Nationalism (Man), and Arthur Garcia, organized the new Communist party of the Philippines along the lines of "Mao Tse-tung thought." Through the participation of some political leaders in Tarlac, this leadership of the new Communist party of the Philippines aligned forces with Bernabe Buscayno (Commander Dante), one of the younger commanders of Commander Sumulong, who was overall military commander of the HMB in Central Luzon.

The New People's Army was organized by Commander Dante. The NPA claims an armed strength of 20,000 men, combat support troops of 100,000, and a civilian mass base of 150,000 to 500,000.

My own estimate is an armed strength of 1,000 to 2,000, combat support troops of 5,000 and a mass base of 50,000. The disparity in the figures has a profound military significance, but the reduced estimate nonetheless represents a grave political problem. As the anarchist Bakunin once claimed, "Give me a hundred dedicated revolutionaries, and I will turn Europe upside down."

The rise of the New People's Army and the reconstitution of what its new leaders called the moribund Communist party of the Philippines lent a revolutionary color to the series of demonstrations, marches, and riots in the city of Manila during the period January to March of 1970. Hysteria was followed by demands for the proclamation of martial law or the suspension of the privilege of the writ of habeas corpus, as Ramon Magsaysay, then national defense secretary, had demanded and obtained in 1950 from President Elpidio Quirino. I followed another approach: the formation of village self-defense organizations now known as the Barrio Self-Defense Units (BSDU). These units, usually under the command of an enlisted man or a noncommissioned officer of the Philippine Constabulary, were maligned upon their organization by the media and the politicians, to the extent of questioning, albeit unsuccessfully, their constitutionality before the Supreme Court. But events have since proved their effectiveness.

On September 16, 1970, Commander Sumulong fell in Angeles City, Pampanga, to the troopers of the Tenth Battalion Combat Team and the Pampanga Provincial Constabulary Command, supported by the First PC Zone Headquarters officers and men. He surrendered rather than shoot it out. His political superior and chief in Central Luzon, Pedro Taruc, was killed while resisting arrest in Angeles City. One month later, the other commanders under Commander Sumulong were arrested or killed. Commander Dante himself was seriously wounded in a gunfight at the boundary of Tarlac and Pampanga provinces. Most of Dante's commanders were eliminated in various encounters.

From January 1966 to August 1971, thirty-four top HMB

commanders under Sumulong and twelve top commanders under Commander Dante were either killed or captured with all or most of their men by the armed forces of the Philippines.*

The remnants of these groups operating in Central Luzon were pushed to the northeast mountains of the main island of Luzon, in the province of Isabela where they continued to operate.

These reverses had been forced on the Communists by a counter-strategy to their Maoist concept of "encirclement of the cities." Thus the Central Luzon Communists were prevented from giving support to the violence of the Communists and radicals in the Manila area. The very success of the counter-strategy, however (and this proves too the effectiveness of the Barrio Self-Defense Units in that they deprived the Communists of "the sea in which they would swim like fish"), made Communist agitation in the Manila area more virulent and desperate.

The prevailing atmosphere of violence and terror created by the Communist and now rightist-supported rebellion was expressed starkly in the brutal tragedy in Plaza Miranda in Manila on the night of August 21, 1970, in which hand grenades were thrown at the speakers' platform full of prominent leaders and senatorial candidates of the Liberal party, who were severely wounded, and a great number of innocent civilians were either killed, critically injured, or maimed.

Whether the Plaza Miranda crime was committed by them or not, the subversives, having suffered reverses in their recruitment,

---

* The most important of these were Cesario Manarang, alias Alibasbas; Zacarias de la Cruz, alias Delio; Domingo Yambao, alias Freddie; Avelino Bagsik, alias Zaragosa; Gregorio Garcia, alias Yoyong; Efren Lopez, alias Freddie; Rufino Bautista, alias Tapang; Marcelo Madrigal, alias Madrigal; Manuel Dimatulak, alias Ligaya; Jesus Sagun, alias Jesse; Policarpio Mallari, alias Bio; Severino Gamboa, alias Barredo; Hermogenes Buco, alias Zaragosa; Faustino del Mundo, alias Sumulong; Pedro Taruc, alias Pedring; Florentino Salak, alias Fonting; Gregorio Ocampo, alias George; Narciso de la Cruz, alias Narsing; Poincar Dizon, alias Bucoy; Ponciano Garcia, alias Ponsing; Fernando Pineda, alias Ending; Petronillo Punzalang, alias Bito; Reliciano Quitoriano, alias Larry.

organization, and the conduct of guerrilla warfare, were now resorting to the classical ruthless but futile recourse of revolutionaries: terror.

Openly contemptuous of the "weakness" of liberal democracies, which extends to them the very rights that they aim to abolish, the Communists reason that terrorism will be met by the beleaguered political authority with ineffectual appeals for calm sobriety. They hope to dramatize to the world the impotence of the government when confronted by revolutionary terrorism.

This move is desperate, for even Lenin himself, the Communist revolutionary par excellence, frowned upon a terroristic policy.

But this very desperation of the Communists offers us no easy comfort. Vigilance and a determined will on the part of the political authority are most imperative. Communist terrorists have no scruples about murdering and maiming the innocent, and if the government is ineffective in meeting their menace, the entire civilian population will be disheartened. As any student of revolution knows, governments are overthrown because they have become impotent.

Quite certainly this sudden employment of terror is being debated bitterly in Communist circles. In the first place, today's Communists are divided mortally between what is called the "revisionists" and the "Maoists." For the past two years the Maoists have been referring to the "Taruc-Lava gangster clique." Charges of immaturity, renegadism, adventurism, and opportunism—standard Bolshevik clichés—have been flying back and forth between the two camps.

The "revisionists," or the Moscow-oriented faction, seem to have adopted the parliamentary form of struggle, using infiltration and every legal means, including participation in elections and the manipulation of front organizations and media, to achieve their ends.

On the other hand the Maoist faction, although not inexpert in the use of media and front organizations, lays great emphasis on violence, and now on terrorism.

These two factions are divided in their approaches to the capture of state power. They are seemingly irreconcilable. But both are dedicated to the establishment of a totalitarian political order.

As I have noted, these factions are expert in the use or manipulation of media. Their vocabulary has been adopted even by people who know next to nothing about either communism or revolution. In some reformist enclaves, it has even become fashionable to consort with these revolutionaries. "Revolutionary," in fact, is now "in."

As Mao Tse-tung counsels his disciples, revolution is not a picnic. This is best heeded by those whose impatience for reforms, no matter how sincere, can lead them to supporting causes that actually mock their good intentions. No matter how much certain sectors of the media may glamorize it, our revolution is not "in the streets," but it can be in the halls of quiet decision makers. The Communists and radicals, not to mention the nihilists who flock to any movement that exalts violence, are engaged in an aggressive and virulent campaign to discredit and denigrate the constitutional convention.

This is not to say that their campaign was unfounded. I was myself dismayed by some of the goings-on in the convention that was called to draft a new Constitution. I cannot commend the procrastination and the aimlessness so evident in the delegates' "work." Elected in 1970, the delegates a year later had not yet organized themselves and elected their officers. Thy devoted precious time instead to recrimination and fruitless debate. Their energies were turned to fault-finding and vilification. They were consumed with the desire for luxurious appointments in their conference hall and large allowances for their staffs.

Yet society itself is afflicted with ills that can no longer be taken lightly. When I spoke of our "sick society" in my state-of-the-nation message in 1971, I had in mind what no doubt the marchers and ranters themselves now see, the disease and the suppuration that had brought deplorable conditions in peace and order, in land tenure, in labor, education, and the social services, and most of all in the political situation.

The poor are, of course, the victims of these social evils. Thus it has been suggested that the structure of society itself should be reformed, since the political order reflects the social structure. But even economic reforms were all but impossible because the political authority had been unable to act, its power being actually wielded by the oligarchy. It is only too clear therefore that before anything else might be reformed, the political authority had to liberate itself, recover its will and sense of purpose, and act in one fell swoop to meet the dangerous social trends in the nation.

The people in the old system are insecure, poor, exploited, and victimized. Those who have the power to alleviate their condition are either insincere or indifferent. Those who cry for reforms would not match their rhetoric with action, while those to whom reforms are a necessity have no other recourse but violent revolution.

If we are to prevent a bloody social upheaval and save the nation from disintegration, we have to offer an alternative to violent revolution. In such a case, the only alternative is a democratic revolution, a "revolution from the center," carried out according to our legal and constitutional principles and traditions.

Only in this constitutional way may we be assured of enduring results. There are, for instance, seven areas in the national life which urgently need honest and sweeping reform, which must be undertaken at once if we are to allow ourselves any more hope of surviving the dangers of the present:

1. Peace and order must be stabilized.
2. We must rethink our labor policies and embark upon a labor program better attuned to development needs.
3. Land reform has been superficial: new, vigorous, total effort must immediately be undertaken to end, on a nationwide scale, the oppressive conditions of tenancy.

4. The educational system must be overhauled and reoriented to the realities of modernization.
5. We must introduce drastic reforms in the economy, especially in monetary policy, in investments, and in agriculture and industry.
6. Social services have been inadequate: immediate reform is necessary to upgrade and intensify the Medicare program, the health program, and the entire effort to cope with ecological problems.
7. We must embark upon a thorough political reform, starting with the system of government itself, and the enfranchisement of more of our citizens, if possible to encompass the entire adult population.

In sum, we are confronted with the problem of revolution in our country. Drastic, fundamental changes in our society are necessary. As I said at the outset, revolution is inevitable.

Here we come face to face with the crux of the matter: What kind of revolution? Is it the revolution that the Communists are shouting in the streets, in their isolated base areas—the revolution that, in desperation, must resort, for example, to the terror-bombing of Plaza Miranda and lead, ineluctably, to a totalitarian state? Or is it a revolution that, however convulsive, rejects violence as a policy and looks forward to the expansion of human freedom?

What, above all, can be the role of government in a revolutionary era? How does a democratic government respond to the rise of radicalism?

What is our revolution?

This book invites all of us to be more serious about our political life, which means primarily a continuing self-education in democratic government. In our study of ancient history, one moral stands out. Athenian democracy was conceived for the purpose of producing free men living freely in a free society. That ideal tends to be forgotten in the contemporary concern over a state that causes the production of food, clothing, and shelter for its citizens. This is a practical and vital necessity, but to exalt it as the ideal may mean the totalitarian society guarantee that this can be done through the sacrifice of "bourgeois" or "merely formal" freedom. Mass poverty is the challenge of developing societies, and it can provoke among the masses an interest in ideologies which hold the promise of abundance. But these ideologies, whenever they are installed in power, succeed in developing national power, without necessarily improving the condition of the masses.

The main offense of those ideologies is against the integrity of the individual. It is asked superciliously, "What is the use of integrity in a hovel?" This falsely presumes that no man can be free, or has a right to be free, until he has become comfortable.

Social and economic democracy must certainly be realized now. For this reason we called the constitutional convention, undertook the reorganization of government, instituted land reform and electoral reforms, all for the purpose of constructing a new social and economic foundation for national unity.

We should foresee, along these lines, the regulation but not the abolition of private wealth and property. Such regulation should not be so stringent as to confiscate property or stifle private and individual initiative, which has historically propelled man's advances in most areas of endeavor. It should include the overhauling of the civil service; the reform of the judiciary, such as the appointments of persons from a list submitted by the Supreme Court and the "forced draft" of lawyers five times a year as counsel *de officio* so no man, no matter how lowly, may be without talented counsel; and the mobilization of the out-of-school unemployed for military or civil duty, which includes employment in government projects, such as the settlement of virgin areas and the organization of cooperatives. The private sector, on the other hand, will play an important role in the revolutionization of society. It can be the action agent in extending those social benefits now given by the governments of welfare states, such as housing, hospitalization, and schooling.

The plans to implement these policies will be worked out by a reoriented political authority, one that will pursue from now on the Democratic Revolution.

Of all these measures designed to revolutionize society, the one most likely to arouse controversy is the regulation of private wealth and property. Unless properly understood, this would seem like a compromise with communism, whose entire doctrine was summed up by Karl Marx in the *Communist Manifesto:* "the abolition of private property." But as I conceive it, the regulation, or more exactly, the *democratization,* of wealth and private property does not constitute an alteration of rights but a definition of obligations. We must understand that although property rights are sacrosanct in our society, they should not take precedence over human rights. The very idea of democratization is meant to preserve rather than to abolish property rights. This can be achieved only if private wealth and property are regulated to the extent that their use and the enjoyment of their fruits serve social no less than individual purposes. I am not by any means contemplating a Communist society, for not only does it strike at the very heart of individual enterprise and initiative, but it also infringes on the very foundation of democracy: individual liberty.

This democratization means keeping faith with our traditions and our Christian heritage. The political goal of laying the basis and expanding the horizons of human freedom is joined in this instance with our spiritual and ethical ideals. We revolutionize society for the sake of man, not for the sake of the State.

In seeking to regulate private wealth and property, I am mindful of the oligarchic excesses caused by their unbridled employment for selfish, not to say undemocratic, ends. The exercise of freedom should not, in principle, be inhibited by economic status, but conditions of mass poverty can so preoccupy human beings with the struggle for life that they would compromise their liberties. In the search for an optimum social and economic condition for the masses I commit myself to the regulation of private wealth and property.

But we are not embarked, by any means, on a journey to the ideal state. Aware of the limits of the possible, we aim to radicalize the social order in a manner that will promote the fulfillment of the individual.

There can never be a perfect society.

But a society which permits human beings to fulfill themselves in a manner that befits their dignity and freedom as individuals is worthy of our single-minded dedication.

We know from history that the crises of societies and civilizations have always been determined on moral terms: the outcome of the struggle belongs to those societies armored by a strong leadership, an awareness of the common danger, unity of action, and, above all, a conviction in the rightness of their cause. In times of stress, in revolutionary times such as ours, the decisive factor is the fighting faith of men and nations.

If we accept life as a struggle, and history as the continuing struggle for freedom, we realize the necessity of revolution, and from that, the imperative of a militant creed.

I believe, therefore, in the necessity of revolution as an instrument of individual and social change, and that its end is the advancement of human freedom.

I believe that only a reactionary resistance to radical change will make a Jacobin or armed revolution inevitable, but that in a democratic society, revolution is of necessity constitutional, peaceful, and legal.

I believe that while we have utilized the presidential powers to dismantle the violent revolution and its Communist apparatus, we must not fail our people; we must replace the violent revolution with the authentic revolution—liberal, constitutional, and peaceful.

I believe in democracy as the continuing revolution; that any revolution is unjustified if it cannot meet the democratic criterion.

I believe that even if a society should be corrupted by an unjust economic or social system, this can be redressed by the people, directly or indirectly, for democracy has the powers of self-rejuvenation and self-correction.

I believe that in this troubled present, revolution is a fact, not merely a potential threat, and that if we value our sacred rights, our cherished freedoms, we must wrest the revolutionary leadership from those who would, in the end, turn the Democratic Revolution into a totalitarian regime.

I believe that in our precarious democracy, which tends towards an oligarchy because of the power of the wealthy few over the impoverished many, there remains a bright hope for a radical and sweeping change without the risk of violence. I do not believe that violent revolution is either necessary or effective in an existing democracy.

I believe that our realization of the common peril, our complete understanding of our national condition, will unite us in a democratic revolution that will strengthen our democratic institutions and offer, finally, our citizens the opportunity of making the most and the best of themselves.

I believe that democracy is the revolution, that it is today's revolution.

This is my fighting faith.

| 2 |

DEMOCRACY IN
THE PHILIPPINES

Philippine democracy, when subjected to social criticism, seems to be more apparent than real because of the wide economic gap between the few who are rich and the many who are poor. This perception has popularized the rhetoric of crisis which, if truly reflective of reality, should justify a feeling of national despair.

But what are the facts? What is the reality? From the outset I will discount the claims of government, for they immediately generate political controversy. There is, however, a disinterested study of Philippine social, economic, and political conditions: a report prepared for the Agency for International Development by a team of specialists from the Rand Corporation in 1971. Its title is suggestive—*A Crisis of Ambiguity: Political and Economic Development in the Philippines.*

Why the crisis of ambiguity? As the report says, the perceptions of national conditions are quite distorted. The Rand specialists, for example, arrived at three conclusions on the political situation that cannot but startle the rhetoricians of crisis.

1. Filipinos believe that government has a positive impact on their lives. In 1969, 46 percent of the Filipinos believed that the national government improves conditions, 35 percent believed that the government makes no difference, and 7 percent believed that they would be better off without the national government. Such figures compare favorably with responses from other countries. For example, in Mexico in 1963 only 18 percent of the people believed that the government made no difference in their lives. Similarly, the Philippines compares well with developed democracies in the perception of equal treatment; 42 percent of the Filipinos expect equal treatment; 35 percent do not, 23 percent don't know.

2. It is hard to find groups of voters who are strongly discontended or demanding a more issue-oriented politics. The poor, the young, and tenants appear not to differ from the rest of the population. In general, all groups prefer honesty, pork barrel, and a candidate who speaks their dialect. No group appears to be demanding a different kind of politics. Without such a general demand the stability of the system is unlikely to be threatened. Without such a demand, however, it is also difficult for politicians to be innovators.

3. These results indicate more political stability in the Philippines than casual observation or the press would suggest. Filipino views of government performance compare favorably with those found in developed countries. Demands for fundamental change are hard to find. Politicians perceive the wishes of their constituents accurately and try to fulfill them.

These conditions directly contradict the rabid pronouncements about our political life, and not a few commentators, honing their perceptions in the city, will find them rather difficult to believe. The Rand specialists could be wrong, or there could be some fault in their rigorous method of observation and analysis—and "after all, they are foreigners." But they did investigate our national community in depth, and a clear indication of their scholarly integrity is their use, out of puzzlement perhaps, of the word "ambiguity."

How could there be such a divergence between perception

and reality? The answer may lie in the alienation of the few who go by opinion from the many who go by experience. The commentators, notably foreign journalists (as the Rand report pointed out), have been conditioned by what they hear, read, and see in the urban centers, where the propaganda of disenchantment and discontentment about many things is strongest. But the masses are existentialists about politics.

To begin with the masses, take the rhetoric of crisis for what it is: the language of political competition and debate, which for all its color during electoral campaigns is irrelevant to the people's actual experience and use of government. Outsiders miss the fact that there is a kind of coterie perception about Philippine political life, and that those who are most rabid in their pronouncements are more intent on *making a case* rather than *describing* a situation. But by majority vote, which is the only vote there is (and demonstrative too of democracy's hard realism of putting its faith in the wisdom of the people), Philippine democracy is stable.

The troubles are by no means few: the rich are few and the poor are many; some fraud and violence do occur during elections, as in other democracies; oligarchs do seek to manipulate political authority; public servants do cheat; workers do get exploited, criminals do commit crimes, beggars do beg. But ours remains a stable political democracy. As the Rand survey shows, while some Filipinos do find life difficult, they expect it to be better and believe that government can accomplish this for them. There cannot be a stronger testimony to our political stability.

Not all critics of Philippine democracy can be completely wrong. They do represent an articulate segment of the population. When they are obviously disinterested and are not simply grinding their axes, they deserve a serious hearing. Their contention that ours is a society of privilege, which in turn institutionalizes corruption, inequity, and even injustice, must make us pause and wonder about the general feeling of satisfaction about the political system. A ready explanation is the freedom that Philippine democracy permits to every citizen. But we must go deeper than this. The system works, but what, beneath the social and political institutions, gives it its viability?

I will call it the political culture, which is a culture that gives a central and crucial role to the politician. It is fashionable to speak of "politics" as a "disease" in our national life, but we must face the fact that a majority of our people depend on the government for their well-being, which inevitably means that they are dependent on political connections to get their due from an oftentimes leisurely and corrupt bureaucracy. The political culture of the majority permits and encourages the use of political influence: thus the criterion of accessibility as the measure of political success. That is the underlying meaning of the Rand finding that "politicians perceive the wishes of their constituents accurately and try to fulfill them."

We Filipinos are said to have a keener, more imperious sense of our individual rights than of our collective, or social, interests. At his best the politician must mediate successfully the claims of the individual with those of society, or as the phrase goes, "reconcile individual inclinations with the public interest." Most often the prudent politician follows the line of least resistance by accommodating as many individual constituents as he can, in the hope that somehow collective or social goals (in a political imitation of Adam Smith's "invisible hand") will take care of themselves. Indeed, the most telling popular indictment against a politician or a public official relates neither to his honesty nor to his ability but to his availability—that is, availability to obtain what his constituents, for one reason or another, believe they cannot get for themselves. The politicians who are able to perpetuate themselves in power are responsive in this respect; their constituents retain them and are more or less satisfied.

This arrangement institutionalizes a populist, personalist, and individualist idea of democracy in the person of the politician. Consider how we translate the democratic principle of communication between the governors and the governed into personal, physical contact. Any Filipino who has ever held or sought public office knows that his constituents resent the so-called *cordon sanitaire* (they want him personally for anything), and that they regard him as the inexhaustible font of personal services, from attending wakes to bailing out errant sons, making his availability so punishing as to sacrifice all privacy, including that of his family. All this is quite apart from his duty of bringing to his community all the government service and patronage that his influence and maneuverings can obtain. I recall vividly a then governor's pathetic justification of his support of an incumbent President; he had to cross party lines, he said, because the welfare of his province demanded it. Those who speak of "party ideologies" condemned him, but, as it turned out, his constituents continued to give him their mandate.

As I have said, our democratic culture is populist, personalist, and individualist. It works because the politicians make it work by precisely responding to the peculiar demands of their constituencies. That the system does not recommend itself to the critics is obvious, for they belong to the 35 percent who believe that government makes no difference in their lives. Although a minority, they are sophisticated enough to prefer a more institutionalized way of conducting the public business, which does not however keep them, when necessary, from resorting to the politician. In short, the system does not conform to the Western image of a democracy more or less operating like an efficient industrial corporation.

The function of a politician as the provider of personal and community services weakens rather than strengthens public institutions and breeds "venalities" on the one hand, and high corruption on the other.

I take this to be a valid criticism of Philippine democracy, despite the fact that because it works the majority are satisfied with it. Right now it is only a minority, concentrated in the urban middle class, which is prejudiced by the political culture. Neither too rich to command influence nor too numerously poor to threaten politicians with its votes, the small middle class, knowing the value of time and effort, find the personalism of politics wasteful and inconvenient. Middle-class rhetoric now colors much of political and social criticism, oscillating, as it were, between radicalism and liberalism. Its apocalyptic "message" resounds in the media, not only because of its dramatic effectiveness but also, and mainly, because of its usefulness in promoting the political and economic interests of organized sectors, mainly oligarchies. This rhetoric propagandizes the need for change despite the difficulty of finding any fundamental demand for change among the majority.

The rhetoric of crisis may be an intellectual perversity arising out of the hyperbolic vocabulary of Philippine politics, but it is not easily dismissed as invalid. Shorn of its polemics, particularly those with an ideological tendency, the language of crisis points to an emergent anxiety about our democracy, which is populist, personalist and individualist. The fact that it has worked very well so far, apparently responsive to popular needs, should not make us confident that it will always work.

The very mobility of our society is based on the peculiarities of our democracy, and being peculiarities, they cannot always be reliable in a changing world.

The Rand report, in establishing our political stability, nevertheless contained an observation that should make us anxious. Pointing out that there is no demand for a different kind of politics, and thus no threat to political stability, it suggests that *the very lack of such a demand also makes it difficult for politicians to be innovators.*

What this means essentially is that there is resistance to change, and that given that resistance, how can there be modernization? How can our society modernize? And we must modernize —we must, in fact, face up to revolutionary changes—if our nation is to continue to survive and prosper.

We note that the majority may complain, as anyone would under certain conditions, but they are clamoring for fundamental change. While this means that they approve of our democracy, it also suggests that the acquiescence arises from our peculiarities, our culture. By weakening public institutions, this culture has a negative element; it is not very efficient for the pursuit of social goals. One reason for the pervasiveness of corruption is that, being part of the system, it apparently allows everyone it touches to benefit. As I have intimated, the corrupt politician who is at the same time accessible to his constituents has more chances of staying in power than an honest one "who has not done anything." The latter probably takes his legislative or executive work more seriously, concentrating on collective goals at the expense of political "fence-mending." He is more often judged by the populist, personalist, and individualist standards of constituency in a precarious present moving toward an uncertain future. He dare not initiate or innovate unless he can be sure that it will not cost him his position. It is easy to condemn him for lack of moral courage, but what good is a businessman without a business, a politician without a constituency? "I must see where my people are going so that I may lead them," an Athenian politician was supposed to have said. There are certain conditions, however, in which this attitude cannot be a useful principle of democratic leadership.

The progressive character of a democracy lies in the free debate over policy and performance—in short, in the existence of an organized opposition. This opposition party absorbs discontent and, it is hoped, mobilizes the people for change. Most often, however, change is just a new set of leaders without a new set of policies. This is not so much an "ideological poverty" in the political parties, as some maintain, but rather the perception by the powerful that there is strong resistance to radical change. This resistance comes not only from the oligarchs, who hold on to their privileges and want more of them, but even from the constituency, which is attached to the familiar blessings of the political culture. For change must entail a certain disorientation and it does imply sacrifice.

The masses, it must be noted now, are capable of sacrifice, particularly when persuaded of its necessity: their very dependence on government can act as the lever of consent.

They feel, moreover, that government has social and economic obligations to them, to fulfill which it must spread the wealth of society. This view certainly is not popular with the most affluent members of society, who are naturally conservative in their attitudes.

But can there be any dispute over the principle that those who have must support those who have not? Those who dispute this had better confront the view that it is, on the contrary, those who have not who have enriched and kept in safety and comfort those who have.

The choice is between democratizing private wealth or "socializing" it. Democratization is the governing idea in these remarks on property by U.S. Supreme Court Justice Benjamin N. Cardozo: "Property, like liberty, though immune under the Constitution from destruction, *is not immune* from regulation essential for the common good. What the regulation shall be, every generation must work out for itself." Socialization, on the other hand, means quite simply the abolition of private property, which is a process that historically has been associated intimately with communism. Under this system, as we know from experience, not only private property is abolished but also human freedom.

The choice between democratization and "socialization" is inescapable; we are doomed to make it. Neither procrastination nor evasion will be of much use in our modernizing society. As the Rand report suggests accurately there is hardly any demand for fundamental change in the various sectors of Philippine society. This information is useful and consoling only when determining, at this early time, the changes that must occur in order to modernize Philippine society. The cry of a tiny minority now, even the misperceptions of actual conditions, indicate revolutionary expectations. More than impatience, complacency holds the perils for the future of our society.

This complacency exists because of the very viability of the political system, which, democratic as it can be, is populist, personalist, and individualist, according to the orientation of our political culture.

What are the dangers of a populist politics? How can there be anything suspect in a politics that is exclusively devoted to the wishes of the populace? The first danger is mob democracy, the kind feared by John Stuart Mill when he proposed informing the common sense of the many with the wisdom of a few. Our experience attests that demagogues could give the masses a false sense of well-being and hope, so that important economic and social questions are approached with the prejudices of the masses in mind rather than their welfare. Few leaders are ready to acquaint the people with the sacrifices and difficulties of development under the principle of freedom: they would make everythink look possible and easy to win a popular mandate. There is, therefore, a confusion of popular sovereignty with popular prejudice, to the advantage of the demagogues and the detriment of the many. But more dangerous than this is the inclination of selfish interests to promote their own advantage while professing to champion the people; the people are at times consequently misled into supporting positions and measures which are actually harmful to them but which seem beneficial at the time that they are being strongly advocated.

The common solution is, of course, popular education—a full disclosure and discussion of facts and issues before the electorate. But this is a long process, and, in any case, the "credible" organs of public enlightenment are the very vested interests that have a great stake in perpetuating populist politics for their own ends.

Who, in short, will protect the people from their "protectors"? The people can do something about their elected representatives and leaders, but what can they do about their self-appointed guardians, who have achieved that eminence by the sheer force of wealth and influence?

Formal power is more easily dealt with than informal power, for the former is accountable and the latter, not.

In a populist political culture, the political rhetoric inflames popular passions while actual performance serves private ends.

The majority of the people, in turn, seem to be more conscious of their own personal interests, and hold that government to be good which successfully promotes them. In our culture the pursuit of these ends bypasses public institutions in favor of the energetic politician. More often, the politician neither legislates nor administers so much as he intervenes and mediates. He achieves a personalized relationship with his constituents as individual persons, more anxious about doing things for each of them individually rather than for all of them collectively. A bridge, a school, or a rural development project, although important, is not enough. Has he been approachable? Has he managed to place a son in a Manila office? Where was he when a fire broke out or a typhoon came? How personally generous has he been in satisfying the needs of certain influential leaders? If he fails in these personalist tests, he fails as a politician.

The individualist cast of the political culture follows from its populist and personalist conventions. All this seems to be historically rooted in what may be called the Filipino character: Jose Rizal himself was moved to point out that in the Philippines, there seemed to be individual but no national progress. Everyone had his own strategy for personal survival, but there was no strategy for national survival.

Are the people to blame for this state of affairs? Hardly, for conditions are such that the majority depend on the government. But *are* the politicians to blame, since they are simply responding to the situation as they see it? I would say yes. Within the undeniably practical limits of political survival, politicians can and should try out some innovations that will transform the political culture from being populist, personalist, and individualist to being more nationalist, institutional, and socialist, in the strict meaning of being more conscious about the means of society and the national community.

This was one of the reasons I supported the call to a constitutional convention to draft a new fundamental law rather than allow the members of Congress to do so. Theoretically, the delegates to the constitutional convention would be free of the demands of political survival.

Make no mistake about it, however. Our political culture is not completely a negative force in our democracy; it exercises a positive influence in our commitment to freedom. Its peril is subtle: the mass dependence on government can work at cross-purposes to the democratic ideal of self-reliant, free individuals. A government can successfully satisfy the material needs of a great many people, but it need not be a democratic government at that. Ours is able to achieve this, at least with the majority, in a state of democracy, but that is not the supreme goal: the supreme goal of a democracy is to actively engage more of the 35 percent of the populace who believe that government has no impact on their lives. This is a naïve belief because government does have an impact. This 35 percent are merely indicating that they do not rely on the government for their personal needs. All the same, they can be sufficiently disinterested about government; they are liberated enough to consider government in the light of principles, purposes, and performance—government, in short, as an instrument of achieving the collective purposes and well-being of human beings.

This 35 percent may include the modern segment of our society, the modernizing—revolutionizing—segment. Its ranks have produced many of the leftist intellectuals, radicals, student militants, and Communist revolutionaries. Hence the poignant bewilderment of parents who ask where they have gone wrong because certainly their militant sons and daughters were not truly deprived in life. They confuse the passion for revolution with the experience of dire poverty. But the passion for revolution is perhaps a passion for solidarity, fraternity, and justice; perhaps it calls forth the noblest qualities of human beings, although its bureaucratization—as in the Communist revolutions—also brings forth their cruelty and lust for power. What we should understand about the revolutionary passions of the young and certain segments of the middle-class intelligentsia is that some of them may indeed desire a society of which they can be proud, an order of things that is approximately the concrete expression of democratic ideals. Certainly these are reasonable demands.

They are, indeed, revolutionaries precisely because of the revolutionary potential of the democratic idea, but they may not be extremists. They must be persuaded that their demands are welcome and workable, unless we are prepared to see them misled by conspirators who will mobilize their revolutionary passions and energies for a revolution that will end all revolutions because it will end human freedom.

To sum up: Philippine democracy exists in a political culture that is populist, personalist, and individualist in orientation. Thus far, this culture has worked very well in its influence on political society. But there is no assurance that this will always be the case because of the modernizing—revolutionary—elements in a society which must, as a matter of course, revolutionize itself as an imperative of national development. The problem, therefore, is the modification of the political culture so that the revolutionizing elements can be absorbed within the democratic system, thus achieving not only what is good in itself but also preventing the kind of revolution that is destructive of human freedom.

/ 3 /

DEMOCRACY AND REVOLUTION

In a book called *After the Revolution?*, an investigation of authority in a good society, Yale professor Robert A. Dahl noted that because democracy has never been fully achieved, "it has always been and is now potentially a revolutionary doctrine." Dahl observed that every system purporting to be democratic is vulnerable to the charge that it is not democratic enough, or not "really" or fully democratic.

"The charge," Dahl concludes, "is bound to be correct, since no polity has ever been completely democratized. Even today what one ordinarily calls democracies are, as we all know, a very long way from being fully democratized political systems."

One may perceive in the relationship between democracy and revolution the challenge of democratic ideals, since like all ideals, these are not completely realized in practice. But there is also the fact that men, as they grow in historical experience, continually reexamine the propositions of their public life, often modifying them, or refining them, to suit changed and changing conditions.

The most famous definition of democracy was, of course, made by the great Pericles:

> Our constitution is named a democracy because it is in the hands not of the few but of the many. But our laws secure equal justice for all in their private disputes. . . . And as we give free play to all in our public life, so we carry the same spirit into our daily relations with one another. We have no black looks or angry words for our neighbor if he enjoys in his way. . . . Yet ours is no workaday city. No other provides so many recreations for the spirit—contests and sacrifices all year round, and beauty in our public buildings to cheer the heart and delight the eye day by day. We are lovers of beauty without extravagance, and lovers of wisdom with out unmanliness. . . . Our citizens attend both the public and private duties, and we do not allow absorption in our various affairs to interfere with their knowledge of the city's. We consider the man who holds aloof from public life not as harmless but as useless.

This definition has led not a few ideologues to say that every democracy aspires to the condition of Athens in the fifth century B.C. But this democracy that Pericles extolled was built on the economy of slaves and the political impotence of women and foreigners: it fell too from the greed of empire. It was a democracy of Greek male citizens who were neither foreigners nor slaves. The modern democrat will hardly call this a democracy.

The most that can be said is that Pericles described a condition of political and social life that envisions a democratic society for all *men*.

Centuries later, however, Robespierre expressed the French Revolution's democratic aspirations:

> We desire a state of things wherein all base and cruel passions shall be enchained; all generous and beneficent passions awakened by the laws, wherein all distinctions should arise but from equality itself; wherein the citizen should submit to the magistrate, the magistrate to the people, and the people to justice; wherein the country assures

the welfare of every individual; wherein every individual enjoys with pride the prosperity and glory of his country; wherein all minds are enlarged by the continual communication of republican sentiments and by the desire of meriting the esteem of a great people; wherein the arts should be the decorations of that liberty which they ennoble, and commerce the source of public wealth and not the monstrous opulence of a few houses.

There are significant differences between Periclean democratic vision and Robespierre's formulation. The latter evokes nationalist ("the prosperity and glory of his country") and social sentiments ("commerce the source of public wealth and not the monstrous opulence of a few houses"). Periclean democracy was confined to the city-state; that of the French Revolution to the nation-state; moreover, Greek democracy was based on a slave economy, French democracy was conscious of the oppression of the lower classes. There was, in the latter a resentment of the oligarchy, while in Greece, oligarchy was regarded merely as another institution opposed to democracy.

With the French Revolution came a political consciousness of the opposition between the rich and poor classes of society. It is true that the Greeks were not unconscious of this, but the notice made was in the form of counsel. Plato, in the *Republic,* says that an ordinary city is in fact two cities, one the city of the poor, the other of the rich, each at war with the other.

Plato made no moral judgments here. He simply would ask the wise ruler to take account of the differences between the rich and the poor. But with Robespierre, the difference between the wealth of the few and the poverty of the many was intolerable, so he would have a democratic state that did away with the "monstrous opulence of a few houses." From here on, democratic theorists have confronted the problem between the rich and the poor with blunt savagery.

In what United States Senator Estes Kefauver called a "remarkable anticipation of the basic presumption of Marxism," one of the more perceptive American presidents, John Adams, said:

> In every society where poverty exists there will ever be a struggle between rich and poor. Mixed in one assembly, equal laws can never be expected; they will either be made by the members to plunder the the few who are rich, or by the influential to fleece the many who are poor.

The great American populist Andrew Jackson asserted that "it is to be regretted that the rich and powerful often bend the acts of government to their selfish purposes."

Moreover, the problem of the rich and poor faced the American founding fathers, the drafters of the American Constitution, with only the political conservatives meeting it headlong; they proposed a property qualification for enfranchisement. The proposal was, of course, turned down, as it deserved to be, but those who proposed the property qualifications had raised a question that is valid to this day: can individuals exercise the political freedom of citizenship without freedom from economic dependence on the will of others? Alexander Hamilton averred that power over a man's subsistence amounted to power over his will.

It cannot easily be supposed that the question and the point of view could come only from an aristocrat, or a landed gentleman fearful of his position. No less than the philosopher Immanuel Kant argued that suffrage "presupposes the independence or self-sufficiency of the individual citizen," and since apprentices, servants, minors, women and the like did not maintain themselves by their industry but by the arrangement, or will, of others, they were "mere subsidiaries of the Commonwealth and not active independent members of it." As passive citizens, therefore, they could be deprived of the franchise.

Confronting the same issue, Karl Marx, the social philosopher, asserted that the "battle for democracy" will not be won until "the working class raises the proletariat to the position of ruling class." All governments now feel his influence in varying degrees, principally with respect to his contention that democracy cannot be conceived in political terms alone but in social and economic terms as well.

Modern Marxists and Communists have since based their criticism of democracy (which, for them, is not "really" a democracy) on its association with the capitalist system. The formula may be simplified in this manner: since only the propertied are socially and economically independent enough to exercise political freedom in a democracy with a capitalist economist system, there may be democracy for them but no democracy for the masses. The solution: abolish private property. Only then will there be genuine democracy.

But does it necessarily follow that when you concentrate all rights in the unpropertied they will be any more capable of exercising political freedom? Will this condition not subject them to the will of a political elite, which at the same time exercises social and economic power over them?

The Marxist tries to meet this objection in various ways. By doing away with private property and, therefore, with the profit motive, a government socializes the fruits of production for the benefit of all: the society will consequently be able to afford housing, clothing, food, and education for all, so that no social class will have better housing, clothing, food, and education than the rest. That sums up the social and economic good for communism.

As for the political good, since no social class lords it over the rest through the instrumentalities of government, no citizen need be oppressed by a political regime which is his, like a second skin. It follows too that a citizen who has different ideas can be motivated only by personal interests; his dissent can only be "counter-revolutionary"—for to what end should he dissent, demonstrate, defy, or rebel, except to indulge antisocial, or personal, feelings? Should this happen, the citizen must be shown the error of his ways; if this fails, sanctions are taken against him which may lead to jail, the asylum, or, in certain cases, to execution. There is no allowance in the Communist society for individual "perversity."

I can see and appreciate the social and economic good of communism, as I have stated. But I find it difficult to understand how its political society can be called democratic when a single party, the Communist party, or a group of men who control it, has a monopoly of political power. "The party knows best," is the simplified dictum of the Communist political order. Obviously, this form of government does not accept the fact, which I shall discuss shortly, that the people have an inherent right to remove their rulers, alter their government, or discard policy. On the contrary, the logic in the Communist view is that the people cannot rebel against themselves. This, of course, is a romantic fallacy.

In actual fact, the people are never the government and the government never the people. What joins them together is the principle of consent. In a Communist polity, the people do not merely consent—they must consent.

That the party cannot be infallible has been proved again and again in Communist states. Evidence of fallacies or errors sought to be concealed include the ruthless suppression of the Hungarian and Czechoslovakian uprisings, the de-Stalinization launched by Khrushchev, who was himself deposed in turn, the concentration camps, and notably the imprisonment and persecution of dissenting writers, artists, and historians. The Communist party may hope to exculpate itself by saying that no organization is without its faults, that Stalin himself, like the popes of old, was a perversion rather than the norm. All the same, the party made Stalin possible because its political doctrine provided no mechanism to check the concentration of power in the hands of one or a few men.

The crucial issue in the definition of democracy is political power: the who, what, when, and how of its exercise. This is crucial because democracy is concerned with freedom. Without freedom, the whole concept of democracy falls apart. If the only test of a system of government is how well it can provide clothing, food, housing, and other services to a people, then a government might just as well be autocratic as democratic.

Political power in a democracy is responsible power. Government and people are joined together by the principle of consent; the political authority, is, therefore, accountable to the people. It is an authority that must explain itself. "Although only a few may originate a policy," Pericles said, "we are all able to judge it." This is the affirmation on which democracy rests.

Of all the established forms of government, therefore, democracy is the only one that recognizes the inherent right of the people "to cast out their rulers, change their policy, or affect radical reforms in their system of government or institutions, by force or by a general uprising, when the legal and constitutional methods of making such changes have proved inadequate, or so obstructed as to be unavailable." The right to rebel is an elemental human right, just as the right to suppress rebellion is an elemental public right.

When a general uprising occurs, it is presumed that the legal and constitutional methods of effecting radical change have already become inadequate or unavailable. But it is an altogether different matter when a minority agitates for revolution although a democratic government exists and the majority seems content. Unless it has become impotent, such a government must, on the one hand, feel obliged to defend itself, even if only against the onslaught of an articulate or vigorous minority; and on the other hand, prove its capacity to initiate changes in response to popular expectations. A democratic government, in effect, engages a revolutionary minority in a competition for the minds of the many. This ability bespeaks the freedom that is the source of democracy's strength.

As it happens, there seems to be a trend of freedom in all of human history; at least one historian, Croce, considers history "the story of liberty." It may be said that Athens had started a process that has yet to complete itself in history, the democratization of human society. Democracy is a revolutionary doctrine because of this; the Periclean vision has yet to be realized. On the other hand, the Marxist vision, to put it in the kindest terms, has been perverted in the process of realization.

Still, men like Herbert Agar have been able to suggest that "we should help every effort to make communism and democracy unite. We may learn that the mixture is impossible; but there is no proof yet."

I can guess that this sentiment is occasioned by the comparative social and economic egalitarianism of Communist states, and the fact that in welfare states such as one finds in the Scandinavian countries, political, social, and economic democracy have achieved a level of development that is a tribute to the ingenuity and discipline of social man. Many modernizing—revolutionary—societies might very well settle, I think, for the Scandinavian model with certain improvements which will be explained later as a present-day democratic ideal. I have my serious doubts, however, about the Chinese model, for it may very well be a desperate political response to the social and economic problems of 700 million people. How much of the vast Chinese mainland really can be "communized"? I personally believe the Chinese model is applicable nowhere else, unless it is to a people of comparable size, history, and temperament: it is a unique case.

Men will always rationalize their political preferences, customs, habits, and commitments, and there will never be a shortage of reasons for restricting individual freedom and liberty in the name of "higher goals." Some of these interests and goals can be compelling, such as national victory in time of war, although in the United States, even this reason is not compelling enough to modulate dissent. But we are here dealing with the difficult and tangled question of democracy, by tradition and theory a political system that is identified with freedom and various institutions designed to safeguard and promote it. These institutions are representative government constituted by free and popular elections and freedom of the press, speech, thought, assembly, and association.

A political society blighted by social and economic inequalities, and administered by a government burdened with corruption and inefficiency, may be weak and unstable, but so long as it possesses the institutions of popular representation, freedom of the press, speech, and so forth, it remains, for all that, a democracy. It may be in danger of overthrow by revolutionary groups, which, in our time, may contend with a well-organized Communist revolutionary hard core; but it cannot in any reasonable way be characterized as fascistic; it is still a democracy. And if such a democracy learns to appreciate the dangers not to itself alone but to the people who established it, if it can still muster the courage, the resolution, and the wisdom to save itself, it will be revolutionary.

The Liberal Revolution

When we speak of revolution, we ordinarily think of that revolution which liquidates an entire ruling class as a precondition for the establishment of a new social order. This is the Jacobin type, named after the Jacobin party of the French Revolution. But there is another type of revolution, one which is carried out by the assimilation of the revolutionary classes into the existing order, resulting as in the case of the other type, in a different social order. This is the liberal type of revolution.

As described by Walter Lippmann in his book *The Public Philosophy*, the liberal revolution presumes

> the existence of a state which is already constitutional in principle, which is under laws that are no longer arbitrary, though they may be unjust and unequal. Into this constitutional state, more and more people are admitted to the governing class and the voting electorate. The unequal and unjust laws are reversed until eventually all the people have equal opportunities to enter the government and be represented.

This was the working theory of the British democratic revolution in the eighteenth century, and this was how, according to Lippmann, the principal authors of the American Constitution envisaged the enfranchisement of the entire adult population.

There are thus two approaches to revolutionary change, the liberal and the Jacobin, which, in modern terms, divide into the constitutional and armed struggles, or peaceful and violent revolutions.

The demands of the parliamentary or peaceful revolution may start out as less ambitious than those of armed revolution. This was clearly shown in the Philippine revolution of 1896. Jose Rizal and the propagandists invited Spain to institute liberal changes in its Philippine colony, but since the colonizing country was stubborn, the Filipino masses took to arms to overthrow the colonial government. Had Spain acceded to the demands of the propagandists instead of persecuting them, the ends sought by the natives could have been achieved without armed revolution. Spain rightly perceived, however, that the granting of liberal reforms would lead to more and more reforms, and ultimately, to the revolutionizing of Philippine society. She, therefore, become more oppressive and so provoked a revolution in the name of changes which were historically inevitable. Spain chose to go against history.

A situation exists in the Philippines today which has similar implications. While the country is no longer governed by a foreign ministry, its society still retains certain feudal and colonial characteristics. It is for this reason that articulate groups are agreed about the necessity of radical political, social, economic, and cultural changes. They demand a revolution but at the same time they *fear,* while a small minority hopes for, a violent revolution.

Those who hope for a violent revolution are often revolutionaries and agitators committed to a particular ideology. If they are Communists, they see no substitute for a Communist revolution. The many, however, would be content with a radical change.

Another group, pointing up a mechanical division of political society between the governing and the governed, regards as genuine only those revolutions which come "from below," which means the masses taking direct action against their government. In their view, the government can only reform—but cannot revolutionize—society. They betray, in this respect, an anthropomorphic and ossified notion of government.

A democratic political society has no ruling class as does a monarchic political society. In a democracy, political leadership is open to all classes; its "ruling class" is constituted by those politicians who have won mandates from the people to manage public affairs. A system of free, popular, and periodic elections precludes any automatic right to the exercise of public power.

But it may happen that the aim of free and popular elections is frustrated through the control, corruption, and manipulation of the political process. The democratic order can be subverted by forces within the society in the pursuit of private gain. Not all subversions, it must be noted, have public aims, such as the Communist conspiracy to establish a totalitarian state. History is full of examples of democratic regimes which have been subverted by powerful social and economic groups determined to promote their sectarian interests.

A political authority so corrupted, so subverted, and so manipulated is obliged to defend itself and the public good. The assumption here, of course, is that the political authority has not lost its power to act, that it has not been conquered by the manipulators.

When the consciousness of the political authority coincides with the revolutionary demands of the masses, a revolution by government itself becomes a matter of necessity. This revolution is more likely to be *liberal* than *Jacobin*.

The Challenge of Revolution

Few societies, if any, are spared, to a greater or less degree, the challenge of revolution. There are two reasons for this: the modern temper and the actual conditions of societies themselves. The power to control and change his environment is a cardinal belief of modern man, and revolution is the ultimate expression of this outlook—the modernizing outlook. On the other hand, societies that have experienced economic and social changes exercise tremendous pressure on their political authorities, which makes for a "revolutionary situation." These social and economic changes are not only status changes, or improvements in the living conditions of certain groups in society; they are changes—or an awakening—in the political consciousness of these groups, such as colored, ethnic, and cultural minorities, including women, peasants, workers, students; in sum, the so-called "revolutionary classes." They are in rebellion against the established order; their demands constitute an explosion of political participation, which is characteristic of revolution. This situation is particularly challenging to so-called developing societies which, properly speaking, are modernizing societies. In actuality and by definition, modernizing societies are revolutionizing—indeed, revolutionary—societies.

It is idle to talk in this context of the threat of revolution; what must be considered rather are its challenges. The revolution is not about to come; it is here. It is not a potential but an actual problem. The meaningful question, however, is: Revolution for what?

Many of us do not see the actuality of revolution because we wait for the classical sign: the nationwide clash of arms. But the violence of revolution is there, in the language, emotions, and marches of the rebellious groups, except that these do not fall within the common definition of revolution. If there is one thing that present discontents have done away with, it is the legalistic attitude toward sweeping social change. General violence, as a matter of fact, is not as relevant to revolution as change.

Recent memory brings to mind a bloodbath which can hardly be called revolutionary: Indonesia. On the other hand, the students' overthrow of the Syngman Rhee regime in South Korea was revolutionary: that the liberal, democratic government which followed was later replaced did not make it less revolutionary; it only meant that the revolutionaries themselves, the students, were less clear about their revolution. The pattern of authority was not unlike that of the great French Revolution: a moderate rule ending in the Napoleonic thermidorean reaction. To understand, therefore, the condition of modernizing—revolutionary—societies, we should attend not to the signs of violence but to the signs of change.

In the revolution being waged today in the Philippines, violence has not occurred in a dramatic battle. However, incidents of violence have occurred in a sustained, continuous, and apparently planned sequence.

The New People's Army, or the Maoist faction of the Communist party—the Army ng Bayan of the Moscow-oriented or traditional faction of the Communist party of the Philippines—actually engaged in open hostilities against the armed forces of the Philippines.

There are also other independent groups who have at one time or another conspired or plotted a *coup-d'état*. Even the alleged moderates have used coercion or intimidation as well as outright force in open support of the operations of Communist groups and their front organizations. The question therefore arises: Is violence necessary?

In Communist doctrine and in the very nature of the Jacobin type of revolution, violence is not only necessary, it *is* the revolution. For the purpose of a Jacobin revolution is to wipe away society and its ruling clique. This means the liquidation of the oligarchs, the economic imperialists, as well as the political authority, and their replacement by a dictatorship of the proletariat, or a totalitarian state ruled by the Communist party.

On the other hand, violence is never used in a liberal or constitutional revolution, except to defend the government from its own liquidation, which is the immediate purpose of a Jacobin-type of revolution. This is manifest in the existing Constitution and inherent in the fundamental principle of self-defense.

The Constitution provides that the President may proclaim a state of martial law or suspend the privilege of the writ of habeas corpus when there is any invasion, insurrection, or imminent danger thereof.

However, even during the employment of such extraordinary power to suppress riot or disorder, the rights of citizens as well as residents of the country who are not participants in the Jacobin-type revolution should be and are respected. This applies even when some persons may be arrested and kept in custody for a period of time without charges before a court, or under martial law in a situation bordering on war where in effect the armed forces of the Philippines assume the powers of government. This was shown by the manner in which the order of the late President Elpidio Quirino was implemented in 1950 when he suspended the privilege of the writ of habeas corpus.

It is true that the government used violence and force in the implementation when pursuing the armed elements resisting arrest. Although such violence and force was legal, it was nonetheless violence and force.

But the distinguishing feature was that it was utilized only against those who had identified themselves with the Jacobin-type of revolution. All other citizens and residents of the country continued to enjoy their individual freedom as enshrined in the Constitution as if the whole country was at peace. The local police proceeded through their daily routine of preventing crime, apprehending criminals and prosecuting them, and otherwise enforcing the law. The courts continued to function in the redress of grievances, in the protection of private rights, and in the maintenance of peaceful relations between individuals. The local and national governments continued to administer the laws and the civil service continued to hold office in the normal atmosphere of unhurried bureaucracy. And yet for all that, about 1,000 leaders of the Communist party, including the Communist politburo members headed by Jesus Lava, were arrested and detained, and the 14,000 fully armed soldiery known as the Hukbalahap, which was the army of the Communist party under Supremo Luis Taruc, were liquidated in a series of battles.

When violence starts in a democracy and threatens the security of a government which is by and large stable, and whose leaders still retain the mandate of the people and have not lost the will and the capability to survive and protect the people who had entrusted the political authority to them, then the contest posed by the new political ideology passes from the minds of men to the arena of combat. In a society with an environment similar to the Philippines, the military, although often criticized, is still looked up to by a majority of the people for the protection of their persons and properties. For the military is the strongest organization in such a situation. And since it is still the strongest armed force in such a society it will triumph in a conflict brought about by violent revolutionists. From these premises, a conclusion must follow, that violence is ineffective and undesirable.

The experience of the past two years indicates that when the Communist manipulators were able to mount a quiet, peaceful demonstration, no matter how inflammatory their oratory and slogans, they evoked sympathy from the people who may have valid grievances. On the other hand, these Communist manipulators lost ground when violence was clearly and openly perpetrated and initiated by them. This was the case in the University of the Philippines, where they captured the university premises, including its radio station. The leaders demonstrated a crudity, cruelty, and total disregard for the sensibility of the citizenry. On the other hand, the political authority showed graceful generosity and paternal concern not only for the university and its inhabitants but also for the citizenry by avoiding the open employment of arms and brute force which was the most convenient recourse to take. Even from the viewpoint of the true revolutionist, violence is undesirable because an embattled government that has strengthened its armed forces seeks to transfer the ground of conflict from the arena of ideas into the arena of force when it is frankly and admittedly superior. In short, violent revolutions are passé. The Jacobin-type of revolution does not belong to this decade.

All that the democratic government need understand, then, despite its failures or shortcomings, is that the revolutionary challenge to democratic government is nothing more or less than the challenge of its own ideals.

Considered in the light of new conditions and deepened or expanded perceptions, subjected to a social setting in which new demands confront established institutions, these ideals must necessarily arouse a revolutionary allegiance.

Modernization, revolution, change. These are the equations in societies which, like ours, have experienced social and economic development. But the important question is whether ours is a society whose "processes of political modernization and political development have lagged behind the processes of social and economic change."

Samuel P. Huntington suggests that political modernization "involves the extension of political consciousness to new social groups and the mobilization of these groups into politics." On the other hand, political development "involves the creation of political constitutions sufficiently adaptable, complex, autonomous, and coherent to absorb and to order the participation of these new groups and to promote social and economic changes in the society."

In the Philippines as elsewhere, it thus seems axiomatic that the revolutionary demand for a different form of government, a point raised by Hannah Arendt, must meet the democratic criterion. A revolution that replaces a regime with one which restricts rather than expands the areas of human freedom may still deserve the name of revolution, but it is not an act of liberation. What form of government can be a substitute for a democracy?

On this point lies the whole revolutionary issue. A democratic government may confront the imminence of revolution because of those social and economic inequalities in developing or modernizing societies. Under these conditions, the democracy that the people enjoy is a precarious one. A revolution can justify itself then only as a movement towards fuller democratization: a revolution that sets its sights in the other direction can only be antidemocratic. Such a revolution can justify itself only by its success, if indeed that is possible.

A democratic government faced with such a revolution has two alternatives: suppression, which, if carried too far, will justify charges of fascism; and accommodation to those revolutionary demands whose realization cannot but strengthen the democratic system. The democratic government, in effect, competes with the subversive forces which aim to manipulate revolutionary expectations for their antidemocratic ends. The government itself then becomes revolutionary, promoting a revolution from the center—in sum, a Democratic Revolution.

4

REVOLUTION FROM THE CENTER

An intellectual attachment to old political categories will find in the idea of a government-initiated revolution a contradiction in terms. A government, according to the old wisdom, cannot make revolution because it cannot revolt against itself. The common axiom derived from this semantic proposition is that there can never be "revolution from above."

History and tradition—not to say modern political thought —pitilessly refute this Jacobin prejudice.

The Jacobin attitude postulated from experience an oppressive ruling class that was so intolerable it had to be destroyed. As the encyclopaedist Holbach saw the French nobility of the eighteenth century: "We see on the face of the globe only incapable, unjust sovereigns enervated by luxury, corrupted by flattery, depraved through unpunished license, and without talent, morals, or good qualities." This governing class and its government had to be overthrown by a people united in revolution.

But there was, around the same time, the English ruling class, which had one vast difference from those of the French: its government became responsible and responsive to popular demands. The English nobility preferred to lose their privileges rather than their heads, probably because of the penchant of the English then for beheading their monarchs.

This latter case was a "revolution from above"—through the assimilation and enfranchisement of the masses, literally lifting them to a higher level and, hopefully, a nobler station.

Here is an instance of a political authority that responded to popular demands, that acknowledged, in short, the inevitability of social change. It placed itself at the center of popular aspirations, giving them a surer direction.

Modern political thought also puts the Jacobin prejudice to rest. Governments are now judged according to their willingness and capacity to act as the instruments of social change. The people—the governed—look to their governments for leadership not only in the political order but also in the social and economic fields. The government has ceased to be a mere policeman, governing best because it governs least.

Only when a government has failed in these roles is it rejected or repudiated by its people.

This reasoning is a bit involved, if not confusing, to those who are unfamiliar with the democratic tradition. The openness and candor with which inequities and defects in a democratic society are discussed can easily delude the totalitarian mind into thinking that everything is hopeless, that the people are too oppressed, and that the only solution is to destroy the society. They do not count on the healing, self-rejuvenating power of a democratic system, its capacity to act under pressure of the true sovereign, the people.

Government in a democracy stands at the center of—not above—the political community. It governs, and the men in government may constitute a governing class, but only in the democratic sense that the masses, sovereign as they are, cannot govern. As Jefferson pointed out:

> The people are not qualified to exercise themselves the Executive Department; but they are qualified to name the person who shall exercise it. . . . They are not qualified to legislate; with us therefore they only choose the legislators.

For this reason, democratic government is accountable to the people, and its place is at the center of public life. It listens and responds to the deepest needs of the people. Confronted with revolutionary aspirations, democratic government must give them shape and direction so that the people, to whom it is accountable, may achieve them without great damage to their welfare and solidarity.

The simple-minded view that government cannot lead a democratic revolution—"for there is no revolution from above"—does not take into account the fact that history is change, that conditions change, and that government evolves in theory and practice. Countries develop their own peculiarities and traditions. Only thirty years ago, the semifeudal, semicolonial conditions in China made a Communist revolution inevitable; free elections in Chile elected a Marxist president, who was not inclined to put the bourgeois parties to the sword. Philippine democracy, on the other hand, was the dream of the Philippine revolution of 1896 and it evolved under American colonialism. That *the people is all* is an article of faith in Filipino political thought, whatever gap there may be at times between faith and practice.

The government under this doctrine does not conceive of itself as the head, the crown, the apex, of the national community. It is not at the summit but at the core; it is the power center surrounded by the people, to whom it proposes and whom it leads—standing *in front* of them but not *above* them. The old, traditional picture of government as top man on the totem pole, true of colonial times but no longer true now, perpetuates the misunderstanding of democratic government. It betrays an adherence to useless political categories, useless because they are dated and because they do not apply to the peculiar doctrine of Philippine democracy.

It may finally be said that the masses do not originate revolution: they respond to the call and leadership of a revolutionary minority. But a revolutionary minority in a democratic society, whatever its shortcomings, may have some other purposes than the liberation of the masses; the system of government that it hopes to establish may result in less rather than more freedom for the people. A democratic government, then, is obliged to make itself the faithful instrument of the people's revolutionary aspirations.

This is the entire concept of a revolution from the center, a Democratic Revolution.

The Origins

We need not go beyond our historical experience to establish the origins of the Democratic Revolution. The fundamental nationality of a revolution determines its success. Exported revolutions can only fail, as many of our self-proclaimed revolutionists have yet to understand. It is certainly wise to learn from the experience of others, but it is also unwise, if not traitorous, to fashion ourselves after—or submit ourselves to—foreign models. We have a revolutionary tradition that we can well be proud of, a tradition that, moreover, continues to exercise its influence on our serious political thought.

The Democratic Revolution, derived as I have shown from a general theory, is also Filipino in concept and inspiration. It is faithful to our historical aspirations and experience, rooted, as it were, in the historical demands of the Filipino people which gained full expression in the revolution of 1896. We are, in many ways and under changing circumstances, still waging this revolutionary struggle.

What are the aims, the demands, of this struggle? As expressed by the propagandists and ideologues of the last century, who were "articulating the inarticulate thoughts of the Filipino people," these were all summed up in the desire for a political authority that would be the instrument of national liberation, the promoter of the people's intellectual and moral development and their economic and social well-being. They envisioned a society based on moral principles, governing in turn the people's economic and social relationships.

This kind of society, as Jose Rizal pointed out, could only come about with the unity of people and government, since "a fatuous government would be an anomaly among a righteous people, just as a corrupt people cannot exist under just rulers and wise laws."

Apolinario Mabini, the "brains of the revolution," completing the formulation, considered revolution an imperative of *social regeneration,* the radical change not only of institutions but also of *our ways of thinking and behaving.* He called for an "external" as well as an "internal" revolution, for in his view, as in ours, the moral education of the people is a necessity, and therefore they should establish society on firm foundations, in the process purging themselves of *their* vices. The revolution of 1896 was not merely a clash of arms leading to physical liberation: it was a cleansing experience, a *moral* act.

What, indeed, happened in the revolution of 1896? A group of landlords offered to put up a bank to lend money to the revolutionary government with large tracts of the national patrimony for collateral; military leaders and civil officials subdivided territories among themselves; Andres Bonifacio was charged, among other outlandish accusations, with having received money from the enemy, the Spaniards; Antonio Luna, whose military qualities Rizal admired greatly, and at whose death Mabini commented, "the revolution is dead!," was assassinated by soldiers of the revolution; the so-called "constitutionalists" drafted a charter which placed power in the hands of what "constitutionalist" Felipe Calderon frankly called an "intellectual oligarchy," because they feared the masses who were bearing the brunt of the revolutionary struggle. On the threshold of creating a new society, the *ilustrado* class established an all-powerful Assembly which revived the Spanish system of taxation and returned to its colonial owners the friar lands which were precisely one of the causes of the "revolt of the masses."

In his personal recollections and numerous writings related to the Philippine revolution, Mabini showed an acute awareness of the full moral dimensions of the task of revolution. This is an awareness that has asserted itself again and again whenever we speak of the necessity of radical change in Philippine society. Mabini's *purge* (let us call it that) disappointed and frustrated him when in one brief glorious moment he saw his people rise in revolution only to witness the "colonial vices" betray their hopes.

Without the recognition of our own deficiencies and corruption, whether these are brought about by colonialism or not, we cannot understand the meaning of the Philippine Revolution, or, for that matter, the Democratic Revolution which has become the necessity of the present. The exclusively institutional revolutionists, many of whom borrow their insights from alien sources, ignore this "internal" task postulated by Mabini, either out of convenience or out of expediency. It is true that colonialism has corrupted the peoples that it has touched and that the task of regeneration must begin with the liquidation of those institutions that perpetrated and perpetuated the colonial orders. But more than this, a point is reached where the subjugated peoples themselves must change their ways of thinking and behaving, their outlook and attitudes, to be truly and completely free.

A native elite stepping into the shoes of a foreign elite may constitute an improvement over the colonial order, but it is not the most significant step in the process of decolonization. Revolution should be national, otherwise it is just a *coup d'état* of color; this is particularly true if the native elite is nothing more than a "Westernized" segment of the population. Mabini rather than Marx spelled out the meaning of revolution for the Filipinos: "Any agitation promoted by a particular class for the benefit of its special interests does not deserve the name [of political revolution or evolution]."

However, the ascent of the *ilustrado* class to the leadership of the Philippine revolution, which was launched by the masses under the *Katipunan,* was accepted as the unity of that class with the people. The masses needed leaders and officials who had the means—the logistics—with which to carry out the struggle. In this sense, the so-called rule of the "intellectual oligarchy" was an essential element in the revolutionary and political tradition, the "revolutionary vanguard." It would establish the kind of political authority desired by the ideologues: the instrument of national liberation and popular intellectual and moral development.

It is also idle to speculate now what the fate of the *ilustrado* "republican" government would have been had the revolution succeeded completely. Under the American occupation there followed a brief period of education in self-government under a modified—some say a stronger—presidential system. The commonwealth era had a colonized government waiting to be free, so that it could fully be the instrument of national liberation and development. It was the consensus that when the hour of independence came, the Filipinos would full emerge a unified people, a nation in every sense of the word.

But the Filipino nation emerged at a time of great division, and this was reflected in turn by our early postwar politics. There was a division on nationalist and social issues, which, in their original form, were the bases of the revolution of 1896. At the same time, partisan politics emphasized the rhetoric over the substance of what is best called popular radicalism. Deliberately or not, every political utterance, particularly in the campaign to win votes, equated the failures of an administration with the fundamental alienation of people from government. The political culture, which I characterized earlier as populist, personalist, and individualist, ironically enough sanctioned the condemnation of the very politics which it encouraged. In sum, radical rhetoric and reactionary reality, but with the burden of blame on political authority and not on the operations of economic and social forces.

The approval by a great majority of the people of their government can only suggest that the government is responsive to their needs, and yet the rhetoric says the opposite. There is some truth in the saying that administrations have fallen on the issue of graft and corruption. Yet with the supposedly cleansing process of election and repudiation the issue of graft and corruption has been raised at every election. Why? The facile reply is "politics." But this is a simple-minded view of the complex reality. Our corruption is social; it is not therefore a simple administrative problem. Corruption exists because of the intervention of wealth in politics, in the same way as militarism and clericalism are the interventions of the military and the organized church in politics. Thus in examining the imperfections of political authority, we go beyond the authority itself to the wider realm of the society or national community that influences it.

The corruption of political authority lies not in itself but in the source of its power. Colonial governments are corrupt, for example, because they are established on the pretended superiority of one people, or race, over another. The colonized are objects rather than citizens. Now a democratic political authority, whose source of power is the people, is corrupted when the people themselves, or an influential minority among them, attempt to use its institutions or the authority itself for their private advantage. At this point the oligarchs begin to infiltrate the democratic political order; this is the root cause of social corruption. The effective practice of the few becomes a model to the rest, hardening in the end into a way of life, a "culture."

The result, however, is by no means an autocratic or despotic political society. Oligarchs are not interested in political power as such but in economic gain and social privilege. They do demand a minimum of peace and order within the community but they can and do secure their persons with a private force. It is not that they wish the poor to remain in misery but that the improvement of their lives should not interfere with the oligarchical profit. Thus the oligarchs may have human sentiments and social sympathies as others do, they may not deny the humblest citizen the right to try and influence government for his own ends, and on that basis they consider themselves democratic. That they have more of the means, more of the economic power with which, in Andrew Jackson's words, "to bend the government to their will," is, in their view, no fault of theirs. It is rather their reward for enterprise, ability or good fortune, even if these were originally abetted by inheritance.

There is no hard evidence, except for doctrinaires and the socially committed intelligentsia, that the poor of the nation resent the ways of the oligarchy. Our conservative ethic is such that so long as one's fortune did not come from outright thievery and graphically illustrated exploitation, it merits the honors and respect of men. We confront here a personal, simplistic ethic that is a corruption of the individualism which holds a man solely responsible for his life. It does not take into account the fact that no single individual can be responsible for the social conditions into which he is thrown by the accident of birth. Thus this poverty of social thought popularizes the notion that the poor are poor because they are not industrious or lucky. Certainly there are instances in which this is true, but judged from the sociological perspective, mass poverty and oligarchical wealth are the result of social arrangements.

This, in all candor, is the disease of our democracy: an ethic that has a simplified view of the illegitimate accumulation of wealth, while the wealth of the economic personnel are legitimately amassed. It ignores the fundamental fact that the political personnel cannot enrich themselves without the connivance of the economic personnel, since corruption, to be successful, must satisfy the greed of both the corrupt and the corruptor. "Sharing the benefits" has become the greatest impetus to social corruption at all levels. The efflorescence of social corruption has also abetted the sad phenomenon of the poor extorting from the poor.

In the institutional sense the oligarchs, for being privileged, are guilty of bringing about this state of affairs. In the cultural sense, however, everyone is guilty. Social corruption exists because of general consent and toleration. This is the full moral perception of the revolution that has been bequeathed to us by Mabini. Here is the meaning of the "internal" revolution which he considered indispensable to "social regeneration."

To understand this is to understand one of the noble reasons for democratic government—which is to end "the elevation of the few over the degradation of the many," which, by the way, is the essence of an oligarchical society.

A people may have the most responsive political authority but unless they are faithful to its tenets and use its institutions wisely, that authority will be eroded by the few who will manipulate it for private gain. The political authority will then suffer from a diminution of force and of moral authority. A revolutionary situation cannot but follow from this erosion of force and confidence, with the poor realizing or being made to realize that their poverty has been caused by the oligarchical society. This is the reason why revolutionaries, for all their elaborate theories, anchor their appeal on the age-old conflict between the rich and the poor. Their success, however, in fomenting this class war often depends on the decay of the political order.

But history has shown that revolutions based on this premise may have abolished classes formally but have not appreciably made men more equal and more free. Dictatorship had to be enforced in the name of freedom and revolution. The main reason is that the deposed governments have been weak, thus necessitating as a successor a despotic rule, not only to further the aims of the revolution, but also—and above all—to prevent another bloody upheaval. As Franklin Delano Roosevelt wisely observed, dictatorships do not grow out of strong and successful governments but out of weak and helpless ones. "The only bulwark of continuing liberty," he added, "is a government strong enough to protect the interests of the people, and a people strong enough and well enough informed to maintain its sovereign control over government."

Our own revolutionists understood this perfectly. Mabini and Calderon differed as to which branch of government should have the greater power—the executive (hence "absolutist") or the legislative (hence "constitutionalist")—but both recognized the necessity of a strong political authority. The point is so obvious it would need no emphasis were it not for a minority view that democracy is equivalent to "weak government and strong people," which is a misunderstanding not only of democracy but also of our own tradition, not to mention the very concept of government itself. The power of government, based on common consent, holds a human community together. Diminish that power and the community falls apart.

Implicit in this principle is the integrity of the political authority. An inordinate influence on it by any segment of society, promoting its interests at the expense of the whole, compromises the authority's ability to promote the common welfare. When government finds itself in this position, it must either finally succumb or liberate itself. A government that is captured by a special segment loses its legitimacy, since it cannot profess to exist by common consent. It may continue to command force, but its use of it would be repressive. On the other hand, should government decide to liberate itself, it becomes an initiator of revolution, and its use of force is legitimate rather than repressive. Democracy, as observed earlier, is a self-revolutionizing, self-rejuvenating political system.

But a doctrine is not enough: the decisive factor is the popular commitment to it. The revolutionary education of the Filipinos stopped at the threshold of "internal" revolution. It must resume now at a time of great social and economic changes. By anchoring the Democratic Revolution in our very own traditions, I have shown, I believe, the source of our capacity for "social regeneration." True, we are crippled by a social corruption that erodes our moral strength. But we also know its causes. Above all, we are aware of the revolutionary necessity.

This necessity dates back to the anticolonialist struggle of 1896 for a political authority that would be the instrument of national independence, a promoter of the Filipino's moral and intellectual development, his economic and social well-being. This demand continues to this day, and through the years government had been trying to satisfy it through all the vicissitudes of development. The demand has become more acute owing to the growing complexities of the modern world.

Thus revolutionary change has a special urgency.

The time is limited and the choices are few. We can either take the revolution into our institutions and thus give it a democratic direction, or, out of confusion, lack of will, or indifference, we can leave it in the streets and the countryside, where it can flourish wildly and bear, in the end, bitter fruit. No responsible government, particularly a democratic government, will elect the latter course deliberately. It has to assert its mandate.

The Democratic Revolution is therefore a rededication to the historical aspirations of the Filipino people, but it makes demands not only on the political authority itself but on the very foundation of that authority: the people.

The Agenda for Change

The dominant characteristic of our society which demands radical change is the economic gap between the rich and the poor. We find here a wide consensus that includes the rich themselves. This gap is the constant theme of political oratory and social criticism. There is a general ageement that this gap must be narrowed, if only for the sake of social stability.

Now the stability of Philippine society is founded on precarious ground: the effectiveness of government as a patron of the poor. We must distinguish here between the social services that government provides out of the allocation of the scarce resources of society and the patronage that it dispenses for political purposes. The latter suggests a kind of privilege for the poor in order to insure their consent to the established order of things. This is precarious because no government can remain a patron without institutionalizing a general dependency that is not only a burden but a threat.

While the government must care for the unfortunate members of society, this cannot be its social mission. The social mission of government, given widespread poverty, is to turn wards into free men. Unless this is done, they will soon constitute a separate nation of the poor. We come then face to face with the problem of property. As soon as the poverty of the many and the wealth of the few is raised as a social issue, only two demands can be heard: either to regulate (or democratize) private wealth, or to abolish it.

Our society, it appears to me, has reached that point where it must decide consciously, and quickly, between the democratization of weath or its abolition. We should not imagine that our society can postpone making its choice in the hope that time and good fortune will set things right. The intellectual, moral, and religious traditions of mankind have never looked kindly on the private possession or enjoyment of property. These traditions have a particular sharpness in the modern world because of a general consciousness that poverty is neither a fate nor a punishment but a social condition that can and must be changed.

There was a time, of course, when property was strongly defended. John Locke held that its preservation was the reason men entered into society. Pope Leo XIII, the author of the *Rerum Novarum,* pronounced that the fundamental principle if one would alleviate the conditions of the masses was the "inviolability of private property." Edmund Burke said that "the power of perpetuating our property in our families is one of the most valuable and interesting circumstances belonging to it, and that which tends the most to the perpetuation of society itself."

On the other hand, St. Ambrose declared that "property hath no rights." The pagans blasphemed God because they "hold earth as property." St. Chrysostom called the rich man a thief. Clement of Alexandria called property "the fruit of inequity." Proudhon, the only Socialist Jose Rizal ever heard of, said "property is theft (*La propriete c'est la vol*)." St. Thomas Aquinas advised men to consider their possessions as common to all, "to share without hesitation when others are in need." Lincoln asserted the primacy of human rights over property rights. And Daniel Webster warned that the freest government cannot long endure when the tendency of the law is to create a rapid accumulation of property in the hands of a few, and to render the masses *poor and dependent*.

No political or social theory of modern times holds property to be inviolable or to be privately enjoyed. The most conservative theory reflects the judgment of Theodore Roosevelt, who announced sixty years ago that "the man who wrongly holds that every human right is secondary to his profit must now give way to the advocate of human welfare, who rightly maintains that every man holds his property subject to the general will of the community to regulate its use to whatever degree the public welfare may require it."

As Pope Paul VI reminds us all, in his encyclical *Populorum Progressio:*

> . . . Private property does not constitute for anyone an absolute and unconditional right. No one is justified in keeping for his exclusive use what he does not need, when others lack necessities. In a word, according to the traditional doctrine as found in the fathers of the church and the great theologians, the right to property must never be exercised to the detriment of the common good.

The Marxist revolutionary, however, goes a step further: he demands the abolition of property.

These ideas are certainly not new to the Filipino mind, which has been shaped spiritually by Christian ethics and politically by the democratic—radical and liberal—traditions.

They have colored the political and social utterances of the past seventy years. Whether or not they were meant to, they have gained popular currency. No political or economic leader is so conservative now that he would not at the proper time demand that the national leadership—or the political authority —come out with a program for the "equitable distribution of wealth." But let us understand that no democratic government can disturb the property relations of society without the aid of revolutionary legislation. It must necessarily encounter the most determined resistance from the powerful few who own or control a large portion of the national wealth, and who, above all, intervene in the political sphere.

The process of radical change, although constitutional, is a convulsive one. The force of law is no less violent for being legal. Violence must be controlled in a revolution by constitutional means, and only a strong democratic government can give any such assurance. And in this endeavor, the clearest and deepest consent of the people is imperative.

Only at his own risk, however, may the reader construct my words as an advocacy of welfare statism or some form of socialism. My deepest concern is with the political system that goes by the name of democracy and not in any social or economic *ism* which may or may not postulate a certain political order to realize its aims. I am interested in those economic and social issues which affect the exercise of freedom in society, and which, in effect, encourage or hinder free men in making the most of themselves. *Mine,* finally, is an anxiety over a political society that is imperiled by the fatal social disease of elevating the few over the degradation of the many, caused, in turn, by deep economic and social inequalities.

It is only through improvisation—in which we include all the hopeful "changes" in political leadership—that our political society has succeeded in postponing the consequences of inequality. Demagoguery, on the one hand, and the politics of patronage, on the other, have been providing the seasonal expectations and cyclical contentment that have thus far kept the lid on armed mass revolution. And precisely because of these, the drain on scarce resources and the conspiracy of the mighty against change, the legislation for meaningful social reforms remains in the books. There is a sense, indeed, in which Philippine politics is but a game of "musical chairs," a game of changing personalities but not of policies. The political process is unduly influenced by a plutocracy, sanctioned by popular consent, whose idea of national progress does not go beyond the increase in their economic power, and, indirectly, their political power.

In this sense, we only "play at democracy." If politicians importune the rich for money to win the votes of the poor in order to serve better the rich the result is sham democracy and a glaring poverty in social ethics. We add to this the hypocrisy of radical rhetoric.

But no society can indefinitely deceive itself by allowing freedom of radical expression while ignoring its tenets in practice. It is true that the hyperbolic language of democratic politics produces in the minds of the masses a certain amount of skepticism about the claims and promises of their political leaders. However, the incessant repetition of radical views and radical slogans must in time breed a radical political consciousness.

Let us note that ten years ago any public figure who expressed anything like the "radical transformation of society" would promptly have been called a subversive or a Communist sympathizer. Now it is no longer easy to distinguish the subversive from the radical democrat: their language tends to be similar. Self-professed Maoists do not often know what Maoism really is. The Marxist view of society influences the utterances of non-

Marxists. There is an embarrassing abundance of radical ideology, or to be exact, ideologies.

We have been playing at democracy and perhaps even playing at revolution.

But the time has come when we can no longer play at either.

Through the years of rhetorical radicalism, the masses have been undergoing a political education in mass democracy. It is doubtful, however, if their political education includes an appreciation of the complexities of modern nationhood. The agitators' job is done when they have demonstrated the causes of mass misery and poverty and insinuated the remedy of revolution. The rest possibly is left to political partisanship, the method of which is the organization of discontent for winning elections. But unless free elections result in substantial social changes, discontent will be organized to capture state power.

The constant hammering into the minds of the masses of the necessity for a new society must create an urgent demand for its realization. And unless the political authority is capable of creating that new society, it will be repudiated and the task entrusted to another. A democracy like ours dare not risk this, for the result may mean the end rather than the expansion of human liberty.

We cannot allow our political society to become the victim of unrealized aspirations. Having aroused the hopes of the masses for a new society, the political authority must embark on the task of creating it.

The Primacy of the People

It is for the people that we embark on the Democratic Revolution in order to alter or transform society. We have a more or less clear understanding now of what we mean by Democratic Revolution. Are we as clear, however, about the term "the people"?

In an essay written at a time of democratic crisis, the distinguished American journalist and public philosopher Walter Lippmann sought to resolve the ambiguity of the term, "the people." He pointed out two different meanings: "When we speak of popular sovereignty, we must know whether we are talking about The People, as voters, or about *The People*, as a community of the entire living population, with their predecessors and successors."

The assumption that the opinion of The People as voters can be treated as the expression of the interests of *The People* as historic community was, to Lippmann's mind, unwarrantable, and he considered the crucial problem of modern democracy to have arisen from this false assumption. He attributed to this the enfeeblement of the democratic order.

> Because of the discrepancy between The People as Voters and *The People* as the corporate nation, the voters have no title to consider themselves the proprietors of the commonwealth and to claim that their interests are identical to the public interest. A prevailing plurality of the voters are not *The People*. The claim that they are is a bogus title invoked to justify the usurpation of the executive powers by representative assemblies and the intimidation of public men by demagogic politicians. In fact demagoguery can be described as the sleight of hand by which a faction of The People as voters are invested with the authority of *The People*. That is why so many crimes are committed in the People's name.

This distinction reflects Edmund Burke's view of *The People* as "connected generations of persons joined in partnership" not only "between those who are living" but also with "those who are dead and those who are to be born." *The People* then are a corporation, an historic entity, into which individuals come and from which they go.

Our political discourse does not make this distinction. We have always assumed the enfranchised majority to be *The People*, or, more broadly, the masses of the entire population. To say then that the pleasure of this majority or the masses is the pleasure of *The People* is the same as saying that the pleasure of the House of Representatives is the pleasure of The People.

For The People (so distinguished) are, at best, self-proclaimed representatives of *The People*.

The question, however, is whether this complicated distinction is necessary to serious political thought. I think that it is, and all we need do is to ask the meaning of the term, "the People of the Philippines" as embodied in our Constitution. The framers of our present Constitution were certainly not drafting it for the interest of those who ratified it at a specific period in history. If they were, the whole charter would have been so particular that it would have lost its validity right after it was made. Nor did the recent constitutional convention consider only the interests of The People as voters, as the masses, or even *all* of the people at this time in history. For on this very hour this majority, the masses, and the entire people are changing: many are dying and many are being born. And it is certainly anomalous to say that *The People* of the Constitution are whatever people there may be at the time of its ratification. Constitutions are changed not only because of new social, economic, or political conditions, but because the interests of *The People* cannot be anticipated for all time.

We begin to realize, then, the short-sightedness of our approach to popular sovereignty, the arrogance of our self-regard, when we confine the people's interest to what we, at present, regard to be our interests. Our populist, personalist, and individualist culture must give way not only to collective responsibility, but beyond that to our historic responsibility. As a people we exist not only in the urgent present but in the continuum of history. We shall live, labor, and die as individuals. But as a people, we are part of that historic stream of generations that are *The Filipino People*.

The sure evidence, therefore, of political maturity, of the highest political sophistication, is the recognition of our historic "personality." It is what makes us one nation, one people, for it impresses upon us the scope of our historic existence and thus bestows upon all of us mankind's highest responsibility.

The Western or westernized political theorist may suppress a smile at the suggestion of an Indonesian leader that democracy was "the unity of God with his servant," but deeper examination of the implications of *The People* as a historic community should reveal to him its profound truth.

On the other hand, how many times have we confessed weariness over the words, "our heroes and patriots died for us," as if they were just cliché and not an expression of historic actuality. We do exist and die for those who will come after us, and by our actions we either serve or betray them—those coming generations which are, in their totality, *The Filipino People*.

Nothing less than this high moral consciousness must guide the democratic revolution as it reaches out for a new society.

5

THE REMAKING OF SOCIETY

The Old Society

There is a sense in which ours is an already new society: it is the caesarean delivery from the foreign conqueror. All the developing countries of the world are interchangeably referred to as "new nations" or "new societies." But they are "new" only in the sense that the developed nations are "old." It is all a matter of chronology that has little analytical use for us in "the new world." There is among the caesarean "new societies" much of the old that we must understand. And among them the Philippines is unique, for our precolonial traditions, unlike those of our Asian neighbors, have long been buried and forgotten.

It has been said, perhaps in bitterness, that no Taj Majal, no Angkor Wat, no Great Wall, stands among us to remind the colonial intruder of his insolence in affecting to "civilize us" in exchange for exploitation. In the long struggle against colonialism, our Asian neighbors held their cultures and their traditions aloft against the conquerors: many a colonial administrator and settler lost his head, in more ways than one, in trying to live among "a strange race." There is no similar record in colonial Philippines, so some writers say; about the only insanity inflicted on the colonizer was the insanity of greed, which reached its dramatic climax in the friar assassination of Governor Bustamante. On the whole, it was not an uneasy head that wore the colonial crown in the Philippines. Not the master but the subject was corrupted by "foreign ways."

It is quite revealing that among the articles of faith of the propaganda movement was Rizal's contention that the Filipinos had a culture of their own before the coming of the Spaniards. He was trying to prove an identity which the Spaniards denied. That we had the propaganda movement at all, in the sense of proving to our masters our worth rather than naturally assuming it, belied our cultural subjection, a situation spared the Indonesian, the Chinese, or the Burmese, and similar to that of the Black Americans.

Mabini's bitter allusion to inherited colonial vices is traceable to this condition. The government employee who makes his pile before he is dismissed from office or the syndicate that covers up corruption in the service, is not a modern, postindependence counterpart of the colonial system but an extension of it. The same may be said for the knowing tolerance of social corruption and the public show of moral outrage over what it privately indulged in in good conscience. It is not that we are corrupt, hypocritical, and unheroic as a race, or even as individuals, but that we become so the moment we "step into" society. Social mimesis, let us call it: our behavior is an imitation of society—the old, colonial society.

How else do we account for the bitter suggestion that we could not even make an honest revolution of 1896? It is most assuredly an apocryphal tale, but when the governor general who could quell the "insurrection" was asked by the Spanish

Crown what he needed, the former disregarded troops and am-munition and simply said, "gold." I have been assured that the story was not made up by Spaniards but by Filipino revolu-tionaries themselves.

Long before the British came, India had an ideology rooted in the long and continuing search for the origin and the meaning of life, a tradition that exalted meditation above action, the primacy of spiritual over material concerns. She had the Hinduist and Buddhist religions. She had a long tradition of village politics, the basis of the *samiti,* or general assembly, of the Vedic period, and of republicanism, the institutions of which developed around the eighth century. Gandhi's nonviolent revolution is an original form of protest, but it had its roots in indigenous ideology.

China, on the other hand, has a rich political tradition. The concept of the "Mandate of Heaven" anticipates the people's democratic right to revolt when the ruler has become unjust or ineffective. The *pao chia* system is a device for collective responsibility, and it is, quite possibly, the ancient crutch that supports the Communist concept of democratic centralism, as the "Mandate of Heaven" provided the indigenous power of the Communist revolution. The legalist school of government no doubt establishes ancient support for the totalitarian regime.

We understand, of course, that India and China had their size and ancient civilizations going for them before the period of colonialism. But these civilizations exerted an influence all over Asia that barely touched the Philippines. The influence of Islam, on the other hand, with its socially conscious tenet that its devotees cannot sleep soundly when there is a hungry man within a hundred miles, was arrested in Sulu.

The inaccessibility of the Philippines gave her the Christian religion and the panoply of Western democratic thought, the nineteenth-century enlightenment ideology of Jose Rizal, and the individualistic ideology of our contemporaries. What would have been our political culture, one wonders, if as an ancient base for freedom we had had a modified or even a corrupted form of the Chinese *pao chia* system? Could we have acquired readily the political habit of reconciling our private inclinations with the public good, our individual wishes with collective purposes? Or would ancestor worship have been transformed into a sense of historic responsibility?

But we must now take leave of these exciting speculations and look at ourselves more objectively. While it is undeniably true that four centuries of colonization left their mark on us, our very awareness, our own decision to be free, can only mean that we are prepared to account for ourselves. We cannot be forever holding other peoples responsible for our present condition. The foreign overlords are gone and Filipinos have taken their place: a native oligarchy has displaced the foreign one. The fact that we were colonized can no longer excuse us.

This society that we live in is of our own making. The fault is not in our stars but in ourselves.

Revolution, then, in whatever terms it is framed, under whatever principle, is fundamentally a moral act.

The Oligarchic Society

Ours tends to be an oligarchic society. This simply means that the economic gap between the rich and the poor provides the wealthy few the opportunity of exercising undue influence on the political authority. But it does not mean that all the rich and all the privileged constitute an oligarchic class, for many of them—in government, business, and even the clergy—are socially conscious enough to acknowledge the necessity of revolutionizing the social order. When I speak, therefore, of oligarchy, I refer to the few who would promote their selfish interests through the indirect or irresponsible exercise of public and private power.

What, to begin with, do we mean by "oligarchy"?

The Greek political thinkers who coined the term understood

oligarchy as the rule of the few, as opposed to the rule of the many, which is *democracy*. Aristotle considered oligarchy and democracy to be the principal conflicting forms of government, their distinction being defined with the understanding that the few are the rich and the many the poor. The principal issue is not whether the few were wiser than the many—the issue of aristocracy, which, according to Plato, found its perversion in oligarchy. Rather the historic conflict between oligarchy and democracy is over the political privileges of wealth, the rights of property, and the protection of special interests. As Plato observed, oligarchy arises when "riches and rich men are honored in the State."

Ancient political theory thus recognized the antagonism of the rich and the poor as the root of political conflict in any state. The Marxist theory of the class struggle is, in this sense, but a recent acknowledgment of an immemorial fact. Not that the rich and the poor are in a constant state of belligerence (for they can and do exist in harmony), but that their antagonism rises to the surface whenever the wealth of the few is used to the prejudice of the welfare of the many.

The concentration of a community's wealth in the hands of a small minority must result in an oligarchic society. When this society exists side by side with a democratic political authority, as in the case of the Philippines, the consequence is an oligarchic order, or an "oligarchic democracy"—a term employed in reference to the democracy of Athens, because only a very small percentage of that city-state's population—to the exclusion of women and slaves—enjoyed political rights. In our case, every citizen enjoys political rights, which, however, are not *effectively* exercised because of social and economic inequalities.

How is this so? In the first place, the intervention of wealth in the political sphere produces corruption. And when this practice permeates the whole of society itself, the result is social corruption and moral degeneration. We have seen in a previous chapter how this could lead to the failure of a glorious revolution. Now we realize that this condition can also promote a political culture which equates freedom with self-aggrandizement, and the politics of participation, so essential in a democracy, with the pursuit of privilege.

A society based on privilege is the inevitable result, to the extent that the masses themselves, following the example of those above them, seek their own middling and often illusory "privileges." Corruption at the top is matched by social corruption below. The oligarchic elite manipulates the political authority and intimidates political leaders; the masses, in turn, perpetuate a populist, personalist, and individualist kind of politics.

The permeation of society by oligarchic "values" is also accomplished through the control of the means of mass communication. It is no longer a secret that the displeasure of the oligarchs is communicated through radio and television commentaries and newspaper columns. The media have become the weapon of a special class rather than serve as a public forum. The so-called "editorial prerogative" has been used to justify what is best described as "selective journalism."

The control of the media has perpetuated the simplistic politics that have been obstructive of meaningful change, the "radical change" more honored in the pretense than in the fulfillment. It has been remarked how media owners soon reverse their social—progressive—ideas when it comes to their own labor problems. One must note that the popular prejudice against any increase in taxes, even when these are earmarked for development projects, has primarily been the handiwork of the media.

The freedom of the press is sanctimoniously invoked whenever the work of the media is criticized. But is their hospitality to the most spurious statements and the most outrageous allegations a fair step in, say, improving the quality of political debate or keeping the people well informed? Do the media not promote the decadence of the masses by reducing the discussion of national issues to the level of entertainment? The usual excuse is the "low taste" of the masses, but pandering to it, exploiting it, assuming this judgment to be true, cannot deserve the abused name of "public service."

Quite revealing is the fact that the very radicals with whom the media pretend to sympathize make allusions to the "reactionary press." The sweeping accusation is that the press will lengthily and noisily commit itself to the peripheral issues of our society but not to the fundamental ones, for example, the question of private property.

There can be no other interpretation of the cry for "radical change" than the alteration of the manner with which we recognize the right to, and enjoyment of, private property. But the media have maintained their "high objectivity" by not commenting on the issue; they have contented themselves with reporting the statements of constitutional delegates and other public figures, thus displaying a noncommittal attitude that is uncharacteristic.

Yet the issue is inescapable. As I have said earlier, there are two alternatives: socialization and democratization.

However, we have yet to hear a voice from the media concurring with the proposition that the existing property laws, derived largely from our Spanish past, perpetuate the oligarchic society and ensure, in turn, the continuing corruption of the political authority. But what does radical change, the revolutionization of society, mean if not to strike at the roots of the present social system?

The truth is that government, the political authority, has become the easy scapegoat of the social and economic elite, absorbing the criticism and denunciation of the oligarchs while surreptitiously doing their bidding. After all, insofar as the oligarchy is concerned, changes in political leadership are merely a shift in political personnel. Political change is a process that consolidates privilege, which further entrenches the oligarchic order. Thus the ever-widening economic gap—inevitably, a cultural and political gap—between the rich and the poor.

Who suffers from bureaucratic favoritism? Who is made to

bear the cost of corruption? Who cries the loudest about high prices, but who pays for them? The bureaucracy offers no problems to the oligarchs, who have placed their men in it. The oligarchic bribegiver passes on the cost to the consumers. The oligarchic merchant "adjusts" to the price levels; in any case, what he suffers is a decrease in profit and not a sacrifice of his basic needs. Who is disadvantaged by the political order? Oligarchs either "buy" politicians or become politicians themselves.

The masses alone suffer. But perhaps they can still endure their suffering. The oligarchic propaganda is that somehow, with the election of "good men"—good men who please the oligarchs—mass poverty will come to an end.

In a perceptive book, *The Perils of Democracy,* Herbert Agar voiced a warning that has to be quoted in its entirety:

> We should not flatter ourselves that we can serve freedom by making men more kind or more unselfish. Various religions have tried this without noticeably increasing the proportion of the high-minded. We have no time to cure the human race; but good political institutions can make society more wholesome in a single generation—leaving men as they are, but protecting their weakness and encouraging their respect for justice.
>
> Thus the burden is thrown back upon us. The aimless search for "better men in politics" or a "higher political morality" can go on indefinitely. It requires no effort beyond lip service, which is restful. *But the search for a clearer definition and a deeper understanding of the politics of freedom is laborious and urgent.*

The search for "better men in politics," a "higher political morality," is the oligarch's ready answer to the problem of change. Not institutional change, not the restructuring of society, but "getting rid of politicians," the accursed of society without whose interventions, however, the needs of the masses could not have been satisfied by government, even if haphazardly. In this sense, the maligned politician, serving his own desire for power, is the stabilizing element of the oligarchic society, promoting the special interests of the privileged on the one hand and lulling the masses with patronage on the other. But why is the oligarchic master contemptuous of his political servitor, his stabilizing factor? Simply because there are more of him elsewhere—and because the politician is a servitor. But the politician accepts his status out of his own design: in time, should he stay in the oligarchical conspiracy, he too can become his own oligarch.

Under this system, the search for "better men in politics" is largely a pious sham. And when that sham is discovered, when it can no longer sustain itself by pandering to the few and humoring the rest, the masses must simply seize power and take the law into their own hands.

All this will depend, however, on the capacity of the political authority to reassert its will, which is the will of the sovereign people. It is the political leadership that is called upon to revive the atrophied will of the political authority. A reorientation must proceed; society must be revolutionized.

Ideology and Society

There is a school of thought which asserts that the changing of society raises the question of ideology. In fact, it is a criticism of our political society that its inadequacies may be traced to "ideological poverty." The criticism necessarily implies that ideology, as a system of thought and belief about society, is a unifying force, an organizing principle for the pursuit of collective ends.

If, indeed, we do not have an ideology, how do we go about acquiring one? And what should our ideology be? A consideration of the ideologies of other developing nations could perhaps yield us some answers.

At the outset we note three goals that we have in common with the new nations of Asia, Africa, and Latin America. These are nationalism, modernization, and democracy. Let us see how these goals fit into the ideological framework.

The nationalism of the Third World is new in that it departs radically from Western, or the old, nationalism. The impact of Western nationalism on Asia, Africa, and Latin American was imperialism; the impact of the new nationalism on the West is decolonization. The old nationalism colonized and exploited other people so as to develop its own societies. That is why Marxist hopes for a world proletarian revolution were grossly disappointed: the condition of the working classes of the metropolitan cities vastly improved because of the benefits of imperialism. It has been observed that all the demands of the *Communist Manifesto,* except the abolition of private property, have been realized in the capitalist countries of the West, thus weakening the appeal of communism. But we can go even further; the welfare and socialist states of the West have been established not by social revolution but by imperialism: colonialism built Western socialism. But the new nationalism, even with socialism or communism as a goal, cannot pursue the development of its own societies by imperialist means; it can only, if it chooses, "colonize" *its own*.

Salvador de Madariaga once asserted that there is such a thing as government colonizing its own people. This is a valid criticism of the totalitarian state, which strengthens and develops the society out of the exploitation of its own people. The mobilization of Cubans for the great sugar harvest and the Chinese people for the Great Leap Forward and the Great Proletarian Cultural Revolution, collectivization, and the rest, are instances of "colonization." But the moral issue is not exactly the same, for the exploitative government justifies itself with the socialization of wealth.

This, in fact, is the problem of the new nationalism: it has to develop its own societies in far less time and more rapidly than the old nationalism developed its societies with the exploitative machinery of imperialism. The leaderships of the new nationalism are, on the other hand, faced with the problem that no Western leader has had to face in two or three hundred years, the problem of a Moses, Solon, Lycurgus, and Hammurabi. Out of this difficult and complex condition have arisen the various ideologies of the developing nations.

There is common among these ideologies a commitment to democracy, on the one hand, and socialism (with the exception of the Philippines, Liberia, and Malaysia), on the other. But it is a democracy that no Western democrat would regard as such, and a socialism that will not satisfy the consummate Socialist. There are, to begin with, collective, guided or basic, and elitist democracies, or to cover a wider range, Mao Tse-tung's New Democracy. Ayub Khan sums up the more or less general concept of democracy in his four prerequisites:

1. It should be simple to understand, easy to work, and cheap to sustain.
2. It should put to the voter only such questions as he can answer in the light on his own personal knowledge and understanding, without external prompting.
3. It should ensure the effective participation of all citizens in the affairs of the country up to the level of their mental horizon and intellectual caliber.
4. It should be able to produce reasonably strong and stable governments.

The Western witness to the operation of these prerequisites in the developing societies is liable to dismiss the word "democracy" as either a fraud or a convenient label for an actually repressive ideology. For he will see one-party political systems, authoritarian rule, weak assemblies, press censorship, and militarism. But let him go back to the experience of his country at a similar period, and he will understand that the militarism of some new nations is as much the instrument of national unification as it was for the then developing Western countries; moreover, the new militarism looks inward, not outward for imperialist purposes. As for the other restrictions on freedom long customary among Western democracies, they follow from the principle that a strong government needs strong leaders, and from the historical fact that the Western democracies were not less "despotic" at a similar period of national development.

What we have in these various ideologies, which incorporate the term "democracy," is not so much a concession to political fashion, an attempt at popular deception, or a distortion of the real meaning of democracy, as an honest attempt to win assent to what their authors consider to be "the limits of the possible." Ideologies are often used to justify the leadership—even its errors and failures—to the people, but if that were their only purpose, ideologies would not be formulated at all. It would be sufficient to turn the military on the people. The Duvalier kind of despotism is, however, an anachronism and an aberration in modern politics, whether totalitarian or not, and the incessant communication between the leaders and the led, the striving for mutual identification, is a prelude to full democracy.

The ideologies are thus described better as "limited democratic ideologies," representing historical stages in the development of democracy in a certain country, similar, indeed, to the development of Western democracies, except that in the former case, the stages are formulated, espoused, and submitted to the people for acceptance and consent. This method, I think, is dictated by the necessity of controlling "the revolution of rising expectations," which if allowed full play may very well threaten stability. It is a device, in sum, for the more or less orderly, more or less peaceful and constitutional transformation of society.

This is as true of Communist states as of non-Communist states.

The non-Communist states have, however, a special problem with their domestic Communists, and this sometimes accounts for the ugly features of certain regimes. The Communists are quick to take advantage of "the revolution of rising expectations"; they ride on and manipulate the demands of rising nationalism and radicalism, treating the liberalism of one regime and the repressiveness of another with equal agility, eager to exploit both as opportunities for the eventual capture of state power. The Communist challenge, which blends happily with the inevitable demands of nationalism and radicalism, could very well act as a gadfly to the conservative tendencies of a developing society and would be welcomed as such—except for its explicit objective of overthrowing by armed revolution the existing political authority.

The *Communist Manifesto* asserts that Communists disdain to conceal their aim of armed overthrow of bourgeois society, but in fact, they conceal this behind nationalist fronts and constitutional radicalism. They are committed to armed revolution not as a last resort but as a final act, thus revealing bad faith in the human community. Let them be a constitutional party and they will be welcome in a free society, but it seems that this is possible only with a moribund party such as the American Communist party or in an industrialized country such as France, Italy, or Britain.

For the moment, however, communism is the violent, non-constitutional alternative to a genuinely democratic revolution—"a revolution within a revolution," in the democratic sense a counter-revolution. More than its doctrinal appeal, which relies heavily on nationalist passion, particularly in countries which are sensitive to colonialism, communism's imminent danger lies in its technique of revolutionary warfare.

To a certain extent, therefore, the ideologies of non-Communist countries, in spite of—or probably because of—their socialistic tendency, contain nuances of anticommunism, if only because the Communist states of Russia and China are regarded as big powers. This is understandable because the developing nations have reason to believe that the big powers use them as pawns in their international games. Moreover, the big powers are often considered to be the destabilizing factors in the world order; they exhaust their resources in conflict and prevent the establishment of international peace and harmony, which is the indispensable condition for the rapid and orderly development of the poor and small nations. This attitude among the developing nations suggests their becoming the world's first political communities that do not have to resort to any form of imperialism, inward or outward, to achieve their development. Sustained by the idea of the practicability and inevitability of world order, they contain the seeds of history's most profound revolution. Their conditions may yet give birth to a world ideology that is not merely a subtle expression of the desire of one powerful nation or another for dominance.

Quite certainly the new nations, if allowed to develop without the threat of subversion or domination and the Trojanism of some classes of economic aid, will eventually create societies which may well be the monuments to the creative intelligence of mankind. But they must at present develop themselves under severe and often discouraging conditions, largely relying on their political wits.

As for modernization, the issue turns on the question of "models"—Indian or Chinese? Insofar as the economic principle is concerned there is a strong family resemblance. Like China, India is committed to a "real socialist basis of society." The difference, as Nehru saw it, was in the existence of parliamentary institutions in India. But India is a "collective democracy" and China is a "people's democracy." Necessarily, Nehru thought that the establishment of a socialist society in India would be gradual, although he did not think that the Chinese mode of development was much faster.

The only Asian countries which make no concession, however rhetorical, to socialism, are Taiwan, South Korea, South Vietnam (which are best described as "militant" democracies), Malaysia, and Japan. It is interesting to note that the ruling Alliance party of Malaysia, which postulates "property-owning democracy," considers ideology "dogmatic" and prejudicial to "pragmatism." This has some sanction in political theory which

Andrew Hacker distinguishes from ideology in this graphic manner:

Theory	**Ideology**
Philosophy: a disinterested search for the principle of the good state and the good society.	*Philosophy:* a rationalization for current or future political and social arrangements.
Science: a disinterested search for knowledge of political and social reality.	*Science:* a distorted description or explanation of political and social reality.

In Hacker's sense, ideology is a justification of the present or future state of affairs. Its effectiveness depends not on its truth but on its persuasiveness, and where theory is either true or false, ideology is either effective or ineffective. It is the equivalent of Cassirer's "myth" and Plato's "royal lie."

But as any serious scholar knows, there is a bit of ideology in every theory and a bit of theory in every ideology. The line is not easy to draw. The common observation is that while a theory is abandoned the moment it is shown to be false, an ideology is not; moreover, it is often impervious to refutation, since ideology presupposes "a conditioned mind," which cannot see things in any other way.

Be that as it may, the prevailing ideology in the Third World is a limited socialist or "collective" democracy.

Considering that we share the same goals of nationalism, modernization, and democracy, why has the Philippines never formulated a limited socialist-democratic ideology? One reason is the nature of our "apprenticeship" in democracy. From the earliest days of the American occupation, everyone assumed that Philippine independence would be restored at a definite date. In barely a century personal freedom, individualism, and private initiative became deeply ingrained in the society as enduring values.

The "free enterprise" economic system, on the other hand, found favor wih the advanced classes in Philippine society. For many years this system, along with the democratic political order, offered a high social mobility.

Another reason is that the leaders of the Philippine struggle for independence, owing to the autonomy of Commonwealth politics, did not have to go into exile to pursue their objectives. In the case of the other new nations, their leaders were exiled, and most of them were drawn to the socialist groups in Europe, which of course were firmly opposed to imperialism and colonialism. From these socialist groups the exiled leaders learned the technique of mass political organizations.

Thus the dominant principle in Philippine political society is by contract "unlimited" democracy and a "free enterprise" economic system. However, there is a socialist and communist minority whose organizational aim is to politicalize the masses —that is, forge them into a mass revolutionary party. This minority provides the friction in society, the antagonism between the classes, insofar as their objective is the armed overthrow of the existing political and social order. Their appeal, now as before, rests on the glaring economic gap between the rich and the poor.

This social and economic setting of Philippine democracy calls for radical change. Because the political culture abets the *status quo,* that too must be changed radically. The question is whether these objectives necessitate the formulation of an ideology. Now an ideology should reflect the historical experience, hopes, fears, and expectations of a people. No two nations are exactly alike, no two revolutions identical. Living as we do, therefore, in a revolutionary age, the ideology for the remaking of society or the making of a new society must necessarily reflect the tendencies of the time.

In this sense, an ideology need not be a rationalization or a distorted explanation, let alone the justification of special or class interests; it must fill a general and vital need of human beings in a given community. My formulation (in chapters 3 and 4) of the Democratic Revolution is markedly theoretical; however, it was not undertaken for the academic exercise. The purpose was to offer an understanding of the times and a practical national guide. The theory, therefore, of Democratic Revolution is the ideology that seeks to transform society. Democracy, in sum, *is* the revolution.

On this basis do we look forward to a new society.

Toward the New Society

Whether the intention is to recast, radicalize, transform, or modify the social order, the result will inevitably be a new society. But it is easy to get transported with utopian visions. Herbert Marcuse suggests in his *Essay on National Liberation* that the utopian socialism is now relevant and realizable because of superindustrialism. That may well be so, but for us in the poor nations of the world, the vision must be according to our measure.

Until the superindustrial nations of the world can miraculously agree on an effective plan to infuse the Third World with their affluence, the new nations will have to design their societies according to the indubitable fact of their poverty. In the present world order, these nations cannot develop themselves fast enough to catch up with their problems. Poverty is the principle of life in Asia, Africa, and Latin America. Their peoples will not wait for economic development and political and social change to follow one another in a grand, stately sequence. This was possible in the era of imperialism; it is impossible now.

The communications revolution has widened human horizons to a considerable degree without providing the world's poor with the means, the technology, and the resources to reach out for them. Ironically, the world's poor look to their governments—their leaders and pacesetters—to provide these means for them.

Add to this the unceasing criticism by the Western press of these embattled regimes; the sanctimonious condemnation of the corruption of one society and the inefficiency of another, compounded with the noises made by the local elite, whose perceptions are colored by alien standards, and one appreciates the nearly hopeless plight of besieged societies.

But there is no use lamenting the conditions. The essential thing is that they must be faced, that something must be done about them within the limits of the possible, however restrictive these may be.

The conservative who asks how "a small pie" can be divided among so many millions may believe he is being hard-headed, but to the deprived masses, he is merely anxious about preserving his share. On these terms—and not on any "socialist bias"—the principle of private property is challenged in the developing countries.

Another hard-headed view is that economic development demands strictly economic decisions, that among these is to adjust to the fact that industrialization would require the exploitation of the working masses. When prices rise, for example, there should not be an increase in the minimum wage. But the economics of the masses is a political reality: the masses cannot be exploited without provoking a revolutionary situation. Not even Poland, with all the tight control of a Communist state, could escape the ire of the working masses.

Whatever "the size of the pie," therefore, the democratization of wealth and property must proceed, if the alternative of socialization, or the abolition of private property, is to be avoided. Democratization simply means the "sharing" of private wealth with the entire society, and this calls for the regulation of property for collective human ends. Private wealth and property are not abolished, for this would stultify private initiative and turn man into a pure collective being. (As Winston Churchill wisely observed, "no man is wholly an individualist or wholly a collectivist.") But the unbridled use of wealth and property mocks the ends of human society, for it accomplishes "the elevation of the few and the degradation of the many."

In this profoundly social century, the wealth of the few, like the power of the few, is a violence on the poor; it becomes, when exercised irresponsibily, a new barbarism. Just as power can be democratized by popular representation, free speech, and other free institutions, private wealth should be democratized by regulation for the worthy ends of human society. The Communist answer to the violence of wealth is its abolition, but this alternative also strikes the very heart of human initiative; more than that, it tends, in the pursuit of collectivist ends, to restrict the precious area of personal freedom. I should be emphasized at this point that our concern with private wealth and property is based on democratic principles, for while communism destroys personal freedom, the unrestricted control of wealth and property by a few private individuals similarly restricts the personal freedom of the rest. As Alexander Hamilton observed some two hundred and fifty years ago, the man who has control over another man's subsistence also exercises control over his will.

We envision, therefore, a new society in which equality of opportunity is not a fraud but a fact. An oligarchic society may sincerely believe in equality of opportunity, but so long as there is a wide economic gap, the opportunity does not in fact exist. True equality of opportunity begins at the *starting line,* when a human being is born. This simply means that a few should not be born "with everything" while the many start life with nothing.

When we proceed from this premise, everything else follows: the radicalization of society begins.

Part Two

THE NEW SOCIETY

| 6 |

THE HOUR OF DECISION

I did not become President to preside over the death of the Philippine Republic.

This much was my resolution when the last word of *Today's Revolution: Democracy* was written on September 7, 1971. At that time I had already suspended the privilege of the writ of habeas corpus in some parts of the country. One year and fourteen days later, I signed the proclamation placing the entire Philippines under martial law.

The sequence of events might very well suggest to the reader that I had been deliberating over the martial-law decision for more than a year. There is an element of truth in this. But until the evening of Sunday, September 17, 1972, I continued to hope that we could proceed toward change and reform and realize in modest measure a Democratic Revolution, without having to accept the martial necessity.

On that long night, I sat alone in the private study of

Malacañang, the presidential residence, contemplating one document that stood out among the mass of papers on my desk. This was an extraordinary document because it was spurious. In earlier, less troubled times, it would have been dismissed quickly as a cheap and ludicrous political stunt. But within the context of the national condition and taken together with other documents, it revealed to me the reality and the scope of the danger to the Republic of the Philippines.

The spurious document was *meant* to be a true copy of a "plot" recommended to me by two dedicated generals, Fidel Ramos, chief of the Philippine Constabulary, and Fabian Ver, chief of the Presidential Security Unit and the Presidential Guard Battalion. The plot was for the "military to stage a series of bombings, kidnappings and assassinations 'to sow violence and terror in order to lay the groundwork for the imposition of martial law.'"

As a "true copy," the document did not require the familiar signatures of the two generals; for the purpose of propaganda, it was sufficient that their names were mentioned. In any case, this "technicality" would not prevent the news media from exploiting it the next day. The purpose was to portray me, the President of the Republic, as plotting, with the assistance of the military, against the very government and country I was sworn to serve; in the eyes of the people, I would be a conspirator and a traitor.

I was, of course, indignant. My impulse was to call in my press secretary to have him give a serious warning for the news media that this time my detractors had gone too far. But my instincts told me not to act out of passion or anger. It then occurred to me that the real intent of the spurious document was to provoke me into calling the news media, to establish it as a *fact* that I had telephoned them regarding the document. The story would be even more sensational, because a quick, angry reaction would create the impression that I was suppressing *what might well be genuine*. This realization incensed me even more, but most important was for me to understand the motive or motives behind the intricate plot.

I was not unaware of the determined hate-campaign against me in the news media of the time. More than any President I had suffered abuse at the hands of my opposition, my critics, my enemies, and all shades of commentators. As a politician I was inclined to take all the accusations, however vicious and irresponsible, as a sad if necessary part of democratic politics in our country. So long as I could answer the charges whenever necessary, the facts if not the truth would emerge. I also knew that it was becoming increasingly difficult to present the government's side. The news media, especially the commentators, were beginning to act as a political opposition rather than as a responsible observer of men and public events.

All the same, I had to find out why the propaganda against me, my family, and my administration had sunk to the lowest level, portraying me as a conspirator and a traitor. It was evidently extremist, but for what reason? In the first place I knew that the political opposition was confident about the national elections, which were merely fourteen months away. I recalled that in my own campaign in 1965, my strategy was merely to exploit the issues already current against the incumbent administration without having to fabricate new ones, certainly without doing anything so vicious as branding the President and high-ranking members of the military establishment as conspirators and traitors.

I have never spared myself in dealing with critical matters. In this instance, I faced squarely the possibility that my enemies did not desire merely my political downfall: they wished me dead by an assassin's bullet.

Now, if this were simply the purpose, the problem was personal and not an affair of state. As a matter of fact, I had earlier steeled and somewhat secured myself against this possibility. When I first heard of an elaborate assassination plot against me, I demeaned myself without, as much as possible, demeaning the presidency, by paying a visit to one of the leading oligarchs at his seaside residence. My purpose was to upset the plot's time-table by a gesture of reconciliation that distressed my friends and supporters and disillusioned a great number of our people. Still, I took this calculated risk to protect the integrity of the presidency. The assassination of one President could very well lead to the assassination of the next, and so on. This was one "first" that I was willing to forego.

The assassination, then, was not the new element in the spurious document. There was another possibility: that of a forced resignation in view of the "fact" that I was conspiring against my own government! By this time bombing incidents and assassinations of town officials had already occurred. The seeming impotence of government against these outbursts of terror and violence was now going to be presented as proof that government itself instigated the lawless acts. Given a little more time and sustained propaganda, the people could, it was hoped, be manipulated into believing that this was the truth. My forced resignation could then be accomplished through mass demonstra-tions, which would in turn precipitate a *coup d'état* by certain political leaders and elements in the military establishment. There was no other way: this was the new, disturbing element introduced by the fabricated document.

If the entire attack had been mounted against me personally, it was curious, in my judgment, that my detractors would at the same time discredit two generals. The evident intention was to implicate the military and thus destroy every shred of confidence in both the civil government and the armed forces. An im-mediate result would be the division of the government and the armed forces into two opposing camps. The consequence would be a *coup d'état* and an incipient civil war, with my forced resignation or assassination as the extraordinary occurrence mentioned in the July-August plan of the new Communist party of the Philippines.

I found this conclusion inescapable. If the intention were

to destroy me alone, the spurious document should have carried a forged signature of mine *directing* the two generals, Ramos and Ver, to conduct a reign of terror so that I could impose martial law. However, the fabricators chose to make the two generals the proponents of the plot, a device which suggested that my enemies were bent on undermining popular confidence in the discipline, dedication, and harmony of the military establishment.

On that long night on Sunday, September 17, 1972, I pored over every document on my desk, scrutinized every evaluation of raw and refined data, every bit of classified as well as unclassified information, and discerned little by little the anatomy of a plot against the government of the Philippines.

The Martial Necessity

Taking advantage of popular complacency about actual conditions, the political elite had arrogantly reduced to a comic opera the annual testimony of the defense establishment before the Philippine Congress. The media elite, on the other hand, castigated the military allegedly for concocting "budgetary Huks," or imaginary armed dissidents, for the purpose of increasing the budget of the department of national defense. But it had always been for me a source of scandal that the very Congress which spent the people's money in indiscriminate investigations of "subversives" in various organizations was also the most relentless and vigorous agency in exposing the military to ridicule whenever the latter testified about the state of rebellion in the country.

The fact is that there has been a continuing state of rebellion in the Philippines since the birth of the Republic. I do not have to cite the testimony of ranking members of the armed forces of the Philippines or of the intelligence community to support this statement. There is the decision of the Supreme Court promulgated on December 11, 1971, in the case of *Lansang et al. v. Garcia, etc.,* in which the question of the constitutionality of the proclamation suspending the privilege of the writ of habeas corpus was at issue. This decision was arrived at cautiously by men of prudence and wisdom.

That the strength and intensity of activities of the Communist movement rose and fell according to the strategy of world communism and the local circumstances need not blind us to the fact that it has been, and remains, a continuing threat to the well-being of the Republic. Any President before me could have confronted the martial necessity, as, in fact, Elpidio Quirino did in suspending the privilege of the writ of habeas corpus in 1950. But the political assumption was that the armed forces could contain the armed Communists while the entire society remained what it was, a fertile ground for the sowing of subversive and rebellious ideas and intentions.

To be sure, the perception by the armed forces of the state of rebellion was more acute than that of the civilian authority. The reason for this is obvious: it was the armed forces which offered lives in the fight against the insurgents. In return, their leaders and officers had to face the annual comic ceremony before the Congress.

That the military had made mistakes in the subtle war against the insurgents cannot be denied; or that in certain instances their members abused their authority, which prompted reforms. But nevertheless the effectiveness of the armed forces was affected by the seeming lack of support given them by the civil authorities.

Thus, for many years there was a comic war in which earnest blood was shed and serious treasure was expended; while Philippine society continued to be corrupted by privileged wealth and public power, the armed forces had to contend with an enemy which could not be defeated by bullets alone.

Nevertheless, under a deeply ingrained discipline, the military pursued its assigned function of protecting the Republic. Every year, as one of its duties, it prepared its "contingency plan";

during my term, this was OPLAN *Sagittarius,* which was given a sinister implication by the opposition. As a matter of fact, my detractors and enemies derived the logical implications of their spurious document from this "contingency plan." In any case, the armed forces were protecting the government of a society which seemed indifferent to its own salvation.

These were the reasons for our complacency about our social conditions and our arrogance towards our armed forces. This attitude encouraged the subversives, despite their periodic containment, to carry on their work and acquire the revolutionary sophistication that they needed to succeed.

To the Communist revolutionary, the road to power is an essential *vigilant* waiting game. The successful Communist revolutionary is a disciplined man who fights while he waits and waits as he fights. His life is a combination of struggle and perseverance; to him, the so-called struggle for liberation is a persistent nibbling at the rotten framework of society until the final confrontation, the outcome of which has been predicted. As I saw it, on the night of September 17, 1972, the hour of the Communist revolution had come, not because its adherents had increased (which they had) but because the so-called pillars of the society that the revolution would destroy were themselves conspiring to bring about its destruction.

Before me were reports and documents naming places, dates, and occasions of meetings between insurgents and persons in high and strategic places, in politics, industry and media; of secret meetings among retired generals; of money used to support any student demonstrations so long as they were disruptive; of assignations with Communist leaders in metropolitan Manila; of foreign nationals engaged for the dastardly work of assassination; of high-powered arms smuggled into our shores.

Taken at their face value, these documents told different and unrelated stories. One was that the insurgents had certain well-placed friends and supporters; another was that an unscrupulous band was smuggling high-powered arms; still another was that the demonstrations were being used for political purposes; and, of course, that a group was plotting my assassination. The people involved in these schemes could have nothing whatsoever to do with one another; they were simply going about their business, even if these happened to be illegal.

But with the spurious document before me, I could not dismiss the thought that they were all somehow related, and that if I reached out for more information, called for more consultations among my various friends and advisers in the military, the judiciary, and in the political and economic fields, I could identify the suspicion that was nagging me.

I made several phone calls and demanded answers to endless questions. I did not expect anyone to have a clear picture, but the vague patterns I obtained from several sources crystallized in the commanding heights of the presidency, the one office in any country which has the available resources for a unified view.

I wanted to know, first of all, why a group of otherwise responsible men would plot the assassination of their President. Mere hatred was not enough. Revenge was too obvious; it could only be for profit or gain. What was to be gained? Power would seem to me the most seductive motivation. But what would be the immediate consequence? So that the Vice-President of the Philippines would succeed me? I could not go along with this explanation. For a powerful group, apart from the Communists, to profit from my assassination, the plan must go beyond my death, which was secondary, a mere occasion. An occasion for what? The *capture* of government.

It could not have escaped the plotters that my assassination would be avenged. They must have been well aware of this consequence, and must have prepared for it. This could only mean, therefore, that the plotters were fully prepared for the violence that would be provoked by my death.

This was the only possible logical explanation why reactionaries and radicals, rightists and leftists, could get together, as they did, with of course their own respective plans for dealing with the situation. The reactionaries needed the radicals to harass the government with their demonstrations in the cities, and with their armed comrades' terroristic sorties in the country-side. The growing confidence and boldness of the Communist revolutionaries and their front organizations were reflected in the military encounters with the New People's Army in several provinces, the space and time devoted to the Communists' littlest pronouncements in the news media, the blatant cries of "revolution" in the streets of Manila and in the corridors of our universities, and the public courtship of the marchers by our highest officials. Far from being concerned with the state of social order, the political and economic elite involved in politics cried for reforms which could not be achieved because of the obstruction and opposition they themselves raised. They publicly cried for reforms while privately they opposed them, thus contributing to the general frustration and the continuing advance of the rebellion.

Yet the rightists and reactionaries were not organizing for suicide; they were not offering their necks to the Communist hangman. Clearly, what they wanted was to blame the anarchy and disorder on the President and to have him forcibly deposed and assassinated. In the ensuing confusion and bloodbath their supporters in the military establishment would assist in a *coup d'état* and in one swift stroke risk further bloodshed with the imposition of their own illegitimate martial law. Who was to object to this? No one would make an outcry over a martial law that *had* to be imposed, ostensibly to stop the bloodshed. Has there been any outraged cry over the martial law of Indonesia? The simple reason is that after so much bloodshed, the most ruthless order would be desirable.

But how about the Communist revolutionaries? Were they blind pawns in the reactionary game? It could not have been unknown to them that man for man, weapon for weapon, they were inferior to their reactionary allies, and that, in the end, these would turn against them.

The Communists themselves had no illusions about the good faith of their temporary allies. They relied on the chaos and the inevitable suppressive measures to advance their thesis that the society was fascist and thus was unworthy of popular support. Theory and experience have taught them that a rightist coup would be the dying gasps of a semicolonial, semifeudal, reactionary society. If the reactionary Right was willing to help them, this was acceptable to the Communists, who believe in Lenin's dictum of giving the class enemies "enough rope with which to hang themselves."

Both the reactionary Right and the radical Left found a common focal point and symbol for their plans: Ferdinand E. Marcos. By concentrating on the singular person of the president, the conspirators on the one hand, and the revolutionaries on the other, were able to concretize for their propaganda purposes the complexities of social unrest and the justification of their aims. This is a standard technique of propaganda warfare: the creation of a scapegoat, a sacrificial lamb.

On the basis alone of the Communist insurgency, I could have proclaimed martial law earlier.

The Supreme Court of the Philippines, in its decision already referred to, dated December 11, 1971, in the case of *Lansang et al.* v. *Garcia, etc.* (G.R. No. L-33964), traced the history of this rebellion, thus:

> As regards the first condition, our jurisprudence (*People* v. *Evangelista*, 57 Phil. 373; *People* v. *Evangelista et al.*, 57 Phil. 354; *People* v. *Capadocia*, 57 Phil. 364; *People* v. *Feleo*, 57 Phil, 451; *People* v. *Nabong*, 57 Phil. 455) attests abundantly to the Communist activities in the Philippines, especially in Manila, from the late twenties to the early thirties, then aimed principally at incitement to sedition or rebellion, as the immediate objective. Upon the establishment of the Commonwealth of the Philippines, the movement seemed to have waned notably; but the outbreak of World War II in the Pacific and the miseries, the devastation and havoc, and the proliferation of unlicensed firearms concomitant with the military occupation of the Philippines and its subsequent liberation, brought about, in

the late forties, a resurgence of the Communist threat, with such vigor as to be able to organize and operate in Central Luzon an army called HUKBALAHP, during the occupation, and renamed Hukbong Mapagpalaya ng Bayan (HMB) after liberation—which clashed several times with the armed forces of the Republic. This prompted then President Quirino to issue Proclamation No. 210, dated October 22, 1950, suspending the privilege of the writ of *habeas corpus,* the validity of which was upheld in *Montenegro* v. *Castañeda,* 91 Phil. 882. (See also, *Nava* v. *Gotmaitan, Hernandez* v. *Montesa,* and *Angeles* v. *Abaya,* 90 Phil. 172). Days before the promulgation of said Proclamation, or on October 18, 1950, members of the Communist Politburo in the Philippines were apprehended in Manila. Subsequently accused and convicted of the crime or rebellion, they served their respective sentences. (*People* v. *Nava,* L-4907, June 29, 1963; In re *Jesus Lava* v. *Gonzales,* L-23048, July 31, 1964; *People* v. *Nava,* L-5796, August 29, 1966; *People* v. *Lava,* L-4974, May 16, 1969.)

The fifties saw a comparative lull in Communist activities, insofar as peace and order were concerned. Still, on June 20, 1957, Rep. Act. No. 1700, otherwise known as the Anti-Subversion Act, was approved, upon the ground stated in the very preamble of said statute —that

". . . the Communist Party of the Philippines, although purportedly a political party, is in fact an organized conspiracy to overthrow the government of the Republic of the Philippines, not only by force and violence but also by deceit, subversion and other illegal means, for the purpose of establishing in the Philippines a totalitarian regime subject to alien domination and control;

". . . the continued existence and activities of the Communist Party of the Philippines constitutes a *clear, present* and *grave* danger to the security of the Philippines (emphasis ours); and

". . . in the face of the organized, systematic and persistent subversion, national in scope but international in direction, posed by the Communist Party of the Philippines and its activities, there is urgent need for special legislation to cope with this continuing menace to the freedom and security of the country . . ."

In the language of the Report on Central Luzon, submitted on September 4, 1971, by the Senate Ad Hoc Committee of Seven— copy of which Report was filed in these cases by the petitioners herein—

"The years following 1963 saw the successive emergence in the country of several mass organizations, notably the Lapiang Manggagawa (now the Socialist Party of the Philippines) among the workers; the Malayang Samahan ng mga Magsasaka (MASAKAK) among the peasantry; the Kabataang Makabayan (KM) among the youth/students; and the Movement for the Advancement of Nationalism (MAN) among the intellectuals/professionals. The PKP has exerted all-out effort to infiltrate, influence and utilize these organizations in promoting its radical brand of nationalism. (See page 22 thereof.)"

Meanwhile, the Communist leaders in the Philippines had been split into two (2) groups, one of which—composed mainly of young radicals, constituting the Maoist faction—reorganized the Communist Party of the Philippines early in 1969 and established a New People's Army. This faction adheres to the Maoist concept of the "Protracted People's War" or "War of National Liberation," Its "Programme for a People's Democratic Revolution" states, *inter alia:*

"The Communist Party of the Philippines is determined to implement its general programme for a people's democratic revolution. All Filipino Communists are ready to sacrifice their lives for the worthy cause of achieving the new type of democracy, of building a new Philippines that is genuinely and completely independent, democratic, united, just and prosperous.

"The central task of any revolutionary movement is to seize political power. *The Communist Party of the Philippines assumes this* task at a time that both the international and national situations are favorable to taking the road of *armed revolution. . . ."* (Emphasis supplied.)

In the year 1969, the NPA had—according to the records of the Department of National Defense—conducted raids, resorted to kidnappings and taken part in other violent incidents numbering over 230, in which it inflicted 404 casualties, and, in turn, suffered 243 losses. In 1970, its record of violent incidents was about the same, but the NPA casualties more than doubled.

At any rate, two (2) facts are undeniable: (a) all Communists, whether they belong to the traditional group or to the Maoist faction, believe that force and violence are indispensable to the attainment of their main and ultimate objective, and in accordance with such belief, although they may disagree on the means to be used at a given time and in a particular place; and (b) there is a New People's Army, *other,* of course, than the armed forces of the Republic, and antagonistic thereto. Such New People's Army is *per se* proof of the existence of a rebellion, especially considering that its establishment was announced publicly by the reorganized CPP. Such announcement is in the nature of a public challenge to the duly constituted authorities and may be likened to a declaration of war, sufficient to establish a war status or a condition of belligerency, even before the actual commencement of hostilities.

We entertain, therefore, no doubts about the existence of a sizeable group of men who have publicly risen in arms to overthrow the government and have thus been and still are engaged in rebellion against the Government of the Philippines.

Nevertheless, I was inclined to evade the martial necessity despite the growing cogency of the military estimate of the national condition. I reasoned that with the suspension of the privilege of the writ of habeas corpus and the continuing sophistication of the armed forces in the art of counter-insurgency, the Republic could exist, as it had long existed, with a more or less controlled state of rebellion. I was somewhat under the influence of the liberal view that a certain dose of subversion in society was a spur to social reform. But this presupposed an agreement of fundamentals on the part of the ruling cliques in society.

With the rapacity of the reactionary Right, which itself would promote and welcome disorder to realize its ends, this liberal approach to rebellion appeared imprudent. In the past, despite the reactionary nature of the oligarchy, the news media and other public forums repudiated violence as a means of achieving narrow political ends. For this reason the Republic could exist with a more or less contained state of rebellion.

On January 7, 1972, upon the advice of both military and civil government officials, I lifted the suspension of the privilege of the writ of habeas corpus. As had been predicted by those who opposed this move, the lifting of the suspension marked the escalation of the efforts of both the leftists and the rightists, as well as of the Muslim secessionists, to employ violence, terrorism, and subversion against the Republic of the Philippines.

We had succeeded in penetrating the secessionist bands of the Muslims in Mindanao and had received confirmation of the intelligence report that intensive training was being undertaken for a possible large-scale offensive against military installations and personnel in Mindanao and Sulu as early as 1971. We also received disturbing reports, later confirmed, that firearms in large quantity were being shipped into the country through the southern backdoor from foreign sources.

Kidnappings and robberies became common not only in Manila but also in other centers of population in the country. In the City of Manila the water mains of the potable water distribution system were bombed and destroyed, cutting off the water supply in several instances. Power became the favorite target of saboteurs. Explosives were their favorite weapons. Crowded areas began to be bombed, resulting in casualties among innocent bystanders. Even the City Hall of Manila was not free from such attacks.

The communications system was occasionally paralyzed. Bank robberies and kidnappings were so intensified that many of the well-known families sent their children abroad, then later followed in precipitous flight from the Philippines to foreign lands for security. In many instances investments and property were sold at a loss.

Anarchy had taken over from the local police as well as the constabulary, who were prevented by both political interference and corruption from taking any initiative in preserving order.

The plans of the Maoist Communists were formalized in what is referred to in intelligence reports as the "Tarinsing documents," which were captured by the military from a Maoist field headquarters in the town of Cordon, Isabela, a province in the northeastern part of the Island of Luzon. Outlined in them were the plans of the Communist party and the New People's Army to concentrate not just the usual type of violence but assassination, terrorism and kidnapping in the City of Manila, in preparation for a general program to bring about what Communists have always referred to as a "revolutionary situation."

The government had also penetrated the group of former officers of the armed forces of the Philippines who were conspiring to mount a *coup d'état* and take over political power after the liquidation of the President.

The diary of one of the conspirators, a ranking colonel in the reserve force, had been taken into custody. It revealed the details of the plan, including the identities of persons in and out of government and the armed forces of the Philippines who were coprincipals in this plot.

Several documents from our foreign informants came into the hands of the intelligence authorities which confirmed the dangerous nature of the Muslim secessionist movement and its infiltration by the Maoist elements.

All this was strengthened further by reports of *datus,* or traditional chiefs, of hill tribes in the mountains of northern, eastern, and central Mindanao, in the southern part of the country, who reported a seven-month seminar and training being conducted by subversives in Mindanao.

At about the same time, after the departure of one of our state visitors, President Suharto of Indonesia, a serious assassination plot against me was confirmed with the government's penetration of the group of participants in the conspiracy.

The sophistication of weapons utilized, the entry of foreign explosives experts and criminal elements (American and British) demanded the closest scrutiny and surveillance of this group.

After the capture of the "Tarinsing documents," the floods of July and August which inundated almost all of Central Luzon, including Manila, compelled me to proclaim a state of emergency, as several hundred casualties were reported. The destruction of the road system, and of the levees, river dikes and flood control system throughout the big plains with an area of about 200 kilometers by 100 kilometers, shifted our attention to the immediate and urgent requirements of survival and rescue. The emergency required my immediate departure for the field and my stay there for several months.

On or about July 4 occurred what is now referred to in government reports as the Digoyo incident. The *MV/Karagatan*, a ship that had come from overseas, landed about 3,500 firearms of the M-14 variety with corresponding ammunition, as well as medical and radio or electronics supplies in the village of Digoyo, in the Municipality of Palanan, which is on the eastern side of the Province of Isabela, facing the Pacific Ocean. Discovery before the firearms, ammunition, and other equipment could be brought inland and cached or distributed among the subversives resulted in military operations that ended with the capture of about 900 rifles, some rockets and rocket launchers, as well as radio equipment, and the destruction of some of the camps of the subversives in the jungles of the Sierra Madre mountain range in Isabela Province.

However, reports were confirmed of successive landings south and north of this area before the Digoyo incident. Inasmuch as the captured enemy personnel had confessed that the firearms, ammunition, and other military supplies came from foreign sources, the subversives obviously no longer depended on domestic sources of supply alone but on foreign suppliers as well. This posed a much greater danger to the Republic.

While I was in the field attending to the emergency created by the floods of Central Luzon, the secretary of national defense, Juan Ponce Enrile, reported to me that the leaders of the Communist party of the Philippines had met with a leader of the opposition political party (Liberal party). At the meeting they had discussed "a possible 'link-up' between the Communist party of the Philippines and the Liberal party in terms of funding, propaganda, political action, influencing, and utilizing government instrumentalities, including the armed forces, and the 'elimination of opposition' " to this condition. Also discussed was unified action by the two groups to counteract any moves the President might make against those engaged in rebellion.

(The various overt acts which brought about the state of despair and hopelessness that had immobilized not only government but the entire civilian population, are found in Proclamation No. 1081, included in the appendices. These left the countryside and even centers of population like Manila open to the activities of the subversives, and created a situation where the Communist party of the Philippines, through its spokesmen in the media—quoted like spokesmen of heads of state—was contemptuously proclaiming the impending take-over of the Republic by the Communists.)

I rushed back to Manila obsessed with one thought: the need to unite the people of the Philippines against the common enemy, the subversives, especially those who proclaimed themselves to be Maoist Communists. For this purpose I again went through the humiliating exercise of seeking to propitiate some of the oligarchs. I visited them in their houses, broke bread with them, and temporized on their demands for special favors from the government, hoping thereby to delay their fatal decision to place their resources, frankly and openly, at the disposal of the rebellion.

As I was flying by helicopter from the floods of Central Luzon, I was burdened by the thought of an impending famine because of the destruction of the crops in the area often referred to as the granary of the Philippines. I had been notified of the warning from other countries predicting a world shortage in staples such as rice, corn and wheat. Shortages in rice often had caused popular disturbances in Asia as had shortages in bread in other parts of the world. The ensuing riots and disorders often have unseated governments.

My fears were to be aggravated later when the floods were followed by a longer period of drought, which prevented replanting of the former flooded areas, and then by an infestation of *tungro* (a disease that attacks rice plants in Asia).

In Manila I reviewed all the intelligence reports and found many of them alarming. One report indicated that our village self-defense units, popularly known as the Barrio Self-Defense

Units, had been infiltrated by subversives. Even some communication lines of government were being utilized by rebels.

The contingency plan adopted by my administration to meet the possibility of internal threats was known by the code name OPLAN *Sagittarius*. We had taken the usual security precaution of setting up several dummy plans with this code name to identify possible security risks and leaks in our organization. I was disturbed to note that one of the dummy plans had come into the possession of the leaders of the political opposition party and was publicly discussed in the halls of Congress.

The most disconcerting report, however, came from both the secretary of national defense and the chief of staff. They reported that the operations of the armed forces of the Philippines and of national defense authorities were immobilized by a succession of events. The two officials explained that, forced into a corner by these events, they had to promise that the armed forces of the Philippines would not move against the subversives without the approval of the members of the opposition party who were also members of the highest security body in the Republic, the national security council.

Adroit maneuvering by both the political opposition in Congress and the media, which were now hysterically antigovernment, had compelled the Secretary of National Defense to call the executive committee of the national security council to a meeting at which leading members of the opposition Liberal party were present and at which the chief of staff had to reveal the entire scheme, concept, and operations of OPLAN *Sagittarius,* the government contingency plan against rebellion. On this occasion the opposition party leaders managed to immobilize the military authorities, as I have stated.

So while the men actively supporting, aiding, and abetting the rebellion were drawing out all the secrets of government, which included possible counteraction against rebellion, the Republic was now rendered almost impotent to take any action against its enemies, who were incessantly plotting treason.

I called upon the Liberal party for a common stand against

the Communist rebellion and subversion and offered it the possibility of a bipartisan political leadership in government.

My efforts were contemptuously rejected.

I was left with no other alternative than to move on, with the counsel of my conscience, in the exercise of presidential power to its constitutional limits. While I accept sole and complete responsibility for my decision, I cannot escape the sense that events, the thrust of history, and even the will of the people, somehow guided my hand to the deed.

In *Today's Revolution: Democracy,* written in 1971, I stated:

> We succeeded in 1970 in infiltrating the ranks of the Communist party, the New People's Army and the front organizations. Our sources of information are, therefore, highly dependable.
>
> For the past several years I have been studying the histories of countries that have been subverted or overwhelmed by various forms of conspiracies. These included the case histories of the mainland of China, Malaysia, Indonesia, Laos, Cambodia, Vietnam, the African states, Latin America, and most recently Jordan. Even the histories of the Nazi takeover in Germany and the French collapse before the Second World War were studied. This study taught one clear lesson and this was that a government, especially of developing states, can tolerate subversion or internal conspiracies for power up to a certain point. When such a point is reached, the illness of subversion or dissension becomes so widespread it paralyzes the will not only of the people but also of the political leadership. It immobilizes even the most normal faculties and facilities of defense and protection of the state.
>
> The secret of national survival is to mark this point of no return very well and for the political leadership to resolve that this point of deterioration should never be reached.
>
> This I had done as early as 1969 when I watched the growth of subversion in our country.

So, on the long night of Sunday, September 17, 1972, I saw quite clearly that the rightist conspiracy and the Communist rebellion had almost succeeded in rendering the government impotent to meet any crisis, that in fact this hitherto strange combination, given just the shortest time, would pronounce the death sentence on the Republic.

At the end of that September vigil, during which I exhausted all the possibilities in my mind, I found my duty—and the responsibility for the nation's destiny—forced on me by historical circumstances.

There were other options before me. The most tempting one was the establishment of a revolutionary government. This would have been swift, direct, and unremitting, a bold solution to the problems that had dragged the country down to violent disorder. But a revolutionary government would have led to unrestrained bloodshed.

The solution I wanted was one that would also fulfill a need I saw clearly to be a vital part of the entire problem, the need to establish a code of conduct for all—the military, the civil government, and the citizenry.

No matter how I turned the question and the answers around in my mind, one idea persisted, which I had to accept as the impeccable truth. Adherence to the Constitution was indispensable. I knew that we must go beyond the simple need of restoring order, to meet the other and even more important imperative of reforming society. Any reform, however, would be hollow and short-lived if it did not both challenge and satisfy the moral consciousness of our people. The time had come to prove that reform, even radical reform, could and must be attained under the Constitution; and that bloodshed was unnecessary and even prejudicial to our efforts to establish a new and compassionate society.

As will be explored further by a book I am now in the process of writing, *The Constitution and Martial Law*, the Philippine experiment is novel in the sense that it seeks a constitutional means of bringing about revolutionary reforms without the violence and bloodshed attendant to those revolutionary convulsions familiar in man's long history of seeking progress and change in his society.

This is the thrust of the original first book, *Today's Revolution: Democracy*.

Man has always brought about change by bloodshed.

What we seek to initiate is change without bloodshed.

This sounds simplistic and quite easy to accomplish and yet the sad history of mankind disproves this.

But we must formulate our own contribution to civilization and man's claim to a noble destiny. Formulate it and prove it with our own experience.

This would not only be to our profit, but from this venture we could provide mankind some guide or mechanism for the transformation of other societies equally burdened or corrupted by unjust social and economic or political systems.

For me, no less than for our people, the hour of decision had finally come.

THE SEPTEMBER 21 MOVEMENT

My decision launched what I have since called privately "the September 21 Movement," to mark the date I enforced Proclamation 1081. The name also confers distinction upon the groups whose wise and objective counsel was most valuable in the study and the execution of the proclamation; I cannot divulge their identities and composition, for their members should not share the burden of a responsibility that was mine and mine alone. Many of them would have had to obey my lawful orders anyway; but at the time, I wanted not simple obedience but a commitment to, and a full understanding of, the imperatives of national survival.

There is another reason for the appellation. This was the realization that the decision to impose martial law entailed much more than saving the Philippine Republic by restoring peace and order through military means. Everyone recognized the legal basis for martial law; this was the simplest thing of all. National decline and demoralization, social and economic deterioration, anarchy and rebellion were not just statistical reports: they were documented in the ordinary experience and stamped on the mind of every Filipino. But, as a study of revolutions and ideologies proves, martial rule *could not, in the long run,* make the Philippine Republic secure unless the social inequities and old habits which precipitated the military necessity were stamped out.

Hence the September 21 Movement. If martial law is to be of lasting benefit to the people and the nation, if the national discipline that martial law requires is to be justified, a government must lead a movement for drastic and substantial reforms in all spheres of national life. Save the Republic, yes, but to keep it safe, we must start a massive effort, an intense organized undertaking to remake society.

Inevitably, there was excitement over the thought of a new beginning. But there was wistfulness too, for could not the old sick society have cured itself without the extraordinary, seemingly painful step it was now being called to take? Unfortunately, the answer was no. The old society was, in the first place, the social and political elite manipulating what I called in *Today's Revolution: Democracy* a precarious democracy of patronage, privilege, and personal aggrandizement. Now our democracy was not even precarious any longer; it was besieged, on the brink of ruin. The sense of doom was not alleviated by the realization that the seeds of its inevitable destruction had been planted by the very elite which flourished in it. The old society *had* to go; it was no longer workable and could not be made workable ever again. Meanwhile, this very same society's affliction was devouring the state itself. If the political authority did not act and exercise its emergency powers, the death of that society would come about in a fratricidal clash of arms, a bloody social revolution.

I recalled my own summation of Philippine democracy, that it existed in a political culture which was populist, personalist, and individualist in orientation. My belief then was that

> . . . thus far, this culture has worked very well in its influence on political society. But there is no assurance that this will always be the case because of the modernizing—revolutionary—elements in a society which must, as a matter of course, revolutionize itself as an imperative of national development. The problem, therefore, is how the political culture may be modified so that the revolutionizing elements can be absorbed into the democratic system, thus achieving not only what is good in itself but also preventing the kind of revolution that is destructive of human freedom. (See part 1, chap. 2.)

But on September 21, 1972, the political culture clearly needed alteration rather than mere modification, and the remaking of society was an imperative not just of national development but of national survival. As for the kind of revolution that is destructive of human freedom, it could no longer be stayed without the use of extraordinary powers.

The Philippine Republic had been in a state of siege before, but it was always able to count on a constitutional opposition, which counterbalanced the party in power and replaced it through free, periodic, and popular elections. The methods of the political opposition were always within constitutional bounds and as such fulfilled an important prerequisite of a democratic society. Contrary to the insistent demand of critics, the survival of democratic processes does not require that political parties be distinguishable from each other; what is essential is that their methods of winning public power are constitutional.

In the 1970s, political opposition resorted more and more to unconstitutional methods. Mainly through the machinations of political leaders and their oligarch friends, funds were provided for radical demonstrations and private armies were created and supplied with high-powered weapons smuggled into the country. The political opposition connived and synchronized their activities with outright subversives. This made the *end* of winning public power justifiable by *any* and *all* means, even by threatening the security of the state. *The organization of popular discontent for the purpose of winning an election is democratic, but the sowing of anarchy, social violence, and rebellion is not.* The latter is not an instrument of constitutional opposition but of subversion.

This repudiation of an indispensable element of democracy, the constitutional opposition, forced me to conclude that the democratic order had broken down in the Philippines even before we were confronted with the martial necessity. As a matter of fact, the recognition of this necessity was hastened and became more acute because of it. The traditional and openly unconstitutional opposition, the Communist revolutionaries, had found common cause with the legitimate opposition, which had now become illegitimate, pursuing its ends *outside* of the democratic political machinery.

This analysis finally identified seven sources of threats to the Republic: the Communist revolutionaries, now divided into the "traditionalists" and the "Maoists"; the rightists with their plans for a *coup d'état;* the Muslim secessionist movement in Mindanao and Sulu (the two main islands which comprise our "southern backdoor"); the private armies and the political warlords, who were actually the power brokers in the old society; the criminal elements, which partly promoted and took advantage of the situation; the oligarchs, who sought by all means to maintain the *status quo* and were possibly allied with the rightist conspirators; and the foreign interventionists, evidence of whose funding was confirmed by the government through banks in Japan, Hongkong, and the United States of America.

The manifestations of the rebellion and subversion by both the leftist and the rightist groups, the secessionist movement in Mindanao and Sulu, the conspiracies for a *coup d'état,* and the assassination attempts, as well as other threats to the Republic that necessitated and legally justified the proclamation of martial law, will be discussed in detail in two other books now in preparation. One is a personal account by the author of his actions as President, tentatively entitled *Philippine President's Diary;* the second is a book on the law of the question, tentatively entitled *The Constitution and Martial Law.*

The foreign and domestic news media were faithfully reporting the deteriorating conditions in the country, but no attempt was made to analyze and evaluate them for the general reader. All they would do was to present those conditions and the developments connected with them, not as threats to the nation but as alleged failures of my administration. They disregarded completely the historical circumstances, the perspectives and motivations which had given rise to the perils which we now faced. It took the September 21 Movement to discern the pattern of conspiracy and subversion in the Philippines and thus give shape to, and identify, the fear of law-abiding Filipinos.

We have here a case of weak government and weak people, on the one hand, and power *factions,* on the other, all of which presumed to speak "for the people." Individual elements in the news media acted with various motivations, from downright involvement in the conspiracy to self-aggrandizement, in the form, among others, of "jumping on the bandwagon," that most comfortable means of locomotion among the unprincipled. With these motivations, the news media propagated national disintegration without analyzing its real and profound causes; it was not difficult for them to indulge in the exercise of blaming the government, whose measures and problems they would not deign to recognize. Faced, therefore, with a war which the factions made much of but which they chose not to acknowledge publicly in its full dimensions, the beleaguered government and besieged Republic could not move forcefully and effectively. The consequence was that the people, who relied on the picture presented to them by the powerful factions which had access to, or control of, the news media, had to live with their undefined fears and insecurities; and these, in turn, were ruthlessly exploited for the political objectives of the various unconstitutional oppositions.

Two analogous situations, by *no* means similar in *all* respects, immediately come to mind: the Vietnamese and the Indonesian. In the first, the machinations of powerful factions in a still unreconstituted political society spawned a "united front," precipitating a civil war or a "protracted war" in which the unarmed populace was the battleground; in the second, precipitate action on the part of Communist elements provoked assassinations and such bloodshed as to necessitate the complete military take-over of government.

My conviction has always been this: a revolution, should it become inevitable or necessary, could be undertaken by constitutional, orderly, and peaceful means, with the expansion rather than the destruction of human freedom as *the end*.

I had, however, no illusions about the capacity for bloodshed of either the Communist revolutionaries or the rightist conspirators. The Communists will sacrifice men for a program; the conspirators, who are in actual fact the fascists, will sacrifice men to self-interest. A fair regard for the expenditure of human lives is the difference that sets a democratic revolution apart; it is dedicated to the axiom that the state exists for man, and not man for the state.

The history of modern revolutions has a singular lesson for us: once whole populations have experienced fratricidal bloodshed they become docile and submissive to the dictates of the victorious faction. Thus, Communist regimes coming to power after a period of bloody revolution are able to command and manipulate a weary peple; the case is similar with Fascist regimes. This is *the* reason why weak, parliamentary, or democratic regimes, having once become unable to prevent revolution, are never restored again. Triumphant dictatorships learn from the weakness of democratic regimes and thrive on the consequent popular diffidence over another civil war. The Communist commitment to unceasing struggle is too strong for the modest dreams of an unorganized citizenry; while the politically organized self-interests of Fascists, if downright repressive, can only be resisted by a Communist-led social revolution. In either case, a weak people become nothing more than a pawn in a ruthless, ideologically determined, power game.

Why, then, let us ask ourselves, should we risk our survival, let alone our democratic future, by inaction, on the one hand, and half-measures, on the other? To be indifferent to the lessons of history is a heinous form of treason.

What was crucial, therefore, was a beleaguered democratic government's *will to resist*. The exercise of naked power alone, assuming that this was still possible, would not be enough, in my view, to save the Republic; there would have been a division in government itself, not to mention the military establishment. And the price would be too high for a country to pay. A democratic regime should always act according to its own laws; precisely for the sake of these laws it must act decisively. To put it in another way, a threatened Constitution should provide for itself its own means of survival. Significantly, it should invest the exercise of this *means* in the highest magistrate bound by oath to protect and defend the Constitution. We in the Philippines are blessed to have such a Constitution. Thus Article VII, Section 10, Paragraph 2 of the 1935 Constitution provides:

> The President shall be commander-in-chief of all the Armed Forces of the Philippines and, whenever it becomes necessary, he may call out such armed forces to prevent or suppress lawless violence, invasion, insurrection, or rebellion. In case of invasion, insurrection, or rebellion, or imminent danger thereof, when the public safety requires it, he may suspend the privilege of the writ of Habeas Corpus, or place the Philippines or any part thereof under Martial Law.

This provision, clear and comprehensive enough to protect the Constitution and the Republic from their enemies, indisputably sanctions the martial necessity without interjecting the supremacy of the military; it continues to uphold the supremacy of the civil over the military authority. Thus, except in crimes against the state, the civil courts continue to exercise jurisdiction over the entire legal system.

The Constitution, therefore, provides for its survival in a clear, orderly, and democratic manner; for the instrument used is not only legal but moral in the highest sense. It places the proclamation of martial law under the rule of law.

This resolves the eternal moral question of *ends and means*. The Constitution, being democratic in spirit and content, does not recognize means which are not *integral* with, or do not logically follow from, its ends, even though the end may be self-preservation itself.

Its enemies, on the other hand, have resorted to *exceptional* means, those of terror and violence.

As a constitutional measure, the proclamation of martial law must then take into immediate account the immobilization and dismantling of the unconstitutional opposition: the advocates and perpetrators of rebellion, the conspirators, the separatists, and the various lawless elements, which although not politically motivated, are actually displacing public power. (There is a point at which the scope and frequency of lawlessness becomes *criminal* rebellion, displacing public order with anarchy.) Thus, the apprehension list in the execution of Proclamation 1081 (proclaiming martial law in the Philippines) contained the diverse elements in society which individually and collectively, or in combination, constituted a grave and serious danger to the Republic.

But how many countries have such a constitutional and legal mechanism for a "crisis government"? And how can such a mechanism be utilized to bring about a restructuring of society so as to redress the unjust economic and social system it has fallen heir to?

This is the burden of the political leadership.

/ 8 /

THE REBELLION
OF THE POOR

The immediate judgment on the martial-law situation is best summed up in the report submitted to the U.S. Senate by Majority Leader Mike Mansfield (the report is also known to us as the Valeo report, having been written by Frank Valeo, U.S. Senate secretary, who made an on-the-spot survey a few months after Proclamation 1081):

> *Martial law was declared and is being administered at this time on a constitutional basis in the Philippines.* The military carries out the orders but it is the President who gives them. In this respect, the principle of civilian supremacy remains in the saddle. Barring the assassination of President Marcos, there is little likelihood of its being unseated.

The immediate purposes of martial law have been achieved, "in that a violent opposition has been silenced and a measure of order and discipline has been introduced into Philippine affairs." But this discipline, I must emphasize, is essentially one

139

that was *imposed* and had yet to be tested as an enduring basis of our social life until the plebiscite held from January 10–15, 1973, to ratify the new Constitution and the referendum held on July 27, 1973, on the continuance of martial law and the continuance in office of the incumbent President beyond 1973.

In this connection, the following observation of the Mansfield (Valeo) report is significant:

> To sum up then, beyond the ostensible objective of restoring law and order, martial law *has paved the way for a reordering of the basic social structure of the Philippines.* President Marcos has been prompt and sure-footed in using the power of presidential decree under martial law for this purpose. He has zeroed in on the areas which have been widely recognized as prime sources of the nation's difficulties—land tenancy, official corruption, tax evasion, and abuse of oligarchic economic power. Clearly he knows the targets. What is not yet certain is how accurate have been his shots. Nevertheless, there is marked public support for his leadership and tangible alternatives have not been forthcoming. That would suggest that he may not be striking far from the mark.

What is even more significant, however, is the report's reflection of the view of the September 21 Movement, that beyond the immediate purposes of martial law, there are other aims which "have to do with bringing about fundamental changes in Philippine society." An interlude of martial law that simply eliminated criminality and crushed rebellion and insurrection, although these in themselves are formidable tasks, would leave the country under the same social conditions which produced criminality and rebellion and would thus fail to establish long-term security for the Republic.

The fundamental reason for building a new society involves the outstanding fact of our age: the rebellion of the poor. This is a rebellion over which the might of government can have no avail, for the poor are, in many ways, *the people* for which governments exist.

From another perspective, Gunnar Myrdal, the Swedish economist, calls this rebellion the new nationalism and regards it, in the manner of most Western economists, as the desire of poor nations for economic development. But there is more to this rebellion that enables it to leave the imprint of its specific character upon our time. Quite simply, the rebellion of the poor reverses the traditional situation, in which society sits in judgment of the poor: now the poor sit in judgment of society. It proclaims that the poor, from this day on, will shape the societies in which they must live.

We are just beginning to realize the full significance of this historic reversal of roles between society and the poor. In every age but ours, the poor were generally resigned to their state and only when they were intolerably and particularly oppressed did they break into mass violence. All the same the paradigms of this mass violence were the food riots and land seizures rather than any demand for a new order: they either expended themselves or were presently quelled without altering in any manner the condition of the poor.

The great revolutions of mankind, on the other hand, while proclaiming the rights of man and enlisting the support of the masses, were nonetheless revolutions of the *unpoor:* as Marx showed, they established the dominance of a particular social class. This is not to say that the democratic revolutions of the nineteenth century had a deliberate class bias; simply, the ideological emphasis was political and the advanced revolutionary class of the period was the bourgeoisie. This very condition led Renan to observe that the majesty of the law impartially decreed that both the rich and the poor would be punished for illegally sleeping in the park. This ironic remark is just one among numerous others that date from the earliest societies: it demonstrates the compassion of societies for their poor.

The earnest of this sentiment is society's many charitable or compassionate *acts* for the poor: sharing the wealth, as it were, in every conceivable form and manner. The poor were those creatures that society or its more fortunate members *had to do some-*

thing for. This attitude still persists, but as we shall see, it has been losing its moral force.

> We live in an era in which scientifically, politically and sociologically poverty is an anachronism [writes C. R. Hensman in *Rich Against Poor,* an investigation into the realities of aid]. What man can find out about the earth, what he can get, use, build and manufacture is almost without limit. All over the world the poor have decided that poverty and exploitation are neither inevitable nor tolerable any longer. New forms of human organization for fighting the causes of poverty and living a humanly meaningful existence have been tested successfully. *The persistence of poverty needs then to be explained* [italics mine]. People in the centuries before the nineteenth of the Christian era had their conceptions of Utopia. But they could not have talked (as we can) in a matter-of-fact way about poverty as a transitional, historical phenomenon. It must seem strange to those who are impatient to see that every community and person is adequately fed, clothed, housed and equipped for modern life to realize that for nearly the whole of the history of civilized man poverty was not regarded as a social phenomenon or even a particularly unfortunate condition. Even morally sensitive thinkers with the noblest and most ambitious conceptions of what every man, woman and child was destined to achieve, were with few exceptions not concerned with *eradicating* it. Those to whom the poor yielded their rights and their substance—the rich and powerful were admired and honored. The main cultural tradition has tended to present the poor as less deserving of consideration, respect and service than the rich.

This realization, that poverty is a social product rather than the natural condition of man, was brought about by the rise of democratic radicalism in the West and the struggle against Western colonialism in the East. In the West, Marxism sponsored the proliferation of Socialist workers' organizations. These eventually led to the success of trade unionism, on the one hand, and the continuing existence and varying degrees of success of Socialist parties, on the other. Colonialism and imperialism, to which the Socialists were fiercely opposed, were not exactly unbeneficial to the poor of Western societies. Their societies developed and their living standards improved owing to the not inconsiderable wealth obtained from the colonization of other peoples.

Thus the rebellion of the poor, owing to the indisputable success of Western civilization, found its cause among the victims of colonialism. This rebellion was born out of the anticolonial struggles for national independence. Western colonialism spawned a rebellious elite which earned its legitimacy by espousing the cause of nationalism and identifying itself with the unspoken longings of the poor masses. The poor were told that their liberation from poverty depended on the success of the struggle for national independence. For the poor multitudes, the age of colonialism ushered in the age of commitment.

The dumb protest of centuries found a moral form—rebellion. Excited into common action, awakened to a promise of a better life at least, the poor *committed* themselves to the ideology of nationalism. They looked forward to the establishment, as far as they could conceive it, of a new society.

But the new society did not follow in the wake of national independence. The struggle for it did unite the poor with the various groups of colonial society, but as John Spanier observed in his book *Games Nations Play,* "once the opponent who united them is gone, there is little else to hold them together as a political, economic, and administrative entity; the centrifugal forces then begin to exert their pulls."

We behold at this point the contradictions of transitional societies, that problematical state of being torn between the old and the new: the desire for development opposed by values and institutions obstructing its attainment; the obvious need for unity offset by the anarchic pursuit of interest; the anemic struggle for power of various elites distorting the national consensus; and the aroused popular expectations, without any serious program for fulfilling them.

Social scientists from both the East and West have analyzed thoroughly the transitional societies to explain the poverty of their masses. The explanations may be valid. To the poor, who continue to see certain hideous spectacles unrelieved—the great gulf between them and the few who are rich, the graft and corruption, the discrimination of law and justice, the "ignorance" of the masses—the "explanations" explain everything except *their* poverty.

At this point the poor become a "combustible" people. Awareness of the utter hopelessness of improving their condition, while seeing the few enjoy the abundant life, may tempt them to any action that offers the slightest chance of success. A truism is that the miserably poor are as "reactionary" as the very rich; in any case, they are too abject to revolt. Crane Brinton in his *Anatomy of Revolution* confidently asserts that no one revolts for a standard of living.

Scholarly studies on revolution tell us that it is not among the impoverished and "advancing" poor that we shall find the potential for revolution. But modern communication, not to mention the dedication of agitators, tends to blur these handy distinctions. In spite of what orthodox Marxists and imitators may say, when Mao Tse-tung declared that "poor people want change, want to do things, want revolution," he was not drawing hard-and-fast distinctions among the children of poverty.

Let us remind ourselves that the poor had been enlisted in the anticolonial struggle for national independence on the strength of great expectations for a new society. Now they are being told that the new society will come only after they have made a new commitment: to nation-building. Thus the despair of the cognoscenti over educating the poor about contradictions of traditional societies. We know from experience that the poor, having known the galvanizing power of commitment, are not averse to either pursuing or renewing their commitment.

If there is one thing the poor completely understand in this revolutionary age it is the great potency of the *political act*.

In his study of Burma's search for identity (*Politics, Person-*

ality, and Nation Building), Lucien W. Pye observed that in transitional societies:

> This is also a time of faith in the miraculous powers of politics. The belief has been rampant that all aspects of life will be different with a change in sovereignty, with the elevation of new leaders to old offices, with the manipulation of new slogans and the worship of new symbols. Works of civilization which in other times were assumed to follow only from the patient application of skill and diligence and the acceptance of sustained efforts are now thought to be conceived by the potency of political acts. In the new countries, where politics unlimited is sovereign and where it is believed all problems can be solved by its methods, other activities tend to lose their charm and worth. Thus rationalization in politics has never been greater; never have more people been able to play the game with greater self-assurance that in doing so they are performing a public service. Older nations have been built upon the myth that if each seeks his interests, the interests of all will be served, new countries are trying to be built upon the myth that if each strives to get ahead in government and politics, the public good will be served.

The generalization, although simplified in parts, nevertheless applies to the present self-consciousness of the poor: they do believe in the miraculous powers of politics. Because of the imagined potency of the political act, they are confident that they can begin to shape society instead of merely being shaped by it. Whenever they feel that their societies seem to be unresponsive to their needs, they conclude that the reason is because they are not availing of their political power. Individually, separate from one another, the poor do indeed feel helpless. But they understand their collective power.

Transitional elites know the dimensions of this power, but they have fallen from leadership, all the same, because they failed to come to terms with it. Long used to manipulating the poor, the old elites through sheer radical rhetoric and "generous gestures" would indefinitely obtain for themselves the support of the poor. In many ways, the elites, Westernized as they were, approached the poor from a high horse, on the valid ground that

146 / The Democratic Revolution in the Philippines

they are the many. Thus, they would *do* things for "the people," or "the masses"; they would *"salve their wounds";* and would consequently be surprised, perhaps even embittered, should a counter-elite or competing elite be able, *against all reason,* to win the allegiance of the poor masses in destroying the old order.

It is characteristic of transitional politics to look upon the poor as nothing more than a base of power to be availed of in pursuit of sectarian ends. The common complaint of the poor, for example, is that they are important only during election campaigns. It has been shown time and again that the poor masses regard election campaigns not as genuine opportunities for radical change but as an occasion for "getting back at the crooks." But most of the time the poor during elections are choosing men who belong to an unchanging elite. Realizing this, the poor are inevitably disenchanted with the political process. and disenchantment leads to indifference and cynicism.

Beneath "the power of the few and the indifference of the rest," lurking behind the popular cynicism, is the conviction that things must get better. In the struggle for national independence, "We" were the people and their leaders against "They," the colonialists and imperialists; now "They" are the transitional elites which replaced the colonial ruling class and "We" are the poor.

This situation lends itself readily to the agitation of radicals and revolutionaries of the Right and the Left. However, the Communists, with their highly developed revolutionary theory and practice, are most skillful in exploiting the disenchantment of the poor and their capacity for commitment. As part of their strategy to manipulate the poor, the elites of transitional societies may grant concessions to them; in contrast, the Communists give neither aid nor comfort. Communist revolutionaries tell the poor that they can never get their due under any system in which they are not in command; in sum, the poor must liberate themselves by capturing state power through the Communist revolutionaries. Then and only then will the contradictions of transitional societies be resolved, and their captivity to neo-colonialism ended, a precondition for the creation of a new society very much to the dreams and aspirations of the poor.

Mao Tse-tung's vision, in so far as it goes, presents a hope for the poor:

> In a few decades, why can't 600 million *paupers,* by their own efforts, create a socialist country, rich and strong? The wealth of society is created by the workers, the peasants, the working intellectuals. If only they take their destiny into their own hands, follow a Marxist-Leninist line, and energetically tackle problems instead of evading them, there is no difficulty in the world that they cannot resolve.

This has a powerful appeal on two counts: the actual conditions of transitional societies suggest an impotency for change, while the making of revolution has about it an excitement and glory that revive the old enthusiasms and the hopes of commitment. Carrying a gun, erecting barricades, and shouting revolutionary slogans have a more serious meaning a more hopeful aura, than laboring monotonously in the factory or farm, especially in societies which seem to offer nothing substantial to the poor.

While the making of revolution captures the imagination and simplifies the problem of development, it postpones the necessary and continuing task of nation-building. As soon as the Communists capture state power, they impose on the poor masses a rigorous and totalitarian regimentation to promote their Communist aims. The revolution obviously is regarded as an exciting prelude to the regimentation that inevitably follows: the poor, having committed themselves to revolution and having made it with their blood and tears, are trapped and defrauded into accepting a discipline that they could have given themselves in the first place without the necessity of a Jacobin upheaval.

That the Communists doctrinally insist on the necessity of revolution does not alter the fact that revolution, under Communist terms, serves to indulge the wishes of the poor and expend their violence in order to make them malleable to the totalitarian regimentation of their lives. This is the *fraud* behind the Communist conspiracy, insofar as the role of the poor masses is concerned.

> Every mass movement has its distant hope [Eric Hoffer asserts in *The True Believer*], its brand of dope to dull the impatience of the masses and reconcile them with their lot in life. Stalinism is as much an opium of the people as are the established religions.

The radicals of the Right, on the other hand, ride on the demand of the poor for law and order and clean, honest government—but on their terms and not on the terms of the poor. To the radical rightists, it is a simple matter of applying the force of the state without altering the social structure in any manner. They would welcome martial law, for example, if it meant preserving the *status quo.* Hence the favored weapon of the radical rightists is the *coup d'état* or palace revolution.

No less than the Communists, the rightists speak righteously about the poverty of the masses. But they look upon their "concern" as a form of security for the rich minority and the privileged elites to which they belong. They will do *anything* for the poor except destroy the poverty-creating order. For they themselves are creating the hunger and the poverty, and the amenities of freedom that they so zealously defend are reserved for them alone.

The fraud in the violence of the Communists, on the one hand, and the radical rightists, on the other, is that in either case the poor are cheated of their demands for a new society. There are comparative differences between Communist and rightist regimes, but both are impositions on the poor masses. What prevails in the end is neither the ideology nor the commitment of the masses but the ideologies and commitment of the ruling classes.

After all this is said, the problem remains: how to confront the crisis of commitment of the poor. If the Communists alone can inspire their commitment, then communism will sooner or later prevail in our nation. But if the Communists are weak, though troublesome, then the rightists will exploit the commitment of the poor to the latter's disadvantage.

We know that the poor will commit themselves to an ideology which they believe to be in consonance with their aspirations. They are willing to accept the burdens of making a new society, for it is going to be *their* society.

Therefore an ideology for the new society must base itself on one ruling principle: the interests, objectives, and needs of the poorest of the working people take precedence over those of the rest. It has been suggested that this will require the *structure of a democratic politics,* or the process of genuine development will tend to go awry. National development means the participation of the poor, but such participation can only be expected if the ideology offered to them—the new society envisioned—pledges and fulfills an authentic transformation of the social order.

Thus the work of social transformation begins with the search for an ideology which makes the rebellion of the poor the basis of a new society.

Moral realism requires this ideological basis; the consciousness of the poor is permeated by a profound sense of being oppressed, not simply because the rich oppress them brazenly but because it is *poverty itself* that oppresses them. To be poor is to be without and, therefore, to be *an outsider* in the vibrant and meaningful political, economic, and social life of the modern human community. Above all, being poor is being invisible; violence makes the poor visible.

Of what good is democracy if it is not for the poor?

EQUALITY AND POLITICS

Equality is the fundamental demand of the rebellion of the poor: it should be the ideological force behind the New Society. How this egalitarian demand is understood is crucial to the distinction between the Democratic Revolution and the Marxist-Jacobin revolution.

The Marxist answer to the egalitarian demand is the dictatorship of the proletariat, which Maurice Duverger shrewdly describes as *an accurate continuation of the Jacobin theory of terror:*

> . . . Man is born good but capitalism corrupts him: In order to destroy the system of oppression, exploitation and alienation developed by capitalism, violence must be used. Violence against the state, in the first place, so long as it is in the hands of the exploiting classes: this means revolution. Next, when the working class has taken power, the force of the state is directed against the exploiters and used to destroy every trace of exploitation: this stage is the dictatorship of the proletariat.

In a society such as ours, in which the rich are too few and the poor too many, the Marxist-Jacobin approach has a ringing appeal. For the term proletariat, one simply substitutes the poor. By "expropriating the expropriators," or eradicating the rich, equality is achieved in one bold stroke.

The trouble with this formulation, however, is that the dictator-proletariat is itself *dictated* upon by an all-powerful party, while even among the poor there is a hierarchy of classes, beginning with the "advanced" proletariat, followed by the peasantry, the intellectuals, and the *petite bourgeoisie*. Moreover, there is a contemptible class, the lumpenproletariat, a term reserved for "the scum of the earth."

Stated in Marxist-Jacobin terms the rebellion of the poor is self-contradictory: it is unable to approximate the egalitarian ideal.

The reason for this lies in the heart of Marxism itself; equality is *exclusively* regarded as a relationship between social classes, hence, the solution to bourgeoisie domination is proletarian dictatorship. In sum, while the domination of one class is oppressive, the domination of another is not. But the egalitarian principle states that all men are equal, whatever their class, color, or creed; it is thus a condition of *each and every individual* in society. A man is not just a worker, a farmer, a teacher, or a capitalist: he deserves to be treated justly and equally as the rest not because of the social function indicated by his job but simply because he is an individual human being. But the Marxist-Jacobin equality depends on class, on status, which is contrary to the concept of human equality. For this reason man in a totalitarian state is defined arbitrarily and persecuted arbitrarily by assigning him to a social class.

How could this logical and practical contradiction gain so much power and appeal? Partly because of coercion and partly because of the fascistic tendencies of capitalism in underdeveloped societies. Communism was the only honest alternative in Tsarist Russia and feudal-warlord-colonial China. The democratic revolutionaries in these countries were neither sufficient nor strong enough; there was no sense of democratic revolution.

Democratic institutions, no matter how weak or corrupted by the social system, are a precondition for a democratic revolution, or what is called "revolution from the center." Its central problem, like that of the rebellion of the poor, is equality. Equality, moreover, that is necessarily initiated in the political realm.

Obviously, the fundamental task of drastic political reform is to democratize the entire political system. The high cost of elections, for example, works against the egalitarian principle, for the rich man or the agent of the oligarchic rich has an edge over the poor. The literacy test discriminates against the illiterate, who, in the present-day state of mass communication, need not necessarily be less intelligent and therefore less qualified than the literate. The minimum voting age of twenty-one discriminates against the eighteen-year-olds, who are considered old enough to fight and die for their country. The oligarchic grip on the political authority makes democratic rights work for the exclusive benefit of a controlling class.

The Marxist-Jacobin claims that political reconstruction is impossible without social revolution. On the contrary, political reconstruction can change society, *as we are now changing society through a reorientation of our political authority.*

To begin with, the modernization of the *barangay* system in the form of the citizens assemblies, restores power to the people, where it properly belongs. All citizens from fifteen years of age and above, are entitled, indeed obligated, to lend their voices to the consideration of great national issues. This is a drastic improvement over the old "representative" system, in which the mass of citizens indulged in politics as a spectator sport, applauding and supporting the loudest and shrewdest debater—in a word, the more effective demagogue. In the past, the great issues of the nation were settled among themselves by the political and media elite, with the oligarchy pulling the strings in the background.

A distinction must be recognized between access to political authority and access to the mass media, which are often incompatible with each other. The government was obliged to promote private interests in the guise of safeguarding the public interest. The humble citizen who could not be heard through the newspapers, radio, and television was powerless. The present system provides him with a ready access to political authority through his *barangay*.

Government by publicity has not advanced the national cause; government by physical accessibility should.

How is government by physical accessibility achieved? As I said, through the citizens assemblies. To this may be expressed the objection that only great issues are put before the assemblies; how about the day-to-day exercise of public power? Quite apart from the new private media, new in their orientation, and the government information department (which could not be organized earlier because of the objections of private media, prompted by their desire to maintain a monopoly of communicating information), there is also the new status of the barrio captains as the people's representatives in the municipal councils. Barrio captains, unlike the old representatives, are daily accountable to their constituents for the conduct of local governments. At the same time, their constituents are also members of the *barangay;* thus on both national and local questions, the barrio captains are the people's vital link to government.

This political structural reform is by no means minor. In the context of our experience it is quite revolutionary. The gap between the humble citizen and the center of national power is narrowed down considerably. But what is of paramount importance in this reform is the advent of *participatory democracy*. The masses no longer need wait until the controversies and issues of the day are crystallized for them by the debates of vested groups in the media; they crystallize the issues themselves. In this way, their opinions and sentiments are felt directly by the political authority.

Not a few observers—and detractors—have scoffed at the citizens assemblies, suspecting them of being "manipulated." Quite possibly, in some instances certain ebullient supporters of martial law or plain rowdies bent on mischief tried to assert themselves in certain assemblies. But this is like assuming that primary elections in West Virginia or elections in Cook County, Illinois, represent the entire United States presidential elections. Martial law has changed the moral atmosphere of Filipino society over night, but it has by no means produced the same drastic change in every citizen of the republic. Isolated excesses should not blind us to the fact that with rare exceptions the results of the first citizens assemblies are accepted as *an accurate indication* of popular feelings and sentiments about the questions presented to them.

The citizens assemblies, the modern form of the ancient Filipino *barangay,* or group of families, were activated at the initiative of the present leadership. Now they are an indispensable feature of our democracy. They have seen the humblest sitting in common counsel with the "mightiest," who have one vote like the rest. Previously the latter could have his way simply by bribing a commentator or visiting a politician on the sly. To belittle this *fraternity* is to misunderstand or distort the political objective of the Democratic Revolution: national integration.

The citizens assemblies are still in their crude beginnings of course; at this point, we still must get them to address questions to the government, so as to complete the circle of dialogue in *participatory democracy.* Although a modern rendering of the effective *barangays* of a primitive democratic age, the citizens assemblies must wait to be perfected as an institution of popular control over government.

These assemblies are one of our responses not only to our people's political requirements but also to the crisis of democracy the world over. The friendliest critics of democracy point out that bureaucratization, the rise of technocracy, the increasing complexities of modern life, and the acceleration of technologies and their cost, especially in mass communication, have made the ordinary citizen the creature rather than the sovereign of his public life. The ordinary citizen has lost the sense of control over his government. At the same time he is fed the illusion that he is in control. I do not think however that this illusion is strong, for the ordinary citizen comes to know sooner or later by experience that he is no longer sovereign. If this can happen in industrial and postindustrial democratic states, how much more in one that has been corrupted by wealth and privilege? The humblest citizen should and must be heard without having his sentiments and words distorted by self-anointed spokesmen and "interpreters" of public opinion. The citizens assemblies offer him such an avenue.

Moreover we are adjusting our public life to the new Constitution, which now perceives, where the old Constitution did not, the essentially social aspirations of our national union. The schools and the mass media are not adequate for the purpose of elucidating and disseminating to *all* Filipinos the new constitutional ideas governing our nation. In this fundamental task, the citizens assemblies must play a major role. No citizen should be deprived of knowledge of his country's Constitution by reason of being out of school, or by lack of literacy or lack of access to mass media. The Constitution must go to the people; they do not have to reach out, sometimes at their own peril, to it. If ignorance of the law is indeed no excuse for infraction, the political authority is obliged to see that such ignorance is not made possible, much less promoted, through official neglect. One of the great obligations of all governments in the modern world is the constant dissemination of knowledge—that is, of knowledge which enables the citizen to participate effectively in public life and thereby enjoy its blessings. Every deficiency on this score leaves the field open to the careerists and the demagogues, who will then constitute themselves once more a *privileged political class,* monopolizing knowledge that is meant for everyone.

Finally, the new Constitution and the citizens assemblies

embody in their principles the machinery of practice of a new society. There was in the old society an inevitable conflict between equality and freedom because those who formed the equation of the two concepts had a monopoly of equality and freedom. Inequality breeds injustice and corruption and inevitably breaks the political bond that joins the citizens to their government. Our new covenant based on the equality of all citizens, whatever their station in life, whatever their religious faith and their political belief, signifies that we approach political life as a means of integration and of promoting the general welfare.

The old political system divided our people between the influential and the mass, or the uninfluential, principally on the basis of social and economic status. The new political system unites them into a citizenry with equal individual rights.

Politics in the old society was essentially a politics of conflict, the competition among individuals and groups for social domination. Not surprisingly therefore the poor, the wretched, and the frustrated strove to get what they could out of the politics of conflict, since they never looked upon it as a force for authentic integration. If they behaved indifferently towards government, "coming alive" only during elections or, whenever they could, sought *favors* rather than their *due* from the public service, the reason was because they believed that for the most part government was at the service of the oligarchic and influential few. Their feeder roads, their schools, their bridges, remained unbuilt for one reason or another, while the private roads, schools, and mansions of the rich were constructed with dispatch. There was no controversy about responding to the needs of the influential; there was always controversy about satisfying the needs of the many. This occurred because the influential could *disguise* private greed as public concern.

This state of affairs prevailed principally because of the dishonesty, intellectual and otherwise, in the public forums. The national interest, the common good, were daily betrayed in the name of "principles." But for the masses, the test of principles was the condition of their lives; all the rhetoric did not give them the sense of equality that they have now.

This is something that cannot be taken away from them in the name of the civil liberties of the old establishment. Having known political equality, having known all the freedoms, our people henceforth demand that all freedoms be considered under one supreme criterion; how will they serve the cause of the rebellion of the poor?

Evidently, the egalitarian principle requires a reconstruction of our political values.

The Political Bond

The principle of equality and its earnest enforcement constitute the outstanding characteristic of our emerging new society. Furthermore they are the foundation of its wide popular support.

The popular demand for equality is not completely new. It was an old dream betrayed in the tortuous course of our history. The innumerable revolts and rebellions against Spanish rule (one every two years) and the unifying ideas of the Philippine revolution of 1896 were initial responses of our people to the pretentions of colonial rule, particularly to the pious claim that there was one people under God and that everyone was entitled to just and humane treatment. Equality at that time was not the equality one hoped to have *with* the friars and colonial rulers, but the equality to be dutiful creatures of God and servers of the colonial state. Filipinos aspired not for liberation, but for integration, or in the words of the propaganda movement, assimilation. Underneath the restiveness of the people was the human passion for liberty; but this did not assert itself fully until the colonial regime was clearly indifferent and even hostile to popular feelings.

Upon this *restricted* egalitarian dream, *equality in the colonial state,* the revolutionary ideas of 1896 were forged. This was the earliest political bond among all Filipinos, that is, the native Filipinos apart from the Spaniards born in the Philippines, who for centuries appropriated the name for themselves.

Not the promise of liberty but deliverance from expropriation, not political freedom but the end of day-to-day oppression, brought the Filipino masses to rise up in arms. Where the *ilustrados,* the ideologues of the revolution, applied themselves to the political question, the masses were moved by social consideration. The debate between Elias and Ibarra in Jose Rizal's *Noli Me Tangere* (*Touch Me Not*), the first of two novels by the martyr and national hero, is an *ilustrado* debate between "light and liberty," enlightenment and freedom. In *El Filibusterismo* (the second novel), Rizal portrays in the expropriated Kabesang Tales the social passions of the Philippine Revolution: the right to land and the fruits of one's labors. These, I would suggest, have been lost sight of in our "postrevolutionary" period, during the Commonwealth and the nearly three decades of national independence. Almost exclusively, we have thought of our heritage in terms of the political and constitutional ideas of the Philippine Revolution, forgetting all the revolts which came before it and, determined its social force. We realize only now the unfulfilled and betrayed hopes of the Filipino masses who sacrificed for every revolt and for the revolution and fought every war in our history. We know, of course, that those hopes were social before they were political.

We might have realized these hopes earlier had the Philippine Revolution run its full course instead of being frustrated by the American regime. Our *ilustrados,* in many ways the ancestors of our politicians, might have understood the revolution in the same way that the men of the French Revolution understood theirs:

> . . . The inescapable fact was that liberation from tyranny spelled freedom only for the few and was hardly felt by the many who remained loaded down by their misery. These had to be liberated some more. . . . Moreover, in this liberation, the men of the Revolution

and the people whom they supported were *no longer united by objective bonds in a common cause:* a special effort was required of the representatives, an *effort of socialization* which Robespierre called virtue, and this virtue was not Roman, it did not aim at *res publica* and had nothing to do with freedom. Virtue meant to have the welfare of the people in mind, to identify one's own will with the will of the people—*il faut uné volonté* UNE—and this effort was primarily directed at the happiness of the many. After the downfall of the Gironde, it was no longer freedom but happiness that become the new idea in Europe. [Hannah Arendt, *On Revolution*]

Indeed, by the time of the Malolos Congress in 1898, the men of the Philippine Revolution *were no longer united with the masses by objective bonds in a common cause.* This became quite evident in the social indifference of the Malolos Constitution, which reflected political forms rather than the social passions that led the masses to support the revolution. Few were conscious of the fact that this social indifference left the masses completely out of the emerging political order.

No different were the *ilustrado* successors of the Commonwealth Constitution. In spirit, if not wholly in substance, what we call the "old" Constitution was akin to the American, though the latter was framed in a different social environment: a socially and economically emancipated country. The framers of both Philippine Constitutions were emancipated themselves and the majority had no identity with the many "loaded down in misery." The most that could be said of them in extenuation was their belief that freedom from tyranny would lead to social equality, but there is no historical record that this was in fact so.

The *ilustrado* tradition *politicized* the masses in its own image of the good society. This was disastrous because it converted the social question into the political processes of organization, representation, and litigation, all of which were not effectively accessible to the masses. The only effective form of peasant organization was "subversive," obtaining by violence what could not be achieved by democratic petition. The masses could resort to "political action" only through privilege and patronage. The corruption that riddled political life in the old society was a manifestation of familial, regional, and tribal ties, extending considerably the pernicious "spoils system" adapted from American party politics.

If anything reflects our colonial mentality, it is not the preference for American goods decried by generations of economic nationalists, but the adoption of the American constitutional spirit, which is empty of social content. Unlike French political thought, the American was not conditioned by the social misery of the age. It was essentially a liberation from tyranny, a political act rather than an act of social emancipation. But Filipino political thought, at least in its early stages, most particularly the context of the problem we faced, the restoration of order with Andres Bonifacio, was the expression of the social condition of the Filipino masses.

I have merely given our present social situation a historical perspective. But neither ideological sophistication nor a profound sense of history is required to make us understand that the rebellion of the poor, the rebellion for equality, is what gives our time its specific character. We need the human compassion which moved the men of the French Revolution and our own heroes of the Katipunan. The intention is not, therefore, to make a textbook case for equality, but to awaken us to the fact that now societies no longer judge their poor; it is *their* poor which judge them.

In what other way can the rebellion of the poor achieve the goal of equality except by destroying the society which perpetuates mass poverty? Governments can offer a constitutional and orderly alternative because of their power, which they can use oppressively, on the side of the *status quo,* or redemptively, on the side of equality. On the basis of this necessary choice I understood the declaration of martial law to mean not *only* the preservation of the Republic but also the thorough reconstruction of society.

I have alluded to the immediate support of the people for the *rationale* of martial law. This support could not have come about had they not experienced keenly the egalitarianism of the order. Our people rightly saw that the crime situation had been the consequence of economic hardship and social inequities, and that privileges aggravated it. Thugs, terrorists, lawbreakers, corrupt and abusive policemen and other law enforcers, plus the criminal violence of the prominent, thrived because of social connections, economic domination, and political protection. Almost overnight the privileged wrongdoers, who were rapidly transforming ours into a criminal society, have been immobilized or driven underground. As a result the humblest citizen can now speak truly of his government breaking down the forces of alienation, in which the people were "We" and the society and government "They."

The new situation encourages Filipinos to depend on one another for the achievement of social goals. There is a resurgence in a modern context of the "bayanihan" (or community) spirit, as if in particular response to W. H. Auden's injunction that "we must love one another or die." This human solidarity and cooperation, this sense of community, is more than a moral precept. It is a necessity of our time. The very complexity of life and the enormity of its problems demand of us a fervor for unity unprecedented in the history of peoples and of mankind.

Therefore, we have an emergent sense of solidarity. Now, the essential step is to elucidate on the basis of this solidarity, to build an ideological and visible foundation in our national life. Apparently we cannot depend permanently on the coercive powers of the state, even if they coincide with our desires as a people. We must give to the new political bond the force of our own individual discipline.

"Discipline" suggests a "disciplinarian," and is usually thought of in connection with the martial life: marching in line and instant obedience to command. In many respects this discipline governs a "command society" under martial-law conditions. Obviously we cannot make this a permanent institution in our national life. The great majority of mankind need not be disciplined in this manner in order to live peaceably and responsibly in society, although there might have been periods in human history when this kind of imposition was a matter of necessity.

Still, let us be candid with ourselves. The popular support for the disciplinary measures under martial law indicates that for the vast majority of Filipinos, a disciplined ordering of public life has long been imperative and welcome. The most common criticism of my decision was that I took so long to make it. The decision was not determined by my will alone, but by circumstances. All the same, this further indicates another profound sentiment: our people want to start all over again, to arrive at a new covenant of collective existence.

I will be the first to admit that the present discipline is not exactly the most ideal. There is an element of fear in it, fear of swift albeit just punishment. I take this, as many do, as primitive discipline, or basic discipline, the kind we have been subjected to as children. On the other hand, some elements in society, notably the antisocial and criminal elements, evidently require this kind of discipline. We should be able in the shortest time possible— considering our decency and maturity as a people—to transcend this primitive discipline, the fear of reprisal. We should acquire instead the stronger, more sophisticated discipline which fears for the harmony of society if we violate its laws and norms; in sum, its covenant. We should fear wrongdoing not because of the personal consequences to ourselves but because it might destroy the "balance" of our community and thus adversely affect not only our personal lives but also the lives of others. Only in this way may our covenant with one another become a "lasting institution."

To achieve institutional permanence, the new covenant—the political bond—must take the form of a national ideology. But I part company with those who preach that the lack of a national ideology, in the sense of a political philosophy, produced the ills of the old society. The truth is that we had a political philosophy which viewed politics as essentially a competition for public power and privilege among individuals, political parties, and pressure groups, and only secondarily as a means of promoting the general welfare and the public interest. In the words of Maurice Duverger, ours was "a politics of conflict" and not the "politics of integration." Jose Rizal more aptly called it "the sense of national community." The consensus was that while personal ends should be served, *some* thought should be given to the public interest, and if a politician were to do this, he was better than the common breed. The short-sightedness of this view accounted for its failure and led to the martial necessity.

Many politicians and leaders before me, judging by their speeches, seemed to lament the *autarkic* principle in our political life. Either from ignorance or selfish interests, they were content to accept this "mess" as inherent in the freedom of our public life. This is merely the old voice of privilege trying to reassert itself. A political society which excludes the masses from meaningful participation and considers them as simply *the gallery of consent,* like the audience of popular entertainment, merely assures the perpetuation of organized elites in power and social privilege. These elites are able to speak poignantly of the blessings of "life, liberty, and the pursuit of happiness," while they deliberately keep the vast majority of the people in ignorance and poverty. No one may expect these disarmed elites to support the prevailing state which deprives them of their self-ordained special relationship with the people: they cease to be the demagogic spokesmen of the downtrodden from whose existence they derived their privileged status.

It has been said that enlightened self-interest promotes the public good. But it is difficult to distinguish enlightened from unenlightened self-interest. However, we can distinguish carefully between the private domain and the public realm.

This distinction is easy enough to perceive among those officials and functionaries charged with the conduct of the public business. In the simplest terms, they are not to engage in graft and corruption, fall into inefficiency and incompetence, or be involved in any wrongdoing as provided for by law. As promised in *Today's Revolution: Democracy*, I have reoriented the political authority and may have done so in a rather severe manner: over 6,000 people have lost their jobs or positions in government. Could they possibly just have been forgiven and enjoined not to do wrong again? I think not, if the purpose is to restore our people's faith in government. As it is, there may still be old elements in the bureaucracy, overlooked in the summary process, either "lying low" or still engaging in the old ways and feeling safe in the false thought that *the reorientation is over*.

It is not over: those who serve with me must accept the most ruthless discipline. They must work hard and observe the highest standards of service, otherwise they have no place in the leadership of the New Society. I cannot at this time be moved by their complaint of inadequate compensation—except those who are in the very lowest rungs—for if the masses of Filipinos are still deprived and suffering, all of us must deprive ourselves and suffer with them. This is the tenet of public leadership.

If it is easy enough to distinguish between the private domain and the public realm in the government service, how about *outside* of it? What of the general citizenry, the businessmen, the students, the professionals, and all others in private employment? Obviously, to enjoin them not to tempt our functionaries is futile. Bribery is secret, though not well kept, and both the bribe-giver and the bribe-taker are liable to punishment. Owing to the momentum of old habits, and the mutual benefits afforded both culprits, underground bribery possibly can exist with impunity. The private citizen should be impressed by the sophisticated discipline which fears for the "balance" of society. His indifference to his civic responsibility will, under martial-law conditions, lead to the alternative that martial law is intended to prevent: chaos. Chaos and bloody revolution.

As far as it is able, the government will discipline and punish its own, along with the criminal elements. By accepting this limitation, we serve notice that although ours is a constitutional authoritarian regime, it is not totalitarian, for it will not encroach upon the private lives of our citizens. In this *space of freedom,* the citizen may behave as he pleases in the pursuit of his private happiness: he may order or disrupt his life according to his discipline or lack of it. But once he steps beyond his space of freedom into the public realm, he will risk a revolution that may well impose on him a totalitarian regime. Here again is a case of private privilege perverting the political authority that I discussed at length in the section "Oligarchic Democracy" of *Today's Revolution: Democracy.*

Only up to a certain limit can the government enforce the covenant of the New Society, if that government is to remain honest in its purpose to protect the Republic and inaugurate a new era of freedom. Beyond that limit is the citizen's concern for his whole society, his individual covenant with the rest of mankind.

I am responsible for martial law. I have my own covenant with the New Society for, in many ways, the New Society is a vision that I proposed to our people. But for the final direction of our society, for the entire movement to our destiny, every Filipino is responsible. This responsibility must rest upon an inner discipline, a discipline one imposes on himself not because of coercion but because of a clear understanding of our needs.

With the September 21 Movement, we have passed the Age of Innocence and entered the Age of Responsibility.

Consider well, therefore, this new political bond and heed the warning of an acute observer of modern political affairs:

> As a result of [this] politicization of all aspects of life and of the orientation of all thought and energy toward politics, men increasingly turn to the state for a solution of their problems, though the state could not solve them if it tried. And everywhere in the world this increasing inclination to turn to the state leads to three evils: boundless inflation of the state's size and power; increasing dependence on it by the

individual; and decreasing control over it by the "people" who think they control it, whereas in reality they merely surrender all their powers to it. [Konrad Kellen, translator's preface to Jacques Ellul's *The Political Illusion*]

In conclusion there are public matters which require the initiative of the people. The people have the right to oust a government which has been untrue to the covenant, but if they themselves destroy the covenant, they relinquish their right to rule themselves. Then the edifice of public life crumbles, like the walls of Jericho, at the first blast of the trumpet.

The Age of Responsibility calls not to a few but to the many; everyone is responsible. No one can escape the charge of history.

/ 10 /

THE CONQUEST
OF POVERTY

The New Society is, first of all, a community of equals.

In eleven months of martial law, we have realized *civil equality* —an equality which means "equal treatment." To be poor in this society is no longer to be underpriveleged. True, there is an element of coercion behind this achievement, at least for those who cling to or who wish to revive their privileged status in the old society. An imperative necessity exists to enforce civil equality: as the basis of the new political bond, it is the precondition for attainment of a greater equality, which is *social equality*.

A society in which the majority of the people are poor is, as we have experienced, in constant danger of having its political authority corrupted and dominated by the rich minority. This was the essential point of my analysis of the oligarchic society. In these revolutionary times, such a society cannot last long. That society will endure whose members enjoy equality—in other words, a society which has eliminated economic inequality.

169

The standard response to economic inequality is economic development. According to the conventional wisdom, economic development reduces mass poverty and enriches human life. But the crucial question is, How is economic development to be achieved? We somehow find ourselves debating "models" of economic development, and the usual options are capitalist development and socialist development.

The inevitable conclusion is that we should try to avoid the excesses of either, except we are told that this is impossible. That is the risk of trying to solve our problems according to "system."

Economic development is formulated in terms of capital accumulation and full use of resources at one end and increasing GNP and per capita income at the other. Capitalism and communism present themselves as alternative roads to economic development, the one by the activities of free entrepreneurs making a profit and the other by the national use of resources for "social ends." If we take the ideological versions of these economic systems on their face value—that is, perfect capitalism and perfect communism—it does not really matter which way we go: for either way economic development will be attained and mass poverty will be reduced, if not eliminated, and human life will be enriched.

But there is no perfection on this planet.

The condemnation of communism, for example, is dramatically presented not by an economist but a poet, Octavio Paz, in *The Labyrinth of Solitude:*

> Our lack of capital could be remedied in another way. As we know, there is a method whose efficacy has been proved. Capital, after all, is simply accumulated human labour, and the extraordinary development of the Soviet Union is nothing but an application of this formula. By means of a controlled economy, which avoids the waste and confusion inherent in the capitalistic system, and the "rational" use of an immense work force, directed to the exploiting of equally vast resources, the Soviet Union has become, in less than half a century, the only rival of the United States. In Mexico, however, we have

neither the population nor the natural and technical resources required by an experiment of such proportions (not to mention our proximity to the United States and other historical circumstances). Above all, the "rational" use of workers and a controlled economy signify—among other things—forced labour, concentration camps, the displacing of races and nationalities, the suppression of the workers' basic rights, and the rule of the bureaucracy. The methods of "socialist accumulation," to use Stalin's phrase, have turned out to be much more cruel than "primitive accumulation," which aroused the justified anger of Marx and Engels. No one doubts that totalitarian socialism can change the economy of a nation, what is doubtful is whether it can give men freedom. And this last is all that interests us, and all that can justify a revolution.

But, we ask, is communism essentially repressive and totalitarian?

On the other hand, capitalism is cynical exploitation of labor, amassing profit in every possible way and with impunity. Note, however, that in all the countries where it has been tried (with the exception of the United States), human misery has not diminished. The explanation for this was offered by Paul Sweezy: underdevelopment and development are two sides of the coin of capitalism, the poverty of one is "necessary" to the wealth of the other. Thus underdeveloped nations will never develop within the capitalist global system. Their heroic efforts will end either by their remaining where they are, or their plunging into deeper and deeper poverty.

The world economy seems to conform to this trend: the rich are getting richer and the poor poorer.

If this bleak analysis is correct, then economic development is irrelevant to the condition of the poor masses over a period of time. Whether development be capitalist or communist, the people will have to suffer more before they can suffer less. The question is which *political elite*—fascist or communist—can succeed in imposing its rule on the people. What will count most is the ruthlessness and efficiency of the regime.

This does not imply that political regimes will be indifferent to economic development, for they need some measure of it to perpetuate themselves in power. The more repressive the regimes are, the more they would push the country to development, since they need it to maintain the infrastructure of power. This is what I meant when I said that economic development will be irrelevant to the condition of the masses. The state becomes, in the words of Salvador de Madariaga, the "colonizer" of its own people.

No decent man can accept this rationalization, although it recommends itself to certain political realists, who may see an opportunity for power and seize it should the rebellion of the poor break out in bloody revolution out of sheer frustration. This rationalization aptly is called a *vertical view of society,* for it is the point of view of a reactionary ruling class manipulating and commanding the poor majority of society. Such regimes are costly to maintain in human terms, for generations will have to be sacrificed through forced labor and concentration camps, or other draconian measures to keep mass consumption at the lowest level, in order to attain the economic development that the regimes require. The instruments of repression—and even terror—are not a monopoly of totalitarian socialist states.

We arrive now at the so-called "development dilemma." Economic development is desirable if it increases the welfare and improves the level of life of the poor masses; only in these terms will the pursuit of economic development gain the needed mass support. But the pursuit requires sacrifices from the poor masses —the postponement of consumption, forced savings, etc.—which the masses, were they free to assert themselves, would reject. This would leave the pursuit of development without its needed support. As the "democratic dilemma" states, democracy is indispensable to development, but in a democratic society people will always tend to vote for lower taxes in the same breath that they demand more public services.

Under these conditions, with the so-called "development dilemma" as a ruling principle, a society in which the rich are too few and the poor too many cannot expect development without repression, and for a very long period of time whatever development it attains cannot benefit the masses. In this case the economic system will be a matter of indifference. Capitalism in a democratic polity will be under increasing pressure from the rebellion of the poor and must therefore resort to repressive measures to save itself. Under the same polity socialism will be similarly pressed. In either case, the way out of the dilemma is the armed, even despotic, exercise of power.

This harsh conclusion derives, as I said, from the *vertical* view of society, which assumes that the given society is *prior to,* sometimes even separate from, the individual. Whether capitalist or socialist, society will not change by itself; it is blind to the circumstances which demand change. Men alone can change *their* societies; their perceptions—their perspective—will conceive of and carry out the changes, and not, as we are often told, the play of impersonal forces. If we cannot develop under present conditions governed by the "development dilemma," then we must either change the conditions, reexamine them, or revise or reappraise our notions of development.

We are, after all, concerned with an actual, not hypothetical, underdeveloped society—our own. It is important, therefore, that we extricate ourselves from the mental conditioning produced in us by ideologies foreign to our experience. We must start from the ground up.

Having thus liberated ourselves, we should be able to find that the "development dilemma" is the inevitable product of the vertical view of society, which regards the rebellion of the poor as a force merely to be "reckoned with." At best, society will be reordered according to the calculations and anxieties of those who dominate it. But it should be obvious that nothing less than a new society can come to terms with the rebellion of the poor.

If we abandon—as we must— the vertical view of society and think *upwards* instead of *downwards,* we perceive that a society in which the many are poor and only a few are rich is not only an underdeveloped society but it is not an *authentic human society*.

Men's moral sense and historical experience irrevocably deny authenticity to such a community: firstly, because it is not inevitable; secondly, because it is the product of an undeveloped moral sense; and, thirdly, because in the long run it is socially suicidal.

How then do we proceed after repudiating the "development dilemma"?

A Progressive Society

Gunnar Myrdal, in *Economic Theory and Underdeveloped Regions*, made a brief but cogent observation that lifts the cloud in much of our thinking about economic development. He observed that

> . . . in a progressive society, the improvement of the lot of the people can often be won without substantial sacrifices from those who are better off and is sometimes not only compatible with, but a condition for, the attainment of higher levels in all income brackets, including the higher ones.

This observation is pregnant with implications:

1. "Tainted" but not influenced by the vertical view of society, the statement dispels the capitalist-conservative nightmare of the rich minority being impoverished and brought down to the level of the poor.
2. The statement implies that the pursuit of economic development will be successful because the poor will support it, having a stake in it.
3. The statement implies that this feat can be managed by a *progressive society*.

"But we are not a progressive society, we are economically underdeveloped."

The objection is not valid because it assumes that only an

economically developed society can be progressive. One has only to read the critiques of Marcuse (and others) of the American and Russian societies, the world's most developed nations, to know that under certain criteria material progress does not necessarily make a society progressive. Crucial is the general intellectual and moral receptiveness to new ideas, to progressive change. "Progressiveness" leads to development, though economic development may, but not necessarily, spur progressive thinking. All too often rich societies, like rich people, become complacent about the existing order of things without satiating their appetite for "more of the same."

Social scientists tell us that the attainment of collective goals depends on any number of conditions, but the monumental achievements of mankind were made by men and women spurred by burning visions, unshackled by "inhibiting factors." On the other hand, civilizations have died not because of "conditions" but from the complacency of those who inherited them. In any case our country is not made of stone. A favorite paradigm of the past was that the "Philippines was a beggar sitting on a mountain of gold." In plain words, in terms of resources and capability, the country had no excuse for being a beggar; what was really lacking was the vision and the will.

As has been pointed out, the great task of economic development involves the energies of the many. For the many who are poor, any involvement must meet the test of sincerity; they must participate in whatever boons there are now so that they will *freely* offer their brain and brawn to achieve collective ends.

Are we to take from the rich to give to the poor?

If the proposition is stated in these terms, the poor do not deserve the contempt of our charity. I might say that only the disabled poor deserve it, but that would be a misguided statement. Unless a man be totally disabled, he is capable of some useful work for society. Moreover, the question whether to take from the rich to give to the poor is simplistic. Very few taxpayers ask it when their taxes go to schools, hospitals, roads, and bridges that they probably will have no opportunity to use. In this respect, they are parting with their hard-earned money, or unearned increment, or in the strictest sense, "sharing their wealth." Again the perspective is important: the millionaire who "parts" with three-quarters of his income still has a quarter of a million left while the poor wage-earner, even if he pays only a fraction, will nonetheless have but a few pesos left.

No one—that is, no one except cranks—has seriously suggested that taxes should be abolished so that everyone can keep his money and pay only for the goods he uses: food, clothes, shelter, roads, power, police, telephones, bridges, medical care, etc. This is so because no one is wealthy enough to afford all these goods and conveniences *individually*. Socially and economically speaking, collectivity—pooling resources in the everyday sense—is man's fate. In society every man is his brother's keeper. As Bernard Shaw once wrote in a telling passage:

> . . . St. Paul said, "He that will not work, neither shall he eat"; but as he was only a man with a low opinion of women, he forgot the babies. Babies cannot work, and are shockingly greedy; but if they are not fed there would soon be nobody left alive in the world.

Therefore we should realize that we are not doing anyone a favor by contributing our share—the share proportionate to our capabilities—to the sustenance, or, in this case, the remaking of society. To understand this is to be progressive.

Thus the poor *seem* to contribute less—in monetary terms but not in terms of labor. I said "seem," for in the aggregate, the contribution of the many who are poor does sustain society and also subsidizes the opportunities and comforts of the rich minority.

The solution is not to dispossess the rich in order to elevate the poor. At least at this stage the elimination of economic inequality does not mean that the dockworker is going to reside in an exclusive village, dine on china, ride in an air-conditioned Cadillac, send his children to a private school, and wear imported suits.

Equality in the sense of our progressive society does mean, however, that the dockworker will have his three square meals, a roof over his head, efficient public transport, schooling for his children, and medical care for his family. Without these things, he is trapped in a vicious circle: unproductiveness keeps him poor and poverty keeps him unproductive.

Over a period of time this same stevedore will learn in the pursuit of economic development to aspire to what are called "comfort, leisure, and culture," which go with economic development in a progressive society.

Sad to say there is now a "worker aristocracy": a minority in the labor force can obtain adequate food, clothing, and shelter, and a tinier minority can claim to have obtained some amount of comfort, leisure, and culture. We can choose to call this an improvement for a segment of the poor masses. But again, due to the fact that its number is so small as to constitute an exception, the same problem of social inequality prevails.

Therefore we must review thoroughly and in depth our various existing welfare schemes, the structure of income distribution, in order to strengthen the egalitarian base of the New Society. I am sure that this is what many of our people want: they must lose themselves in the great enterprise of conquering mass poverty.

Our experience with welfare schemes taught us that the "principle of universality"—the indiscriminate distribution of welfare benefits without regard to need—actually works against the egalitarian principle. This form of "equality" dissipates scarce resources without substantially alleviating the condition of the actually needy. There are schools in areas where there are not enough students and from which students may conveniently ride or walk to another place which needed schools; medical benefits for those who could well afford their own physicians simply because they had been "taxed" for the purpose; or, from recent experience, rice for areas which did not actually want it.

It is time that we understood *welfare.* The common misconception is that welfare is merely a more respectable word for *charity* since it is "dispensed" by the state. The truth is that *welfare* is *well-being*. The promotion of the well-being of members and citizens is the reason for the existence of society and the state. For example, when a state puts the building of monuments before the production and provision of food for its citizens, that state has no allegiance to reason. Monuments are important but they do not come ahead of food. Similarly, when the wealth of a society, a great portion of which is in the hands of a few, is dissipated on magnificent mansions, luxurious cars, exotic foods, and other extravagances of "high life," while the majority of the people are virtually homeless, ill-fed, ill-clothed, and ill-educated, that society is a sham because it is outrageously indifferent to the welfare of its members. And this is the inevitable result of social or economic inequality.

Many explanations and justifications have been offered for economic inequality—from the idleness of the poor, the industry of ancestors, and the demands of civilization—but all of them have been refuted by progressive thought. The most recent of these is that the rich, for all their extravagances and frivolities, do provide employment. I had always suspected something spurious about this argument, but before I could probe deeper into it my efforts were spared by a striking paragraph which with wit and wisdom exposed the fallacy. "There is," snapped G. Bernard Shaw,

> no merit in giving employment: a murderer gives employment to the hangman; and a motorist who runs over a child gives employment to an ambulance porter, a doctor, an undertaker, a clergyman, a mourning-dressmaker, a hearse-driver, a gravedigger; in short, to so many worthy people that when he ends by killing himself it seems ungrateful not to erect a statue to him as a public benefactor. The money with which the rich give the wrong sort of employment would give the right sort of employment if it were equally distributed; for then there would be no money offered for motor cars and diamonds until everyone was fed, clothed, and lodged, nor any wages offered to men and women to leave useful employments and become servants to idlers.

There would be less ostentation, less idleness, less wastefulness, less uselessness; but there would be more food, more clothing, better houses, more security, more health, more virtue; in a word, more real prosperity.

Our society is not so poor that it cannot provide for the well-being of all its members; we have only to accept what must be done in order to reduce social inequality. This certainly does not involve dispossessing the rich, or at the other extreme, appealing to their social conscience alone. An economist has disposed of the fallacy that economic development *alone* reduces poverty and enriches human life. These aims can be accomplished only through the intervention of the state, regarded, in this instance, as the collective conscience of society.

There was a time when the rich could maintain themselves against the poverty of the rest, but the rebellion of the poor has reduced this into an illusion. We are moving toward a social order in which before anyone can have more than enough, everyone must have enough.

The determination of what is enough can be a vexing question. A truism states that one man's enough is another man's penury. With the exercise of human reason, determined to be progressive rather than utopian, we can judge what poverty is according to the circumstances of our time. At the minimum, no one must starve. Many of us can still say that "no one starves in the Philippines." We cannot say realistically, however, that no one must be without gainful employment, for in the next few years, we can only reduce unemployment—though substantially, we hope. But we can say: *"No Filipino shall be without sustenance."*

There are prerequisites in order for the New Society to remain an *authentic* society. The political authority will establish the priorities and provide the mechanisms of equalization. But the entire citizenry must provide the work and in some cases accept the sacrifices. We are determined that these sacrifices shall not be in vain. This is our social contract.

The Economic Society

The question arises, What kind of economic system shall we have?

Again, the tyranny of "systems." When I say economic society, the emphasis is on *society*. We must, therefore, arrive at whatever system will make the kind of society we want—the New Society—work.

Capitalism and socialism have so many nuances and definitions that the layman is served best by eidetic definition—that is, by just pointing to the country which represents them, American capitalism or Russian socialism. No two capitalist countries or socialist countries are exactly alike. Within the Communist world itself accusations of revisionism and Stalinism are often heard.

Much of the debate between capitalism and socialism is polemical, and although some of the points are enlightening, nothing is more useful to us than our own experience.

Few people refer to our economic system as capitalist. The most allowed is that our base is private enterprise, which is to say that the economic activities of the society are carried out mainly by businessmen, industrialists, traders, and merchants. In the old society, however, it was not unusual that certain businessmen were in politics and certain politicians were in business. Further, the government itself was involved in certain economic activities, especially those of a scale which private business could not manage. In a rather simplistic sense, there are also "communist" features in our society, for roads, bridges, parks, museums and such things are "held" and enjoyed in common. The proper question to ask of this system was whether it worked. I think that we can answer this in the affirmative, although we are not exactly clear what it *worked for*. Eventually we found that it worked only for the few oligarchs who, in accordance with the old style, were capitalists when business was good but who demanded assistance from the government when business was in distress. They were thus sometime anticapitalists.

Now we are trying to build a society in which economic activity promotes the interests of the individual and the welfare of the whole. Necessarily, the authority of government must be exerted whenever these ends are not being served. Obviously individual enterprise and initiative will play a significant role in the economic society. The distinction between the public and private sectors is formal, since each has its particular duties to the people and their society. But this should not prevent the two sectors from joining together in a common cause. What made the old economic system unacceptable was that the so-called partnership between government and private business resulted in an oligarchy rather than an egalitarian economic society.

This partnership should have resulted in the conquest of mass poverty, for that was its only justification. But the values of the old society were such that the partnership between the public and private sectors was, in many instances, a conspiracy to enrich and increase the power of the few. This is certainly not capitalist, according to the tenet that it is the most efficient and liberal way of making society prosperous. Neither is the solution to this necessarily socialistic.

The solution lies in the moral commitment to the aim of the New Society, the conquest of mass poverty, and in the political will to carry it out.

THEORY AND PRACTICE IN THE NEW SOCIETY

Any man of experience in government realizes the importance of theory in the lives of men and nations. Men act according to a set of beliefs, a "philosophy of life," most of them unconsciously. Societies operate in a system which stems from a framework of beliefs, such as an ideology, or framework of law, such as a constitution. It would be fatal—and certainly not practical—to ignore theory, as the historian Carlyle pointed out to a businessman when he said, "There was once a man called Rousseau who wrote a book containing nothing but ideas. *The second edition was bound in the skins of those who laughed at the first.*"

Theory is a measure of conduct. Theory and practice are judged in their relation to each other. According to J. S. Mill, the great systems—communism and liberal democracy—are indicated by the theories behind them, Marxism and liberalism. The Hungarian Revolution and the Czechoslovakian uprising were

183

undertaken in the name of Marxism; the Sino-Soviet split reflects clashing interpretations of Marxist theory. On the other hand, critics of liberalism describe democracy as "the rule of the politicians," or an "elite *sprung* from the people," thus indicating that democracy itself *is the rule of the few*—the politicians—although in the name of the many. All this suggests that practice often fails theory.

In our case we have the right to be judged by our own theory —our political and social theory. Moreover, this is not the vision of one man alone in our time, but one deeply ingrained in our national consciousness. As I see it, the declaration of martial law had been anticipated long before I made my decision, although many of us hoped that the deterioration would not become that critical. When the necessity presented itself, everyone accepted it.

The severest critics of Philippine martial law—and their number is diminishing—must grant two things about it: its compelling necessity and its uniqueness.

To recapitulate: the compelling necessity arose out of the seven grave threats to the existence of the Republic. These were the Communist rebellion, the rightist conspiracy, the Muslim secessionist movement, the rampant corruption on all levels of society, the criminal and criminal-political syndicates (including the private armies), the deteriorating economy, and the increasing social injustice. I have already explained in detail the "martial necessity" of the decision.

Our martial law is unique in that it is based on the supremacy of the civilian authority over the military and on complete submission to the decision of the Supreme Court and, most important of all, the will of the people. It is unique in that it does not seek to maintain the *status quo* but has instead brought about radical reforms. (In another book, I will discuss the highly technical and constitutional aspects of martial law for the benefit of legal and constitutional scholars, demonstrating that at every level of reasoning, martial law is (1) an imperative of national survival and (2) permissive of constitutional authoritarianism.)

I have always adhered to the idea that all revolutions, no matter what kind—whether Jacobin or democratic, violent or peaceful, bloody or constitutional—depend for their success on the initial and eventual support of the people. Accordingly, I took steps immediately to formalize the acceptance of martial law in the New Society through the adoption of a new Constitution, a plebiscite, and a referendum which would manifest in unquestioned manner the desire of the citizens.

Upon the approval of a new Constitution by the constitutional convention, I organized the *barangays,* or village councils or citizens assemblies, in the barrios (which are the smallest political units in the Philippines). I directed the new Constitution to be submitted to the *barangays,* or citizens assemblies, in a formal plebiscite from January 10–15, 1973. The *barangays* voted almost unanimously to ratify the Constitution, and continue with martial law and the reforms of the New Society.

This action was challenged in a petition filed before our Supreme Court in the cases entitled *Javellana* v. *Executive Secretary et al.,* G.R. Nos. L-36163, 36164, 36165, 36236, and 36283. The issue raised was whether I had the power to call a plebiscite; whether I could proclaim the ratification of the new Constitution. In raising this issue, the petitioners (who, incidentally, were Liberals or political opposition leaders) raised the fundamental issue of the power of the President under a proclamation of martial law to issue decrees.

The issues in turn raised the question of the legitimacy of the entire government. To meet the insistent suggestion that I proclaim a revolutionary government in the event of an adverse decision, I decided to submit to the jurisdiction of the Supreme Court. This I had done in 1971 in the *Lansang* v. *Garcia* case (already cited) when almost the same parties in interest questioned my powers as president to suspend the privilege of the writ of habeas corpus. (See page 118.)

This submission to the Court would also calm the fears of

every cynic who had misgivings about my intentions or claimed that I was ready to set up a dictatorship. Certainly no dictator would submit himself to the judgment of a higher body like the Supreme Court on the question of the constitutionality or validity of his actions.

At the same time I wanted to emphasize that the revolution which I was leading was a constitutional revolution. It was constitutional because it did not depart from the strictures or limitations of the old and new Constitutions.

Questioned most insistently was General Order No. 1, in which I had directed that I would exercise all the powers of government. I had suspended the sessions of the legislators in view of the manifest opposition of the people to the calling of an *interim* National Assembly. I created a military commission to try cases committed by persons charged with treason and subversion as well as related crimes.

Inasmuch as I, and all those who counselled me, were convinced of the validity of my position, I decided to submit unconditionally to the jurisdiction of the Supreme Court by appearing through counsel and answering all the issues raised before this highest tribunal of the country.

The Supreme Court upheld our position and in its decision of March 31, 1973, penned by Chief Justice Roberto Concepcion, ruled in this wise: ". . . all the aforementioned cases are hereby dismissed. This being the vote of the majority, there is no further judicial obstacle to the new Constitution being considered in force and effect." The new Constitution had been ratified by the *barangays* in the plebiscite I had called on January 10–15, 1973.

It will be noted that I had submitted myself to the jurisdiction of the Supreme Court in all cases questioning my authority—in 1971 in the case of *Lansang* v. *Garcia* on the question of the suspension of the privilege of the writ of habeas corpus, and in the case just cited on the proclamation of martial law as well as the other related cases.

There was another question regarding my swift action on the

Constitution, and I can understand how this must have bothered the legal "constructionists" among us. On November 30, 1972, I called a plebiscite after the constitutional convention had approved the new Constitution; this plebiscite was set for January 5, 1973. But on December 23, 1972, I suspended the plebiscite upon the petition of some parties, including jurists, who pointed out that a longer period was necessary to prepare the citizenry and inform them thoroughly about the Constitution. Immediately after I had suspended the plebiscite, I organized the *barangays* and called for a show of hands regarding the new Constitution on January 10–15, 1973. Why did I make this sudden decision?

I know that some old-society politicians thought their "eloquent" and "brilliant" opposition had precipitated my action. This was understandable, for they could not have imagined that a danger greater than their oratory was pressing upon the Republic.

The truth was that martial law had peculiar ramifications in the Muslim areas. At that moment a three-pronged rebellion and conspiracy was in progress that included the Communist rebels, the rightist conspirators, and the Muslim secessionists. The dangers from the Communist rebellion and the rightist conspiracy were checked in Luzon. But in Mindanao as early as 1971 (or even before) other plans were in operation. As early as the summer of 1972, while Luzon was in near anarchy, Mindanao was beleaguered by the activities of some 16,000 Muslim secessionists. Strengthened by foreign material and moral support, encouraged by the seeming impotence of government in Luzon, the secessionist rebels planned an all-out attack to overwhelm government military installations in the Muslim provinces of Sulu, Zamboanga del Sur (including the island of Basilan), Zamboanga del Norte, Lanao del Sur, Lanao del Norte, and Cotabato, and from there take over all of Mindanao and Sulu.

As early as October 1972—less than a month after the proclamation of martial law—the rebels in Marawi City (Lanao del Sur), *confusing their signals,* precipitately started the rebellion, overwhelming some constabulary detachments. They burned the Philippine army headquarters, took over complete control of the city—notably, the Mindanao State University, where the Japanese Ambassador, Toshio Urabe, was almost captured by the rebels—and cut off all radio and road communication to other parts of the province. In late February and early March, the summer plan of 1972 belatedly went into operation in Cotabato when 6,000 rebels overran most of the towns, threatening the IV Philippine Constabulary Zone headquarters in Parang as well as Cotabato City, destroyed the bridges and immobilized all transportation within the province. Before that, Basilan Island was almost completely occupied by several other thousand rebels; Zamboanga del Sur was plunged into a state of turmoil. Again before January, government troops had practically lost the province of Sulu, except for the *poblaciones* (towns proper), to numerically superior rebels and secessionists. Only the superior training and courage of government troops, their heroic and alert leadership, and the support of both Muslims and Christians, organized and doing battle as self-defense and strike forces, turned the tide and recovered most of the beleaguered areas for the Republic of the Philippines.

What bearing do these apparently strictly *military actions* have on my decision for a quick ratification of the Constitution? The answer is that these military events were dominated by a *political plan*. The Muslim secessionist rebels had somehow convinced their financial supporters abroad (openly identified in the international press) that there was a civil war in the Philippines. They argued that the condition was ideal for establishing a government separate from that of the Republic of the Philippines, allied, if necessary, with a neighboring country. This step would be followed by a demand from the United Nations Security Council for the right of self-determination, following the formula that successfully set up Bangladesh as a state independent of Pakistan. The date set for the accomplishment of the plan was January 1973.

The plan was almost a political masterpiece. My options were few. The hostile reaction of the American press to the declaration of martial law destroyed for us any immediate expectation of United States aid—at a time when we badly needed it. The assaults in Mindanao were calculated to divide our forces between Luzon and Mindanao. The political plan, along with its clever, if crude, military strategy, might very well have worked had I vacillated about the risks of immediately ratifying the Constitution. The danger of a supposedly separate and independent shadow government set up in one or another municipality in Mindanao was apparent and would at once place in doubt our sovereignty in the area.

The only possible maneuver dictated by the national interest was to meet this incipient "splinter state" with a government and a republic duly supported by a great majority of the people. *Most importantly, the Muslim citizenry must be included,* operating under a Constitution of their own making and already ratified so as to be enforceable by the government.

Time, of course, was of the essence. The secessionist plan had been set back a few months, but our intelligence sources from the rebel camps were quite certain that the secessionists were determined to follow through their plans—especially that of setting up a separate government—before the end of January 1973.

More than anyone, I knew the vulnerability of the Philippine Republic in the Muslim areas; martial law was a success in the rest of the country, but our southern backdoor was *strategically vulnerable* to the secessionists. An excruciatingly careful estimate of the situation convinced me that if the entire citizenry, including the residents of the Muslim provinces, were to approve the new Constitution by a show of hands through the *barangays,* this would dishearten the rebels and the secessionists, commit the fencesitters, and derail the plan for separation.

I could achieve this advantage only by pushing through the *barangay* plebiscite by the middle of January. Necessarily some formalities had to be set aside, such as the secret or written ballot and allowing a month or two of full discussion on the Constitution.

I was taking a legal and constitutional gamble, but at stake was the integrity of the sovereign state rather than a technicality of law.

No matter how much it was questioned by a few, the result of the plebiscite achieved the purpose I had envisioned. The secessionist plan was upset.

Obviously, neither armed might nor exhortation would have saved the integrity of the sovereign state had the secessionists succeeded in their plan to install a separate "sovereignty." Prudent statesmanship constrained me from revealing to our people the full dimensions of the danger to themselves, their country, and their progeny.

Having proclaimed martial law, I was responsible also for its repercussions. To my mind, the step that I took is a clear case of the Constitution saving the Republic of the Philippines.

Now we have a basis for the formalization of the political base of the New Society. Also, we have the foundation of the legal structure of this society.

Despite all our explanations, I was informed that in some minds the proclamation of martial law on September 21, 1972, had eroded the old structure of law. There was need to rebuild a new one. If any further misgivings arose, the new Constitution was a basis or foundation for the structure of law that would govern the New Society.

To comply with my promise to consult the people periodically on matters of gravest import, I called a referendum on July 27 and 28, 1973, on a single question. Did the people want me to continue beyond 1973, to accomplish the reforms that had been started under the New Society and under the new Constitution? Technically this referendum was unnecessary since the new Constitution, upheld by the Supreme Court, provided that I could stay in office beyond the end of my presidential term under the old Constitution, which expired with the year 1973.

I had directed that the effects of martial law be suspended some time before and up to the referendum, so that the secrecy of balloting in writing which I had ordered might truly be expressive of the will of the people through the *barangays.*

The new Constitution provided that all persons eighteen years old or over, whether literate or illiterate, were qualified to vote in elections. I had gone further; drawing from our custom in ancient times when those who were fifteen years old were allowed to protect the villages and stay on guard while the older men went out to meet the enemy in battle, I authorized fifteen-year-old citizens to vote in the referendum of July 1973, as I had done in the plebiscite of January. The commission on elections which conducted and supervised the referendum of July, however, tabulated the results so that the votes of those aged fifteen to seventeen were separated from the results of the balloting by the other voters eighteen years old or older.

From this point on, the *barangay* officials became the representatives of the people. In my speeches, and in meetings with these officials, I emphasized that they had taken over from the members of the defunct Congress or the *ad interim* National Assembly that was yet to be called under the new Constitution.

When the nation is confronted with a crisis, as when we faced the shortage in rice, the *barangays* are called upon to participate in instilling discipline among our people. This they have succeeded in doing.

Every step taken in the martial-law situation was measured according to the recognized desires and wishes of the greater number of the Filipino people. Dismantling the Communist rebellion and the rightist conspiracy, for example, took the "classical" form of surveillance, apprehension, detention, and public trial, although I immediately granted amnesty to those accepting it. The Muslim secessionist movement was met—is being met—with full consciousness that our Muslim brothers must be integrated into the national community. Considering that all these rebellions and conspiracies are rooted in the social situation, martial law must proceed further to build a new society. As I emphasized in *Today's Revolution: Democracy,* nothing less than a revolution from the center could reshape Philippine society, unless we are willing to submit ourselves to the rule of an alien ideological system. But the democratic revolution could not proceed at the old pace, *in the old society,* simply because that society—left to itself—had become impotent to reform itself.

The only remaining resource was the political will, which resides in the leadership of the government of the day.

As we had planned in 1971 when the program for the renovation of our society was submitted to our people, we are moving in these areas:

1. Peace and order
2. Land reform
3. Labor reform
4. Educational reform
5. Economic reform
6. Social services
7. Political reforms and government reorganization

We had to restore civil order as the bedrock of any constitutional survival. Civil order is merely the rationale of all societies: enforcement of and obedience to the law. When I placed the entire country under martial law, my first concern was to secure the Republic against any uprising, politically motivated or otherwise, and to secure the entire citizenry from the criminal elements, the private armies bred by local politics, and the outlaw bands in the countryside, who might either take advantage of the temporary panic or undermine our efforts to assert the authority of our police forces. It was imperative that we dismantle the appartus of the insurgency movement and the whole system of violence and criminality that had virtually imprisoned our society in fear and anarchy.

Like all the problems of Philippine society, the problem of civil order was awesome, for the evils had been allowed to accumulate through centuries. The inequities of the system abetted crime incidence and the proliferation of criminal elements. In the context of the problem we faced, the restoration of order could not be the work of a day, a week, or a month. But the immediate results of the campaign were unexpectedly phenomenal. The statistics attest to this. A total of 523,616 firearms were confiscated in the first nine months alone (in the old society, according to the military, it would have taken us forty years to collect these). One hundred forty-five private armies were disbanded and disarmed, and a good number of their political overlords were placed under detention. Twelve thousand persons suspected of crimes varying from petty theft to murder were apprehended. Thirty-two million pesos (about $5 million at the rate of P6.5 to the U.S. dollar) worth of illegal drugs were seized, and the members of the vice rings were taken into custody. So successful was the peace and order campaign that the crime rate dipped to zero during the early days of martial law. To this day, the war against the criminal elements continues; I am not content with a substantial reduction of crime but only with its elimination. We see only too well that civil order can be maintained firmly only with the improvement of social and economic conditions.

The campaign to restore order in Muslim Mindanao has been successful precisely because of the understanding demonstrated in dealing with the rebels. At the same time there has been a complementary effort to alleviate social and economic conditions in the Muslim areas. We matched the forceful military solution with attractive benevolence and a socioeconomic development program. Besides meeting fully the threat of 16,000 armed rebels aided by foreign forces and arms, I treated the rebels as brothers. I released the captured leaders of the rebellion. Negotiations for surrender were as important to me as the plans of the military for battle. I attended personally to both. Of course our starting point was the courage and patriotism of the Filipino soldier who, although outnumbered and often initially surrounded by superior enemy forces, upheld the traditions of his race by refusing to give ground and fighting on even unto destruction.

In Mindanao and Sulu of our south, the Moro National Liberation Front, organized and armed as well as supported by foreign sources, has sought to establish an independent state composed of Mindanao, Sulu, and Palawan. As late as February 7, 1974, this Front attracted international attention by sacking Jolo, the capital town of the province of Sulu, causing many casualties, and burning the town to cover the retreat before counter-attacking government troops and the local Muslim Home Defense Forces.

As of March 11, 1974, the Front's main headquarters in the mountains at Batang Puti was captured. The leaders were killed in combat or surrendered, and the organization was dismantled. It is no longer an effective fighting force.

I created a presidential task force headed by the executive secretary, Annapolis graduate and former navy man Alejandro Melchor, to work on channeling most of our borrowed funds from international institutions (running into hundreds of millions of dollars) into the Muslim areas for roads and bridges, settlements, electrification, schoolhouses, credit for both agriculture and industry, and economic projects like fishing, fishponds, and seaweed culture and trade.

Aware of the fundamental place of infrastructure facilities in any development effort, I caused the allocation of some P900 million ($130 million) to road-building and other construction projects right from the start of the Rehabilitation and Development Program (RAD) for Mindanao, a continuing and steadily accelerating organized effort to put that once-neglected region on the same level of progress as the rest of the nation. This amount (of which P250 million has already been spent) consists entirely of Philippine government funds; apart from it, we have sought, and obtained, amounts from foreign sources, including the International Bank for Reconstruction and Development, the Asian Development Bank, and the German government, to augment our domestic funds for roads, irrigation systems, airports and harbors, flood control and water systems, as well as schoolhouses, for the Muslim areas. By late 1973, more than 1,000 kilometers of completed roads had literally brought the thrust of development into once-isolated Muslim lands.

Under the RAD program we have opened up trade between Sulu and Sabah, which allows the entry of goods duty-free.

We have offered scholarships to 4,000 qualified Muslim youths; trained young Muslims for executive positions; authorized the use of Muslim dialects in primary schools and prepared to incorporate Muslim customs, traditions and laws into Philippine law; and recognized Muslim marriage customs and ceremonies. The same program has increased the number of Muslim schoolhouses to twice the number in the Christian areas.

In the economic field, we have established the Muslim Amanah bank, with a P100 million capitalization; set up small- and medium-scale industries such as fishing, seaweed and shrimp culture, the last as a result of the breakthrough achieved by the Mindanao State University in the culture of shrimp fry under laboratory conditions; and liberalized credit for both agriculture and industry.

We have secured a loan of $100 million exclusively for hydro-electric power and its distribution in Muslim areas. Half of this has already been delivered and is now being spent for this purpose.

Several industrial centers have been and are being established in Muslim territory, notably Iligan City and Cagayan de Oro City.

In compliance with an agreement reached after my first meeting with the foreign ministers of Saudi Arabia, Libya, Senegal and Somalia, who visited the Philippines in late 1973, we have appointed Muslim officers to positions of high responsibility in the armed forces and the civil government. The commanding general now for instance, of the Southwest Command (Sowescom) is a native of Sulu, Rear Admiral Romulo Espaldon.

A Muslim officer was named to the position of provincial commander of Sulu. The same policy is being implemented in other Muslim provinces.

The hopeful signs of development in Muslim Mindanao are evident today. The local governments have been strengthened. Infrastructure projects are injecting new life into the economy of the region.

The institution of social reforms, to benefit the broad masses of our people, formed a complementary concern to the restoration of order and the securing of the Republic. The priority program had to be land reform. For decades the necessity of agrarian reform had been stressed to our politicians, but not until the "September 21 Movement" could this reform be carried out realistically.

On September 26, 1972, five days after the proclamation of martial law, I signed Presidential Decree No. 2, proclaiming "the whole country as land reform area," in the belief that the objectives of the agrarian reform program set forth in Republic Act No. 3844 would be realized sooner through this decree.

The following month, on October 21, I signed Presidential Decree No. 27, emancipating the tenants from the bondage of the soil, transferring to them the ownership of the land they till and providing the instruments and "mechanism" for such emancipation.

With these two decrees the government set into motion the massive overhaul of the system of land ownership in the Philippines, and at last land reform ceased to be an unrealized dream in our society.

There were nagging problems, to be sure. The small landowners must be given just treatment. They could not be treated exactly as the big landowners or inheritors of large estates. An amendment to the provisions of Republic Act No. 3844 was made in Presidential Decree No. 251; it created a new system of compensating the landowner. Six modes of payment, all designed to provide fair compensation, were indicated in this amendment. Six hundred million pesos has been set aside for the compensation of the small landowners, who comprise the majority of those whose landholdings had been affected by the land reform decree.

Despite initial difficulties inherent in any program so vast and unprecedented, the land transfer program launched to implement land reform has moved briskly.

As of the end of April 1974 the government had issued more than 250,000 land transfer certificates covering an area of 360,000 hectares worked by 200,000 tenant farmers. These accomplishments, however, covered only rice or corn lands fifty hectares and above in size. Later the land transfer operation was brought down to the twenty-four hectare category. The targets are 1,000,000 tenant-tillers and 350,000 landowners in a total of 1,767,000 hectares of tenanted rice and corn lands.

We are rapidly converting mere sharecroppers into small agricultural entrepreneurs.

At the same time, to ensure that land reform would not stop at mere ownership for the tenant, a system of rural credit has been extended to the Filipino farmers benefitting from the decree, and a nationwide agricultural cooperative movement has been launched. A total of about P300 million in rural credit was extended under a specific project, Masagana 99. The Philippine National Bank with ninety-eight mobile stations actually delivered the money at the farmers' doorsteps by banca (dugout canoe), helicopter, or jeep. About 500 rural banks participated in the nationwide effort to finance the farmers. The cooperative movement, it must be emphasized, should be seen as an integral part of the land reform program. The individual farmer cannot do it alone, if production is not to suffer. To this end, every effort and assistance is being extended by government to mobilize the farmers into viable cooperative communities that can displace the farming estates of the old order. Such government and civic programs as the propagation of the rice varieties of IRRI (The International Rice and Research Institute), the Green Revolution, Masagana 99, and Palayan ng Bayan, are all designed to render assistance to the farmer communities, to increase production, and to enhance the possibilities of cooperative farming. By the end of 1973, all provinces had organized their Samahang Nayon or Barrio Cooperative.

The recent rice crisis was an occasion—unlike in the past—for moral resurgence on the part of the people. For the first time the problem was treated as economic rather than as political. Rice has to be produced or bought; in either case, its surplus depends on our effort. We must put the pressure on traders and dealers to ensure efficient distribution of rice supplies. But as I told our people in August 1973, "the shortage cannot be met with anger and rioting and by damning anyone. If we want to eat, let us work." The people responded. Farms and gardens sprang up everywhere.

We must realistically recognize one principle: it is far better to face problems which arise out of reform measures than to allow the old problems to grow and overwhelm us. Solutions tend to beget further problems. We must meet the problems of reform with vigor and enthusiasm, for we are bound to solve them.

Social reforms also mean the increase of the minimum wage. Again we must understand that before we can talk of higher wages, we must first apply ourselves to production. I sought the counsel of labor itself on this matter and we agreed. Our rewards lie in our productive capacity. However, this principle must never be allowed to justify exploitation of the working masses. This is the enduring basis not only of industrial peace but of social progress.

As for the national economy, one of its basic features is the active "governmental participation and management in economic planning and implementation as laid down by a constitutional office, the National Economic and Development Authority." One of the first steps taken by government was the establishment of a "free flow" policy, in which foreign investments may be repatriated at any time, profits remitted, and "frozen" dollars allowed to be withdrawn. This policy attracted a flow of foreign investors.

It can no longer be said that our economic development efforts are anarchic, uncoordinated, and unplanned. As a consequence, the two most important resources, human and natural, are being properly and efficiently mobilized for development.

The socioeconomic program has become the total answer to our problems.

As I have clearly indicated in the body of this book, the conquest of mass poverty is our fundamental goal. Progress must not be measured merely by the cold, impersonal statistics of the gross national product, but by the individually meaningful and tangible improvement of everyone's well-being. This is the driving philosophy behind the economic program that the Four-Year Development Plan translates into specific, operational terms.

Our objective is the establishment of a balanced agro-industrial economy. But the pursuit of this objective goes hand in hand with the efforts to achieve our social goals.

Thus, while agricultural development has been concerted and unrelenting on all fronts—land reform, food production, cooperatives' development—we have with equal energy taken firm steps to meet the long-neglected need of processing our agricultural products into semiprocessed goods through the establishment of more factories and industries.

The Board of Investments and, later, the Department of Industry have been organized.

I have set aside more than a thousand hectares for a duty- and tax-free Export Processing Zone in Mariveles, Bataan, where factories and a new city are springing up vigorously.

As a counterpart of the Land Reform Program, the cooperative system, national electrification, cottage industries, national irrigation systems, rural credit, compact farming, and other agricultural projects, I have directed an emphasis on the establishment of small- and medium-scale industries in the countryside.

The potential for the rapid growth of small- and medium-scale enterprises is decidedly great. One need only compare our industrial activity at these scales to those of other countries that are similarly situated to see the importance of these industries. Small- and medium-scale enterprises, for instance, form the backbone of Taiwan's export-oriented manufacturing activities.

More important, and this we realized as soon as we started reassessing our old plans, are opportunities offered by these enterprises through their higher labor intensiveness and efficiency in the use of capital resources. More employment opportunities for our extant labor surplus and wider participation in productive activities by more income groups and by regions are possible through a program for the establishment of small- and medium-scale enterprises.

That this is indeed not only a necessary but also a priority program is confirmed by the Comprehensive Survey of Employment by the Commission under the International Labor Organization (ILO) headed by Dr. Gustav Ranis of the Yale University Economic Growth Center.

To finance this important part of our industrialization effort in the rural areas, P500 million has been set aside by the Development Bank of the Philippines.

The purpose has been to spread technology, financing and industrial activity to the provinces and the barrios.

We are likewise giving new importance to other programs. Under the program for basic and resource-based industries are mineral exploration, processing, and wood-based industries. The next four years, covered by the current development plan, will witness the release of more lands with high exploitation potential for minerals. The establishment of a copper smelter-refinery plant is also to be undertaken within the period.

The program for wood-based industries emphasizes greater processing of domestic logs for exports and a gradual reduction of log exports over the next four years. To sustain the wood requirements, intensified reforestation will be undertaken on more than 120,000 hectares all over the country.

In the meantime, the demand for wage or essential goods is expected to continue to expand. To meet this demand adequately, wage goods industries will be given due emphasis. The program will include the upgrading of local textile industries and the encouragement of food processing such as cereals, meat, fish, and dairy products.

Greater interdependence between agricultural and manufacturing industries will also be actively promoted. This will set in motion a two-way flow: agriculture supplying industry with its raw materials, as in the case of food processing; and industry supplying agricultural inputs, such as fertilizers and farm machines.

The promotion of engineering industries is another important aspect of our industrialization program. This calls for a progressive increase of domestic content in engineering products. Thus, in the progressive car and motorcycle manufacturing programs, domestic manufacture of components will be encouraged through subcontracting arrangements with small- and medium-scale manufacturing enterprises. In addition, a ten-year shipbuilding program has been adopted to meet the needs of domestic coastal commerce.

At the same time the government itself participates in the intensive search for oil, gas, and other sources of energy, although in the drilling for oil, service contracts with the oil majors as well as the independents are preferred.

From late 1973 to the early months of 1974, the energy crisis and the worldwide inflation posed a grave challenge to Philippine resources and ingenuity. Owing to the sudden rise of the price of crude oil, our national oil cost leaped from $200 million to $700 million. This additional cost of $500 million, plus another $500 million representing the additional cost of all our imported requirements for development, increased the overall cost of importation of all our requirements from $1,300 million to $2,300 million.

To meet this problem, I considered it imperative that we

maintain the existing level of our foreign exchange reserves—$1 billion—so as to maintain monetary stability. For this purpose, we geared our new planning to the necessity for additional export earnings and for loans from foreign sources. I did not believe in economic retrenchment or the abandonment of the important projects we had already laid out or launched, inasmuch as our inflation was imported and could not conceivably be mitigated by domestic palliatives. I was determined that the momentum of development would not be slowed down or halted even by the crucial and unexpected struggle to cope with the tremendous burdens caused by the problems of oil and inflation. On the contrary, by resolute action at the top and the support of the entire nation, we continued every measure for economic development, with new emphasis on the establishment of export-oriented industries.

We are preventing further migration to the urban centers, if not actually reversing the trend and decongesting them instead, by making the provinces as attractive to investors, industrialists, and workers as the cities, if not more so.

I have created the Zoning and Human Settlement Commission to mark out areas for new towns and plan not only the infrastructure for comfortable living such as housing, schools, markets, roads, parks and amusement areas, but also employment and sources of income.

We have systematized the big industries such as oil, steel, construction, cement, textiles, and food.

I have directed the dispersal of new large-scale factories.

These efforts are premised on the lessons we have learned from past development thrusts. As in the last two decades, we still hold that industrialization is necessary for overall development. But we now realize that the pursuit of industrial development must not be isolated from our other objectives.

Industrialization will be pursued not as an independent and parochial end, but as an integral part of our social and economic objectives. To develop the industrial sector, we have adopted means which will likewise bring us closer to the attainment of our other goals.

As I said on July 3, 1973, when I announced the adoption of the Four-Year Development Plan for Fiscal Years 1974–77, "This is the Development Plan of the New Society—that we are committed to forge for the nation." Its objectives are six: to attain a more equitable distribution of income and wealth, to expand employment opportunities, to promote social development, to stabilize prices at reasonable levels, to accelerate economic growth, and to promote regional development and industrialization.

Our performance in the monetary, credit, and financial sectors made me conclude that the groundwork had been laid and the stage set for the vast undertaking.

A stable monetary, credit and financial system is a *sine qua non* for such an ambitious economic program. A vigorous financial structure capable of sustaining impetus and providing the massive funding and related requirements for such a program is vital before a start should even be contemplated.

Looking back at the record, we may say that September 21, 1972, marked the turning point for the Philippine economy. This is not to say that a miracle occurred overnight. The record shows that martial law was the catalyst that brought into fruition all our efforts at revitalizing the economy. This began earnestly in February 1970 when I approved adoption by the government and the Central Bank of a rigid stabilization program that featured the unpopular "floating rate" system of exchange administration. Attention was concentrated on strengthening the country's monetary and financial structure. Incentives for growth and expansion of exports and promoting foreign investments, both loans and equity, were set in motion. The need for strengthening these areas had long been recognized. Corrective legislation and policy measures, however, suffered from constraints inherent in the old order of anarchy, violence, vested interests, and political orientation. Both foreign and domestic investments faltered for want of faith in the capacity of government to assure them of security, stability and freedom from undue restraints in capital movements. Martial law and the New Society provided the key to performance.

The climate of peace and order, the extirpation of graft and corruption in centers of government control, and the removal of bureaucratic red tape gave rise to an economic performance, particularly in the external sector, unparalleled in our country's history. Our international reserves rose from $221.5 million, the level on September 21, 1972, to $999.13 million as of February 28, 1974, of which Central Bank holdings amounted to $978.18 million, offset by the negative position of the commercial banking system amounting to $142.22 million. If we add to the gross holdings of the Central Bank the $441.19 million in dollar deposits ($342.3 million as of September 21, 1972) in the foreign-currency deposit system which I approved to be established in July 1970, we began 1974 with foreign exchange resources of $1.419 billion available for our current needs. This gave us strength to cope with uncertainties in the international scene caused by the energy and food crises.

The atmosphere of confidence generated by the New Society made possible commendable performances by other sectors of the government, notably the fiscal sector, which consistently registered surpluses in operations against a backdrop of chronic deficits in premartial-law days. This mirrors the results of an efficient tax administration and collection system hand in hand with cooperation of a citizenry now witnessing in concrete, everyday terms the accomplishments of government made possible by the taxes that they pay. A most dramatic turn of events was an increase in the number of income tax filers from 1,500,000 persons to 4,500,000 persons.

The New Society made possible a program of funds mobilization through sustained national savings campaigns by both government and private sectors. Steps were taken to prevent undue expansion of money and credit and to check unwarranted inflation. All this provides and expands credit on a supervised and geographically dispersed basis to assure availability of funds— financial fuel—that will increase food production and promote small- and medium-scale industries, vital factors in the attainment of our national goal of self-sufficiency and supply of goods to every citizen at reasonable costs.

Even before the adoption of the development plan, we had taken steps to halt the deterioration of the economy and set it on the right course. The restoration of civil order enabled us to make tourism an important economic resource. In a large measure economic equality was accomplished through various "tax amnesties," thus taking out of hiding what is truly the "wealth of society."

The climate for foreign investment has considerably improved partly because of the restoration of civil order and partly because of our new policy on repatriation of capital and remittance of profits. Prior to the declaration of martial law, applications for licensing new foreign investments had a total value of P99.5 million. In the eleven months after martial law was declared, applications for new foreign investments totalled P237.9 million, or more than twice the premartial-law figure.

In the past, the two conditions, civil order and our new investment policy, were not present. Certain opposition officials, playing up to the oligarchs and their controlled media, had denounced all foreign investments in the name of nationalism, irrespective of our capital and other deficiencies. Their actual purpose was to obstruct the success of the government of the day, even if this meant misguiding the nationalist sentiments of our people.

If there is one signal achievement of the New Society, it is that the government has been able to accumulate capital resources through both internal and external means. Mobilized properly, these savings will surely go a long way in providing the necessary incentives for both domestic and foreign investments. After all, the primary role of government in any developing country is the accumulation of capital. And today there is an air of energetic activity everywhere. Over the first ten months of 1973 alone, exports increased by 60 percent over the level of the same period in 1972; 23 percent of this being nontraditional exports.

Indicative of the activity in agriculture is the utilization of fertilizer. In the last three months of 1973, the country used twice the amount of fertilizer expended during the whole year before martial law.

More mines were opened in ten months than in the ten years before that.

Oil exploration increased tenfold.

In the labor field, industrial relations have been streamlined to promote development and to assure peace based on social justice. Out of about 6,000 labor disputes and grievances in 1973, 5,000 were actually settled by arbitration. At the same time, the whole range of economic and social policies was reoriented towards employment generation.

The media have been moved out of the government control that is traditional in martial law. They are supervised and controlled by the Media Advisory Council composed wholly of representatives of the private sector. The chairman is the president of the National Press Club, the members drawn from the ranks of the various sectors of media—one representative each from the Manila Overseas Press Club, the print media, the broadcast media and special media. This is media's self-regulatory body.

The test of any theory—or policy—is its practical consequences on the life of the ordinary Filipino. We have not forgotten the expansion of social services: medicare now covers about one-half of our entire population; we have increased benefits for worker-members of the social security system; and we have provided for the infrastructure of development—from roads to bridges, schoolhouses to community hospitals.

This time the state is not doling out "charity" to the poor masses, but is managing the economy in such a way that the ordinary man can enjoy the fruits of his labor and the rewards of social discipline. We are not just "giving away fish, we are teaching the needy how to fish."

In the end we rely on the political will, which makes political reforms imperative. Constitutionalism remains the basis of the present government, constitutionalism that reaches down to the humblest level of the citizenry.

The *barangay* is not the restoration of an ancient political institution, but the basis of a new institution whose origins are indigenous to our race. It is truly Asian in that the Indonesians and the Chinese, for example, have similar institutions which have been adapted to their present needs. Call it "village council" or "village democracy." There is no question that our people have taken to this "revival," which is actually a constitutional innovation, with enthusiasm and responsibility. I look forward to a time when the *barangays*—the citizens assemblies—can legislate for themselves on matters of immediate concern, so that the democratic cry of "power to the people" will have authentic validity.

Out of the *barangay* concept we have realized the ancient dream of political philosophers: the enfranchisement of the entire adult population, regardless of literacy. Through the *barangays* every adult Filipino, from the age of fifteen, may express his will and cast his vote. At the referendum in July 1973, this meant 22.3 million registered voters—twice the registered voters (11.6 million) in the last elections before martial law.

Universal enfranchisement makes the politics of the New Society a real achievement in participatory democracy.

This is the democratic political revolution.

There is another dimension to the emergence of the New Society: the support that erstwhile rebels have given it. Luis M. Taruc, *the supremo* of the Huks, who fought for more than a decade to destroy the old society, and young Communists such as Benjamin Sanguyo, better known by his *nom de guerre*, Commander Pusa (Cat), former deputy of Commander Dante, Supreme Commander of the Maoist New People's Army, and Benjamin M. Bie (Commander Melody), are active supporters of the ideology and tendencies of the New Society. A large number of Marxist and socialist intellectuals have signified their willingness to serve the aims of the New Society in any capacity. I can only conclude that the ideals of the Democratic Revolution transcend all class ideologies insofar as these erstwhile Jacobin revolutionaries are concerned.

The Institutionalization of the Revolution

We have unleashed by executive action * the beneficent forces of a democratic revolution in a society which otherwise would have carried the Republic along on the road leading to its destruction. This was done in the short space of a year, with the sanction of the Constitution and the support of the people.

The crucial question now is how to make the achievements under martial law the enduring basis of a New Society. To put it

---

* This was accomplished by exercising extraordinary powers. The extraordinary character of these powers is similar to those vividly explained in some American precedents (*Moyer* v. *Peabody*, 212 U.S. 78 [1901]; *Luther* v. *Borden*, 7 How. 1, 12 L. Ed. 584 [1849]; *Martin* v. *Mott*, 12 Wheat. 19, 6 L. Ed. 537 [1827]). It is noteworthy that the opinion in *Moyer* v. *Peabody*, which was written by Justice Oliver Wendell Holmes, is cited with approval by two liberal-minded, civil rights-oriented, and prominent constitutionalists, former Senator Lorenzo M. Tañada and Supreme Court Justice Enrique Fernando. In their book, *Constitution of the Philippines* (vol. 2, pp. 523–25), they averred, citing the Moyer decision:

> Once martial law has been declared, arrest may be necessary not so much for punishment but by way of precaution to stop disorder. As long as such arrests are made in good faith and in the honest belief they are needed to maintain order, the President, as Commander-in-Chief, cannot thereafter, when he is out of office, be subjected to an action on the ground that he had no reasonable ground for his belief. *When it comes to a decision by the head of the state upon a matter involving its life, the ordinary rights of individuals must yield to what he deems the necessities of the moment. Public danger warrants the substitution of executive process for judicial process.* [Emphasis mine.]

another way, the Democratic Revolution must be institutionalized; the ideals, policies and beneficent practices of the New Society must find their place in our institutions.

The Republic has been saved by the supreme exercise of political will. But the dangers persist, for the forces of disruption, dissension, and subversion have yet to be completely dismantled. Now, having come so far in establishing the New Society, how are we going to secure it for the future?

At this point we find the link, the inseparable link, between martial law and the new Constitution.

The calling of the constitutional convention was made in response to a revolutionary demand for change. But for martial law, its work, already compromised by vested interests, would have been academic in the face of national peril. Under the conditions in the old society, the convention could not, in any case, have wrought fundamental changes. Martial law enabled the constituent body to draft a charter attuned to the demands for revolutionary change.

It is logical and natural, therefore, for the new Constitution to embody these changes and reflect the spirit of the times in which it was written.

I derived my martial law authority from the old Constitution. From this authority the constitutional convention was able finally to do its work according to the imperatives of national survival. In turn, the convention realized that the new Constitution should provide for the emergency situation so as to secure its force and survival and, more important, its orderly implementation and perpetuation. Thus Article XVII, otherwise known as the Transitory Provisions. (See Appendix A.)

The Transitory Provisions, drafted with full appreciation of the national situation, delineated clearly the powers of the incumbent president during the period of transition to the new Constitution.

These provisions seem to contemplate three stages in the transition from the old to the new government. The first stage embraces the period from the ratification of the Constitution to the convening of the *interim* National Assembly; the second, from the convening of the *interim* National Assembly to the election of the *interim* President and Prime Minister; and the third, from the election of the *interim* President and Prime Minister to the calling of the regular election by the *interim* National Assembly.

During the first stage, the incumbent President of the Philippines is granted the powers and prerogatives of the President under the 1935 Constitution and the powers vested in both the President and Prime Minister under the new Constitution. Section 3, Subsection 2, Article XVII also expressly grants the incumbent President legislative powers.

The transitory provision envisions the possibility of the *interim* Assembly not immediately being called to session by the incumbent President. During this interregnum the constitutional convention specifically provided for the powers of the incumbent President, thus allowing a graceful transition into the period of full enforcement of the new Constitution.

The pertinent provision reads as follows:

Sec. 3. (1) The incumbent President of the Philippines shall initially convene the *interim* National Assembly and shall preside over its sessions until the *interim* Speaker shall have been elected. He shall continue to exercise his powers and prerogatives under the nineteen hundred and thirty-five Constitution and the powers vested in the President and the Prime Minister under this Constitution until he calls upon the *interim* National Assembly to elect the *interim* President and the *interim* Prime Minister, who shall then exercise their respective powers vested by this Constitution.

(2) All proclamations, orders, decrees, instructions, and acts promulgated, issued or done by the incumbent President shall be part of the law of the land, and shall remain valid, legal, binding, and effective even after lifting of martial law or the ratification of this Constitution, unless modified, revoked, or superseded by subsequent proclamations, orders, decrees, instructions, or other acts of the incumbent President, or unless expressly and explicitly modified or repealed by the regular National Assembly.

During the second stage, it may be noted that upon convening the *interim* Assembly, the President need not necessarily call for the election of the President and Prime Minister. For the final stage, with the exception of the powers granted to the President under the 1973 Constitution, executive power passes to the *interim* Prime Minister elected by the *interim* National Assembly.

My belief is that the Transistory Provisions of the new Constitution should put to rest all doubts as to the constitutionality of all the powers I have exercised under the 1935 Constitution. They also confer upon me certain extraordinary powers not found in the old Constitution. In the exercise of these powers, I could choose not to convene as yet the *interim* National Assembly in view of the emergency situation. I have decided on this choice in accordance with the decision of the people voting in the plebiscite of January 1973.

All interpretations of these provisions are that they constitute the best authority for what I call constitutional authoritarianism.

Under the old Constitution, I exercised martial law powers to meet the national emergency; under the new Constitution I exercise extraordinary powers together with or even independently of martial law. These powers, including the power of legislation provided for in Sec. 3, Subsec. 2, Art. XVII, were prescribed by a duly convoked constitutional convention in a Constitution duly ratified by the people in the plebiscite of January 10–15, 1973, which Constitution is now in full force and effect as ruled by our Supreme Court. (*Javellana et al.* v. *Executive Secretary et al.,* G.R. No. L-36143, 36164, 36165, 36236, and 36283.)

The question most often in the minds of international and some domestic observers is how long martial law will last.

My answer invariably has been "for as long as the people desire it." Often I am asked what I desire personally. I hope that the powers exercised under the martial-law authority whether called by such name or not would continue until the reforms in our society are firmly rooted. Otherwise this would have been a futile experiment.

My intention is to submit this issue periodically to the people through the *barangays* so that they may decide when to dismantle martial law.

The clear intent of the framers of the new Constitution is to allow sufficient time for all the political, social, and economic reforms under martial law to become enduring institutions in our national life. This implies some continuity of leadership. For this reason the Constitution, especially the Transitory Provisions, emphasizes that the ratification of the fundamental law carried with it a direct mandate for the incumbent President.

I surmise that the framers of the Constitution, in their wisdom, anticipated this "constitutional crisis" early in the life of the new charter. The Transitory Provisions plugged the loopholes, as it were, and thus gave us the authoritative instrument for governing a well-ordered political society from the start.

Obviously the new Constitution contemplates two great objectives: first, the institutionalization of the Democratic Revolution, as reflected in the decrees, proclamations, orders, letters of instructions, decisions, policies and implementation under martial law; second, the laying of the legal foundation of the New Society. Drafted and adopted in the crucible of the peaceful revolution, the Constitution attests to our continuing struggle for a better and more fruitful life for our people.

But what seem to trouble some of us are the vicissitudes of leadership in this time of crisis. "What," it is said, "if anything happens to the President of the Philippines?" My ready answer is that there will be a new leader of the Democratic Revolution. One of the agreements arrived at by all those who helped me plan the proclamation of martial law and its implementation was that I should provide, immediately after the announcement of the proclamation of martial law, for political succession by Presidential Decree in accordance with the 1935 Constitution. I had done so as early as September 1972. After the ratification of the new Constitution, succession is provided for in accordance with its provisions. But as agreed, I have kept it sealed to be opened only in case of any contingency to prevent it from sowing intrigues, disunity, and rivalries.

Those who fear fratricidal strife need only to be reminded that the Transitory Provisions, in conferring extraordinary powers on the incumbent President, *clearly* reaffirm the supremacy of civilian authority over the military. I dare say the military submits completely to this republican authority. The question of succession is, therefore, a minor problem.

Under the new Constitution, the situation has been clarified further because I am empowered by the Transitory Provisions, by virtue of my legislative powers, to decide the question of succession and caretaker government in the event of incapacity. The options as well as the instrumentalities I could utilize are by no means confined. Under such new Constitution I could decide to leave a political testament that is immediately executory or subject to the approval of other bodies. There are, aside from the *interim* National Assembly, possibly a legislative council, and the *barangays* or citizens assemblies. I can put the question of a successor directly to the people, to the citizens assemblies, to the *interim* National Assembly or to any other body that may legally be created.

We know that men are mortal. But the Constitution is less mortal and the people are immortal. I am resolved that the New Society's existence and growth will not depend on one man or group of men. The New Society will be "institutionalized." And its institutionalization is documented by the Constitution.

The Internal Revolution

It has been said that a revolution may survive any political or economic error but not a moral one. The question then is what moral error or errors we must guard against in the reshaping of our society. There are errors that are particular to one's situation and functions, and errors which are common to all.

Of those common to all, the most conspicuous is the error of complacency. Some of us, whether in the military or the civil government, are beginning once more to strive for privilege, are less efficient, less courteous, and less honest, in the mistaken belief that exemplary performance at the right time, in the hour of crisis, is a permanent passport in the New Society. This cannot be: all of us are on trial every minute of our lives.

The same complacency may be found in society, in what is called "the private sector," for some believe erroneously that only those who serve the government are subject to discipline. They have even started cultivating new ties and new connections for the old purpose of influencing the political authority to follow their will.

The "human nature" of the old society will die hard. Our sure defense against it is continuing vigilance.

We should not fall into the trap of making our temporary command society into a "surveilled" society; this will defeat our purpose.

Happily, our recourse was prescribed by Apolinario Mabini in another revolution, when he said that an "internal" revolution was necessary for the success of an "external" one. What this means ultimately is that we should be able to internalize the Democratic Revolution, make its objectives, principles and ideals *a part of our being,* if we expect to succeed—and make our success an enduring one.

I have gone over the successes of the "external" revolution in the previous chapters, but as anyone can see, there is still much to be done. Many basic plans have not been implemented completely for varied reasons. While there has been an increase in exports by about 60 percent, 23 percent of which are nontraditional products, ours is still substantially an import economy.

Production is still aimed at filling deficiencies. The prime example of this is our recurring deficits in staples, animal feed, and fertilizers. While we have reason to congratulate ourselves on the results of the tax reforms and the public response to our appeals in the tax campaign, and while we have updated completely the Tariff and Customs Code as well as the Internal Revenue Code, we still have to apply taxation as an instrument for the *regulation and redistribution of wealth* in our society. It must be remembered that the Democratic Revolution calls for the democratization of wealth. As I said in *Today's Revolution: Democracy:*

> The choice is between democratizing private wealth or "socializing" it. Democratization is the governing idea in these remarks on property by U.S. Supreme Court Justice Benjamin N. Cardozo: "Property, like liberty, though immune under the Constitution from destruction, *is not immune* from regulation essential for the common good. What the regulation shall be every generation must work out for itself." Socialization, on the other hand, means quite simply the abolition of private property, which is a process that historically has been associated intimately with communism. Under this system, as we know it from experience, not only private property is abolished but also human freedom.

Our most important reform, land reform, must still be effectively pursued, especially as it relates to the small landowners, who should not be treated in the same manner as the cacique-type landlords, the ancient source of the oligarchy. In conjunction with this are the reforms in labor, the training and utilization of our vast manpower resources, and an improved machinery for maintaining industrial peace and justice.

I am not yet satisfied with the gains in the political reorganization of our society. The old political habits, the old alliances between oligarchs and their political retainers, although tamed, must now be uprooted. All of us are confronted now and then with "a nostalgia for the good old days." This is prevalent among those who have lost their old privileges and thus miss their former dominance, now steadily fading.

The most important field for the *internal revolution* is that of education and culture. Here we must admit numerous and grave problems: problems of national identity, problems of reorientation and administration, of renewed vigor, fresh vision, and the firmest resolution to carry through plans and programs. Educational reforms will be the work not of one generation but of several generations working together. We have not yet, in this respect, offered a complete and challenging program for the youth of our country.

I have been advised that many of our youth have undergone traumatic experience with the declaration of martial law. I cannot be convinced of the validity of this claim. I had my own frustrations as a young man in a society that I wanted to change; my disappointments and sufferings did not constitute a traumatic experience: they became the spur to my strivings. Our youth today cannot be too different from the youth of old. They are idealistic and courageous and morally honest. They can find their cause in the ideals of the New Society.

Where once we told ourselves that the elder generations should first prove themselves to the younger, now all the generations must prove themselves to one another. The New Society is the test of the sincerity of our desire for beneficent change.

Besides the youth there are the poor, the unskilled, the unemployed. With them the moral ideals of the Democratic Revolution will find their greatest trial. Our greatest efforts must be for them and with them.

Thus we understand that while there is still a great deal to be achieved in the "external" revolution, there is more to achieve— to challenge us—in the "internal" revolution.

As we have learned from Mabini, the *internalization* of the revolution is an act of moral will that expresses itself in the material pursuits of a people and their cultural, artistic, intellectual, and scientific work. This requires collective as well as individual striving. In the collective, the government has done its share and will continue doing its share towards creating the "infrastructure" of a cultural awakening. A revolution without a humanist dimension, without cultural roots, is merely a struggle for material things. We are struggling for more than the rice in our bellies and the clothes on our backs. We are fighting for our pride as a nation and as individual human beings.

The proclamation of martial law has made this possible.

Martial law was never conceived nor has it ever been utilized to attain revolutionary or radical reforms. On the contrary it was the ultimate weapon for stability—in short, the final power to freeze the *status quo*. Injustices there may be in that *status quo;* it was not for martial law to redress them.

For the Philippines, history dictated this persuasion. The constitutional provision on martial law had been lifted *verbatim* from organic laws adopted by the American Congress for the Philippines (similar provisions were found in the organic laws of the U.S. territorial possessions, Puerto Rico, and Hawaii, as well as Alaska). These were the Philippine Bill of 1902 and the Jones Law of 1916.

They were meant to consolidate the power of the American governor-general over a colony.

The legalist and historian were outraged that martial law, the weapon *against* revolution, should be converted into a revolution for reform!

This conversion was achieved because of the clarity with which our people, no less than the leadership, perceived the common danger and the urgent necessity for change. Among all the peoples of new nations, we Filipinos have tried the hardest—and the longest—to exist on the belief that the Western political forms could live side by side with the iniquities of an unjust social order and eventually eliminate them. Perhaps, if we had enough time . . . and the barbarians were not knocking at the gates . . . There was, however, not "world enough and time."

Moreover, we have embarked upon the experiment with the full knowledge that its outcome will depend on most of us, not just a few who are managing a "command society." The misgivings are large; the most outstanding is the fear of a powerful few holding the many in subjection. But this fear misses the particularity of Philippine martial law: it cannot and will not exist without the clear and *not* manipulated consent of the governed. Our people will accept only sacrifices which are justifiable to them.

It is more than a homily to assert that the New Society is not a promised land that patiently awaits our arrival. More than a place in time or space, the New Society is a vision in our minds: this can be realized only through the strength of our resolution.

I am mindful of the fact that historically authoritarian regimes tend to outlive their justification. I do not intend to make a permanent authoritarianism as my legacy to the Filipino people. It is sufficiently clear to them, I believe, that martial law is an interlude to a new society, that it is, in sum, a Cromwellian phase in our quest for a good and just society. Certainly, the enterprise is worth a little sacrifice.

Leaders and statesmen are understandably wary of repeating the call for sacrifice and of stressing that a common enterprise is the commitment of all. There is a ring of the cliché in such exhortation and yet it is a monotonous theme among all revolutionaries. This is so because revolutionaries are more concerned with conviction than with elegance. Why should we, then, be less revolutionary simply because the Democratic Revolution substitutes, so to speak, the ploughshare for the sword? For whatever the connotation of martial law, its unique expression in the Philippines is the revolutionization of society by peaceful and constitutional means.

If, either by failure of leadership or failure of nerve on the part of our people, we do not succeed, then we shall merely have prepared our country for the deluge. Few Filipinos, I believe, will accept such a prospect, and from this derives my optimism about timely establishment of the New Society. The opportunity may not present itself again in our time.

| Appendix A |

CONSTITUTION OF THE REPUBLIC OF THE PHILIPPINES (1973)

Preamble

We, the sovereign Filipino people, imploring the aid of Divine Providence, in order to establish a Government that shall embody our ideals, promote the general welfare, conserve and develop the patrimony of our Nation, and secure to ourselves and our posterity the blessings of democracy under a regime of justice, peace, liberty, and equality, do ordain and promulgate this Constitution.

Article I. The National Territory

Section 1. The national territory comprises the Philippine archipelago, with all the islands and waters embraced therein, and all the other territorits belonging to the Philippines by historic right or legal title, including the territorial sea, the air space, the subsoil, the sea-bed, the insular shelves, and the other submarine areas over which the Philippines has sovereignty or jurisdiction. The waters around, between, and connecting the islands of the archipelago, irrespective of their breadth and dimensions, form part of the internal waters of the Philippines.

Artcle II. Declaration of Principles and State Policies

Section 1. The Philippines is a republican state. Sovereignty resides in the people and all government authority emanates from them.

219

Sec. 2. The defense of the State is a prime duty of the Government and the people, and in the fulfillment of this duty all citizens may be required by law to render personal military or civil service.

Sec. 3. The Philippines renounces war as an instrument of national policy, adopts the generally accepted principles of international law as part of the law of the land, and adheres to the policy of peace, equality, justice, freedom, cooperation, and amity with all nations.

Sec. 4. The State shall strengthen the family as a basic social institution. The natural right and duty of parents in the rearing of the youth for civic efficiency and the development of moral character shall receive the aid and support of the Government.

Sec. 5. The State recognizes the vital role of the youth in nation building and shall promote their physical, intellectual, and social well-being.

Sec. 6. The State shall promote social justice to ensure the dignity, welfare and security of all the people. Towards this end, the State shall regulate the acquisition, ownership, use, enjoyment, and disposition of private property, and equitably diffuse property ownership and profits.

Sec. 7. The State shall establish, maintain, and ensure adequate social services in the field of education, health, housing, employment, welfare, and social security to guarantee the enjoyment by the people of a decent standard of living.

Sec. 8. Civilian authority is at all times supreme over the military.

Sec. 9. The State shall afford protection to labor, promote full employment and equality in employment, ensure equal work opportunities regardless of sex, race or creed, and regulate the relations between workers and employers. The State shall assure the rights of workers to self-organization, collective bargaining, security of tenure, and just and humane conditions of work. The State may provide for compulsory arbitration.

Sec. 10. The State shall guarantee and promote the autonomy of local government units, especially the barrio, to ensure their fullest development as self-reliant communities.

Article III. Citizenship

Section 1. The following are citizens of the Philippines:

(1) Those who are citizens of the Philippines at the time of the adoption of this Constitution.

(2) Those whose fathers or mothers are citizens of the Philippines.

(3) Those who elect Philippine citizenship pursuant to the provisions of the Constitution of nineteen hundred and thirty-five.

(4) Those who are naturalized in accordance with law.

Sec. 2. A female citizen of the Philippines who marries an alien shall retain her Philippine citizenship, unless by her act or omission she is deemed, under the law, to have renounced her citizenship.

Sec. 3. Philippine citizenship may be lost or reacquired in the manner provided by law.

Sec. 4. A natural-born citizen is one who is a citizen of the Philippines from birth without having to perform any act to acquire or perfect his Philippine citizenship.

Article IV. Bill of Rights

Section 1. No person shall be deprived of life, liberty, or property without due process of law, nor shall any person be denied the equal protection of the laws.

Sec. 2. Private property shall not be taken for public use without just compensation.

Sec. 3. The right of the people to be secure in their persons, houses, papers, and effects against unreasonable searches and seizures of whatever nature and for any purpose shall not be violated, and no search warrant or warrant of arrest shall issue except upon probable cause to be determined by the judge, or such other responsible officer as may be authorized by law, after examination under oath or affirmation of the complainant and the witnesses he may produce, and particularly describing the place to be searched, and the persons or things to be seized.

Sec. 4. (1) The privacy of communication and correspondence shall be inviolable except upon lawful order of the court, or when public safety and order require otherwise.

(2) Any evidence obtained in violation of this or the preceding section shall be inadmissible for any purpose in any proceeding.

Sec. 5. The liberty of abode and of travel shall not be impaired except upon lawful order of the court, or when necessary in the interest of national security, public safety, or public health.

Sec. 6. The right of the people to information on matters of public concern shall be recognized. Access to official records, and to documents and papers pertaining to official acts, transactions, or decisions, shall be afforded the citizen subject to such limitations as may be provided by law.

Sec. 7. The right to form associations or societies for purposes not contrary to law shall not be abridged.

Sec. 8. No law shall be made respecting an establishment of religion, or prohibiting the free exercise thereof. The free exercise and enjoyment of religious profession and worship, without discrimination or preference, shall forever be allowed. No religious test shall be required for the exercise of civil or political rights.

Sec. 9. No law shall be passed abridging the freedom of speech, or of the press, or the right of the people peaceably to assemble and petition the Government for redress of grievances.

Sec. 10. No law granting a title of royalty or nobility shall be enacted.

Sec. 11. No law impairing the obligation of contracts shall be passed.

Sec. 12. No *ex post facto* law or bill of attainder shall be enacted.

Sec. 13. No person shall be imprisoned for debt or non-payment of a poll tax.

Sec. 14. No involuntary servitude in any form shall exist as a punishment for a crime whereof the party shall have been duly convicted.

Sec. 15. The privilege of the writ of *habeas corpus* shall not be suspended except in cases of invasion, insurrection, rebellion, or imminent danger thereof, when the public safety requires it.

Sec. 16. All persons shall have the right to a speedy disposition of their cases before all judicial, quasi-judicial, or administrative bodies.

Sec. 17. No person shall be held to answer for a criminal offense without due process of law.

Sec. 18. All persons, except those charged with capital offenses when evidence of guilt is strong, shall, before conviction, be bailable by sufficient sureties. Excessive bail shall not be required.

Sec. 19. In all criminal prosecutions, the accused shall be presumed innocent until the contrary is proved, and shall enjoy the right to be heard by himself and counsel, to be informed of the nature and cause of the accusation against him, to have a speedy, impartial, and public trial, to meet the witnesses face to face, and to have compulsory process to secure the attendance of witnesses and the production of evidence in his behalf. However, after arraignment, trial may proceed notwithstanding the absence of the accused provided that he has been duly notified and his failure to appear is unjustified.

Sec. 20. No person shall be compelled to be a witness against himself. Any person under investigation for the commission of an offense shall have the right to remain silent and to counsel, and to be informed of such right. No force, violence, threat, intimidation, or any other means which vitiates the free will shall be used against him. Any confession obtained in violation of this section shall be inadmissible in evidence.

Sec. 21. Excessive fines shall not be imposed, nor cruel or unusual punishment inflicted.

Sec. 22. No person shall be twice put in jeopardy of punishment for the same offense. If an act is punished by a law and an ordinance, conviction or acquittal under either shall constitute a bar to another prosecution for the same act.

Sec. 23. Free access to the courts shall not be denied to any person by reason of poverty.

Article V. Duties and Obligations of Citizens

Section 1. It shall be the duty of the citizen to be loyal to the Republic and to honor the Philippine flag, to defend the State and contribute to its development and welfare, to uphold the Constitution and obey the laws, and to cooperate with the duly constituted authorities in the attainment and preservation of a just and orderly society.

Sec. 2. The rights of the individual impose upon him the correlative duty to exercise them responsibly and with due regard for the rights of others.

Sec. 3. It shall be the duty of every citizen to engage in gainful work to assure himself and his family a life worthy of human dignity.

Sec. 4. It shall be the obligation of every citizen qualified to vote to register and cast his vote.

Article VI. Suffrage

Section 1. Suffrage shall be exercised by citizens of the Philippines not otherwise disqualified by law, who are eighteen years of age or over, and who shall have resided in the Philippines for at least one year and in the place wherein they propose to vote for at least six months preceding the election. No literacy, property, or other substantive requirement shall be imposed on the exercise of suffrage. The National Assembly shall provide a system for the purpose of securing the secrecy and sanctity of the vote.

Article VII. The President

Section 1. The President of the Philippines shall be the symbolic head of state.

Sec. 2. The President shall be elected from among the Members of the National Assembly by a majority vote of all its Members for a term of six years from the date he takes his oath of office, which shall not be later than three days after his proclamation by the National Assembly, nor in any case earlier than the expiration of the term of his predecessor. Upon taking his oath of office, the President shall cease to be a Member of the National Assembly and of any political party. He shall be ineligible to hold any other elective office during his term.

Sec. 3. No person may be elected President unless he is at least fifty years of age on the day of his election as President, and a resident of the Philippines for at least ten years immediately preceding such election. However, if no member of the National Assembly is qualified or none of those qualified is a candidate for President, any Member thereof may be elected President.

Sec. 4. (1) The President shall have an official residence and shall receive a compensation to be fixed by law, which shall not be increased or decreased during his term of office. He shall not receive during his tenure any other emolument from the Government or any other source. Until the National Assembly shall provide otherwise, the President shall receive an annual salary of One Hundred Thousand Pesos.

(2) The President shall not, during his tenure, hold any appointive office, practice any profession, participate directly or indirectly in the management of any business, or be financially interested directly or indirectly in any contract with, or in any franchise or special privilege granted by, the Government or any subdivision, agency, or instrumentality thereof, including any government-owned or controlled corporation.

Sec. 5. In case of permanent disability, death, removal from office, or resignation of the President, the Speaker of the National Assembly shall act as President until a successor has been elected for the unexpired portion of the term of the President.

Sec. 6. The President shall have the following duties and functions:

(1) Address the National Assembly at the opening of its regular session.

(2) Proclaim the election of the Prime Minister.

(3) Dissolve the National Assembly and call for a general election as provided herein.

(4) Accept the resignation of the Cabinet as provided herein.

(5) Attest to the appointment or cessation from office of Members of the Cabinet, and of other officers as may be provided by law.

(6) Appoint all officers and employees in his office in accordance with the Civil Service Law.

(7) Perform such other duties and functions of state as may be provided by law.

Sec. 7. The President shall be immune from suit during his tenure.

Article VIII. The National Assembly

Section 1. The legislative power shall be vested in a National Assembly.

Sec. 2. The National Assembly shall be composed of as many Members as may be provided by law to be apportioned among the provinces, representative districts, and cities in accordance with the number of their respective inhabitants and on the basis of a uniform and progressive ratio. Each district shall comprise, as far as practicable, contiguous, compact, and adjacent territory. Representative districts or provinces already created or existing at the time of the ratification of this Constitution shall have at least one Member each.

Sec. 3. (1) The Members of the National Assembly shall be elected by the qualified electors in their respective districts for a term of six years which shall begin, unless otherwise provided by law, at noon on the thirtieth day of June next following their election.

(2) In case the National Assembly is dissolved, the newly elected Members shall serve the unexpired portion of the term from the time the Prime Minister convokes the Assembly, which shall not be later than thirty days immediately following the elections.

Sec. 4. No person shall be a Member of the National Assembly unless he is a natural-born citizen of the Philippines and, on the day of the election, is at least twenty-five years of age, able to read and write, a registered voter in the district in which he shall be elected, and a resident thereof for a period of not less than one year immediately preceding the day of the election.

Sec. 5. (1) Unless otherwise provided by law, the regular election of Members of the National Assembly shall be held on the second Monday of May and every six years thereafter.

(2) In case a vacancy arises in the National Assembly one year or more before a regular election, the Commission on Elections shall call a special election to be held within sixty days after the vacancy occurs.

Sec. 6. The National Assembly shall convene once every year on the fourth Monday of July for its regular session, unless a different date is fixed by law, and shall continue to be in session until thirty days before the opening of its next regular session, exclusive of Saturdays, Sundays, and legal holidays. It may recess for periods not exceeding thirty days each, and not more than ninety days during the year. However, it may be called to session at any time by the Prime Minister to consider such subjects or legislations as he may designate.

Sec. 7. (1) The National Assembly shall, by a majority vote of all its Members, elect its Speaker from the members thereof. It shall choose such other officers as it may deem necessary.

The election of the President and the Prime Minister shall precede all other business following the election of the Speaker.

(2) A majority of the National Assembly shall constitute a quorum to do business, but a smaller number may adjourn from day to day and may compel the attendance of absent Members in such manner, and under such penalties, as the National Assembly may provide.

(3) The National Assembly may determine the rules of its proceedings, punish its Members for disorderly behavior, and with the concurrence of two-

thirds of all its Members, suspend or expel a Member, but if the penalty is suspension, this shall not exceed sixty days.

(4) The National Assembly shall keep a Journal of its proceedings, and from time to time publish the same, excepting such parts as may, in its judgment, affect national security; and the *yeas* and *nays* on any question shall, at the request of one-fifth of the members present, be entered in the Journal.

Sec. 8. (1) Unless otherwise provided by law, each Member of the National Assembly shall receive an annual salary of sixty thousand pesos. The Speaker of the National Assembly shall receive an annual salary of seventy-five thousand pesos. No increase in salary shall take effect until after the expiration of the term of the Members of the National Assembly approving such increase.

(2) The records and books of accounts of the National Assembly shall be open to the public in accordance with law, and such books shall be audited by the Commission on Audit which shall publish annually the itemized expenditures for each Member.

Sec. 9. A Member of the National Assembly shall, in all offenses punishable by not more than six years imprisonment, be privileged from arrest during his attendance at its sessions, and in going to and returning from the same; but the National Assembly shall surrender the Member involved to the custody of the law within twenty-four hours after its adjournment for a recess or for its next session, otherwise such privilege shall cease upon its failure to do so. A Member shall not be questioned nor held liable in any other place for any speech or debate in the Assembly or in any committee thereof.

Sec. 10. A Member of the National Assembly shall not hold any other office or employment in the Government, or any subdivision, agency, or instrumentality thereof, including government-owned or controlled corporations, during his tenure except that of Prime Minister or Member of the Cabinet. Neither shall he be appointed to any civil office which may have been created or the emoluments thereof increased while he was a Member of the National Assembly.

Sec. 11. No Member of the National Assembly shall appear as counsel before any court inferior to a court with appellate jurisdiction, before any court in any civil case wherein the Government, or any subdivision, agency, or instrumentality thereof is the adverse party, or before any administrative body. Neither shall he, directly or indirectly, be interested financially in any contract with, or in any franchise or special privilege granted by, the Government or any subdivision, agency, or instrumentality thereof, including any government-owned or controlled corporation, during his term of office. He shall not intervene in any matter before any office of the Government for his pecuniary benefit.

Sec. 12. (1) There shall be a question hour at least once a month or as often as the Rules of the National Assembly may provide, which shall be included in its agenda, during which the Prime Minister or any Minister may be required to appear and answer questions and interpellations by Members of the National Assembly. Written questions shall be submitted to the Speaker at least three days before a scheduled question hour. Interpellations shall not be limited to the written questions, but may cover matters related thereto. The agenda shall specify the subjects of the question hour. When the security of the State so requires and the Prime Minister so states in writing, the question hour shall be conducted in executive session.

(2) The National Assembly or any of its committees may conduct inquiries in aid of legislation in accordance with its duly published rules of procedure. The rights of persons appearing in such inquiries shall be respected.

Sec. 13. (1) The National Assembly may withdraw its confidence from the Prime Minister only by electing a successor by a majority vote of all its Members. No motion for the election of such successor shall be debated and voted upon until after the lapse of three days from the submittal of such motion.

(2) The Prime Minister may advise the President in writing to dissolve the National Assembly whenever the need arises for a popular vote of confidence on fundamental issues, but not on a matter involving his own personal integrity. Whereupon, the President shall dissolve the National Assembly not earlier than five days nor later than ten days from his receipt of the advice, and call for an election on a date set by the Prime Minister which shall not be earlier than forty-five days nor later than sixty days from the date of such dissolution. However, no dissolution of the National Assembly shall take place within nine months immediately preceding a regular election or within nine months immediately following any general election.

(3) In case of dissolution of the National Assembly or the termination of its regular term, the incumbent Prime Minister and the Cabinet shall continue to conduct the affairs of government until the new National Assembly is convoked and a Prime Minister is elected and has qualified.

Sec. 14. (1) Except as otherwise provided in this Constitution, no treaty shall be valid and effective unless concurred in by a majority of all the Members of the National Assembly.

(2) The National Assembly, by a vote of two-thirds of all its Members, shall have the sole power to declare the existence of a state of war.

Sec. 15. In times of war or other national emergency, the National Assembly may by law authorize the Prime Minister, for a limited period and subject to such restrictions as it may prescribe, to exercise powers necessary and proper to carry out a declared national policy. Unless sooner withdrawn by a resolution of the National Assembly, such powers shall cease upon its next adjournment.

Sec. 16. (1) The Prime Minister shall submit to the National Assembly within thirty days from the opening of each regular session, as the basis of the general appropriations bill, a budget of receipts based on existing and proposed revenue measures, and of expenditures. The form, content, and manner of preparation of the budget shall be prescribed by law.

(2) No provision or enactment shall be embraced in the general appropriations bill unless it relates specifically to some particular appropriation therein. Any such provision or enactment shall be limited in its operation to the appropriation to which its relates.

(3) The procedure in approving appropriations for the National Assembly shall strictly follow the procedure for approving appropriations for other departments and agencies.

(4) A special appropriations bill shall specify the purpose for which it is intended, and shall be supported by funds actually available as certified to by the National Treasurer, or to be raised by a corresponding revenue proposal included therein.

(5) No law shall be passed authorizing any transfer of appropriations; how-

ever, the Prime Minister, the Speaker, the Chief Justice of the Supreme Court, and the heads of Constitutional Commissions may by laws be authorized to augment any item in the general appropriations law for their respective offices from savings in other items of their respective appropriations.

(6) If, by the end of any fiscal year, the National Assembly shall have failed to pass the general appropriations bill for the ensuing fiscal year, the general appropriations law for the preceding fiscal year shall be deemed re-enacted and shall remain in force and effect until the general appropriations bill is passed by the National Assembly.

Sec. 17. (1) The rule of taxation shall be uniform and equitable. The National Assembly shall evolve a progressive system of taxation.

(2) The National Assembly may by law authorize the Prime Minister to fix within specified limits, and subject to such limitations and restrictions as it may impose, tariff rates, import and export quotas, tonnage and wharfage dues, and other duties or imposts.

(3) Charitable institutions, churches, parsonages or convents appurtenant thereto, mosques, and non-profit cemeteries, and all lands, buildings, and improvements actually, directly, and exclusively used for religious or charitable purposes shall be exempt from taxation.

(4) No law granting any tax exemption shall be passed without the concurrence of a majority of all the Members of the National Assembly.

Sec. 18. (1) No money shall be paid out of the Treasury except in pursuance of an appropriation made by law.

(2) No public money or property shall ever be appropriated, applied, paid, or used, directly or indirectly, for the use, benefit, or support of any sect, church, denomination, sectarian institution, or system of religion, or for the use, benefit, or support of any priest, preacher, minister, or other religious teacher or dignitary as such, except when such priest, preacher, minister, or dignitary is assigned to the armed forces, or to any penal institution, or government orphanage or leprosarium.

Sec. 19. (1) Every bill shall embrace only one subject which shall be expressed in the title thereof.

(2) No bill shall become a law unless it has passed three readings on separate days, and printed copies thereof in its final form have been distributed to the Members three days before its passage, except when the Prime Minister certifies to the necessity of its immediate enactment to meet a public calamity or emergency. Upon the last reading of a bill, no amendment thereto shall be allowed, and the vote thereon shall be taken immediately thereafter, and the *yeas* and *nays* entered in the Journal.

(3) No bill except those of local application shall be calendared without the prior recommendation of the Cabinet.

Sec. 20. (1) Every bill passed by the National Assembly shall, before it becomes a law, be presented to the Prime Minister. If he approves the same, he shall sign it; otherwise, he shall veto it and return the same with his objections to the National Assembly. The bill may be reconsidered by the National Assembly and, if approved by two-thirds of all its Members, shall become a law. The Prime Minister shall act on every bill passed by the National Assembly within thirty days after the date of receipt thereof; otherwise, it shall become a law as if he had signed it.

(2) The Prime Minister shall have the power to veto any particular item or items in an appropriation, revenue, or tariff bill, but the veto shall not affect the item or items to which he does not object.

Article IX. The Prime Minister and the Cabinet

Section 1. The Executive power shall be exercised by the Prime Minister with the assistance of the Cabinet. The Cabinet, headed by the Prime Minister, shall consist of the heads of ministries as provided by law. The Prime Minister shall be the head of the Government.

Sec. 2. The Prime Minister and the Cabinet shall be responsible to the National Assembly for the program of government and shall determine the guidelines of national policy.

Sec. 3. The Prime Minister shall be elected by a majority of all the Members of the National Assembly from among themselves.

Sec. 4. The Prime Minister shall appoint the Members of the Cabinet who shall be the heads of ministries, at least a majority of whom shall come from the National Assembly. Members of the Cabinet may be removed at the discretion of the Prime Minister.

Sec. 5. (1) The Prime Minister shall appoint the Deputy Prime Minister from among the Members of the National Assembly. The Deputy Prime Minister shall head a ministry and shall perform such other functions as may be assigned to him by the Prime Minister.

(2) The Prime Minister shall also appoint the Deputy Ministers who shall perform such functions as may be assigned to them by law or by the respective heads of Ministries.

Sec. 6. The Prime Minister and the Members of the Cabinet, on assuming office, shall take the following oath or affirmation:

> "I do solemnly swear (or affirm) that I will faithfully and con-
> scientiously fulfill my duties as (name of position) of the Philippines,
> preserve and defend its Constitution, execute its laws, do justice to every
> man and consecrate myself to the service of the Nation. So help me God."
> (In case of affirmation, the last sentence will be omitted.)

Sec. 7. The salaries and emoluments of the Prime Minister and the Members of the Cabinet shall be fixed by law which shall not be increased or decreased during their tenure of office. Until otherwise provided by law, the Prime Minister shall receive the same salary as that of the President.

Sec. 8. The Prime Minister and the Members of the Cabinet shall be subject to the provisions of Sections ten and eleven of Article Eight hereof and may not appear as counsel before any court or administrative body, or participate in the management of any business, or practice any profession.

Sec. 9. The Prime Minister or any Member of the Cabinet may resign for any cause without vacating his seat in the National Assembly.

Sec. 10. The Prime Minister shall, at the beginning of each regular session of the National Assembly and from time to time thereafter, present the program of government and recommend for the consideration of the National Assembly such measures as he may deem necessary and proper.

Sec. 11. The Prime Minister shall have control of all ministries.

Sec. 12. The Prime Minister shall be commander-in-chief of all armed forces of the Philippines, and, whenever it becomes necessary, he may call out such armed forces to prevent or suppress lawless violence, invasion, insurrection or rebellion. In case of invasion, insurrection, or rebellion, or imminent danger thereof, when the public safety requiries it, he may suspend the privilege of the writ of *habeas corpus,* or place the Philippines or any part thereof under martial law.

Sec. 13. The Prime Minister shall appoint the heads of bureaus and offices, the officers of the armed forces of the Philippines from the rank of brigadier general or commodore, and all other officers of the Government whose appointments are not herein otherwise provided for, and those whom he may be authorized by law to appoint. However, the National Assembly may by law vest in Members of the Cabinet, courts, heads of agencies, commissions, and boards the power to appoint inferior officers in their respective offices.

Sec. 14. The Prime Minister may, except in cases of impeachment, grant reprieves, commutations and pardons, remit fines and forfeitures, after final conviction, and, with the concurrence of the National Assembly, grant amnesty.

Sec. 15. The Prime Minister may contract and guarantee foreign and domestic loans on behalf of the Republic of the Philippines, subject to such limitations as may be provided by law.

Sec. 16. All powers vested in the President of the Philippines under the nineteen hundred and thirty-five Constitution and the laws of the land which are not herein provided for or conferred upon any official shall be deemed, and are hereby, vested in the Prime Minister, unless the National Assembly provides otherwise.

Article X. The Judiciary

Section 1. The Judicial power shall be vested in one Supreme Court and in such inferior courts as may be established by law. The National Assembly shall have the power to define, prescribe, and apportion the jurisdiction of the various courts, but may not deprive the Supreme Court of its jurisdiction over cases enumerated in Section five hereof.

Sec. 2. (1) The Supreme Court shall be composed of a Chief Justice and fourteen Associate Justices. It may sit *en banc* or in two divisions.

(2) All cases involving the constitutionality of a treaty, executive agreement, or law shall be heard and decided by the Supreme Court *en banc,* and no treaty, executive agreement, or law may be declared unconstitutional without the concurrence of at least ten Members. All other cases, which under its rules are required to be heard *en banc,* shall be decided with the concurrence of at least eight members.

(3) Cases heard by a division shall be decided with the concurrence of at least five Members, but if such required number is not obtained, the case shall be decided *en banc*: Provided, that no doctrine or principle of law laid down by the Court in a decision rendered *en banc* or in division may be modified or reversed except by the Court sitting *en banc.*

Sec. 3. (1) No person shall be appointed Member of the Supreme Court unless he is a natural-born citizen of the Philippines, at least forty years of age, and has for ten years or more been a judge of a court of record or engaged in the practice of law in the Philippines.

(2) The National Assembly shall prescribe the qualifications of judges of

inferior courts, but no person may be appointed judge thereof unless he is a natural-born citizen of the Philippines and a member of the Philippine Bar.

Sec. 4. The Members of the Supreme Court and judges of inferior courts shall be appointed by the Prime Minister.

Sec. 5. The Supreme Court shall have the following powers:

(1) Exercise original jurisdiction over cases affecting ambassadors, other public ministers, and consuls, and over petitions for *certiorari,* prohibition, *mandamus, quo warranto,* and *habeas corpus.*

(2) Review and revise, reverse, modify, or affirm on appeal or *certiorari,* as the law or the Rules of Court may provide, final judgments and decrees of inferior courts in—

(a) All cases in which the constitutionality or validity of any treaty, executive agreement, law, ordinance, or executive order or regulation is in question.

(b) All cases involving the legality of any tax, impost, assessment, or toll, or any penalty imposed in relation thereto.

(c) All cases in which the jurisdiction of any inferior court is in issue.

(d) All criminal cases in which the penalty imposed is death or life imprisonment.

(e) All cases in which only an error or question of law is involved.

(3) Assign temporarily judges of inferior courts to other stations as public interest may require. Such temporary assignment shall not last longer than six months without the consent of the judge concerned.

(4) Order a change of venue or place of trial to avoid a miscarriage of justice.

(5) Promulgate rules concerning pleading, practice, and procedure in all courts, the admission to the practice of law, and the integration of the Bar, which, however, may be repealed, altered, or supplemented by the National Assembly. Such rules shall provide a simplified and inexpensive procedure for the speedy disposition of cases, shall be uniform for all courts of the same grade, and shall not diminish, increase, or modify substantive rights.

(6) Appoint its officials and employees in accordance with the Civil Service Law.

Sec. 6. The Supreme Court shall have administrative supervision over all courts and the personnel thereof.

Sec. 7. The Members of the Supreme Court and judges of inferior courts shall hold office during good behavior until they reach the age of sixty-five years or become incapacitated to discharge the duties of their office. The Supreme Court shall have the power to discipline judges of inferior courts, and, by a vote of at least eight Members, order their dismissal.

Sec. 8. The conclusions of the Supreme Court in any case submitted to it for decision *en banc* or in division shall be reached in consultation before the case is assigned to a Member for the writing of the opinion of the Court. Any Member dissenting from a decision shall state the reasons for his dissent. The same requirements shall be observed by all inferior collegiate courts.

Sec. 9. Every decision of a court of record shall clearly and distinctly state the facts and the law on which it is based. The Rules of Court shall govern the promulgation of minute resolutions.

Sec. 10. The salary of the Chief Justice and of the Associate Justices of the Supreme Court, and of judges of inferior courts shall be fixed by law, which shall not be decreased during their continuance in office. Until the National

Assembly shall provide otherwise, the Chief Justice shall receive an annual salary of seventy-five thousand pesos, and each Associate Justice, sixty thousand pesos.

Sec. 11. (1) Upon the effectivity of this Constitution, the maximum period within which a case or matter shall be decided or resolved from the date of its submission, shall be eighteen months for the Supreme Court, and, unless reduced by the Supreme Court, twelve months for all inferior collegiate courts, and three months for all other inferior courts.

(2) With respect to the Supreme Court and other collegiate appellate courts, when the applicable maximum period shall have lapsed without the rendition of the corresponding decision or resolution because the necessary vote cannot be had, the judgment, order, or resolution appealed from shall be deemed affirmed, except in those cases where a qualified majority is required and in appeals from judgments of conviction in criminal cases; and in original special civil actions and proceedings for *habeas corpus,* the petition in such cases shall be deemed dismissed; and a certification to this effect signed by the Chief Magistrate of the court shall be issued and a copy thereof attached to the record of the case.

Sec. 12. The Supreme Court shall, within thirty days from the opening of each regular session of the National Assembly, submit to the President, the Prime Minister, and the National Assembly an annual report on the operations and activities of the Judiciary.

Article XI. Local Government

Section 1. The territorial and political subdivisions of the Philippines are the provinces, cities, municipalities, and barrios.

Sec. 2. The National Assembly shall enact a local government code which may not thereafter be amended except by a majority vote of all its Members, defining a more responsive and accountable local government structure with an effective system of recall, allocating among the different local government units their powers, responsibilities, and resources, and providing for the qualifications, election and removal, term, salaries, powers, functions, and duties of local officials, and all other matters relating to the organization and operation of the local units. However, any change in the existing form of local government shall not take effect until ratified by a majority of the votes cast in a plebiscite called for the purpose.

Sec. 3. No province, city, municipality, or barrio may be created, divided, merged, abolished, or its boundary substantially altered, except in accordance with the criteria established in the local government code, and subject to the approval by a majority of the votes cast in a plebiscite in the unit or units affected.

Sec. 4. (1) Provinces with respect to component cities and municipalities, and cities and municipalities with respect to component barrios, shall ensure that the acts of their component units are within the scope of their assigned powers and functions. Highly urbanized cities, as determined by standards established in the local government code, shall be independent of the province.

(2) Local government units may group themselves, or consolidate or coordinate their efforts, services, and resources for purposes commonly beneficial to them.

Sec. 5. Each local government unit shall have the power to create its own sources of revenue and to levy taxes, subject to such limitations as may be provided by law.

Article XII. The Constitutional Commissions

A. Common Provisions

Section 1. The Constitutional Commissions shall be the Civil Service Commission, the Commission on Elections, and the Commission on Audit.

Sec. 2. Unless otherwise provided by law, the Chairman and each Commissioner of a Constitutional Commission shall receive an annual salary of sixty thousand pesos and fifty thousand pesos, respectively, which shall not be decreased during their continuance in office.

Sec. 3. No member of a Constitutional Commission shall, during his tenure in office, engage in the practice of any profession or in the management of any business, or be financially interested directly or indirectly in any contract with, or in any franchise or privilege granted by, the Government, or any subdivision, agency, or instrumentality thereof including government-owned or controlled corporations.

Sec. 4. The Constitutional Commissions shall appoint their officials and employees in accordance with the Civil Service Law.

B. The Civil Service Commission

Section 1. (1) The Civil Service embraces every branch, agency, subdivision, and instrumentality of the Government, including every government-owned or controlled corporation. It shall be administered by an independent Civil Service Commission composed of a Chairman and two Commissioners, who shall be natural-born citizens of the Philippines, and, at the time of their appointment, are at least thirty-five years of age and holders of a college degree, and must not have been candidates for any elective position in the election immediately preceding their appointment. The Chairman and the Commissioners shall be appointed by the Prime Minister for a term of seven years without reappointment. Of the Commissioners first appointed, one shall hold office for seven years, another for five years, and the third for three years. Appointment to any vacancy shall be only for the unexpired portion of the term of the predecessor.

(2) The Commission shall, subject to such limitations as may be provided by law, establish a career service and adopt measures to promote morale, efficiency, and integrity in the Civil Service.

Sec. 2. Appointments in the Civil Service, except as to those which are policy-determining, primarily confidential, or highly technical in nature, shall be made only according to merit and fitness, to be determined as far as practicable by competitive examination.

Sec. 3. No officer or employee in the Civil Service shall be suspended or dismissed except for cause as provided by law.

Sec. 4. (1) No elective official shall be eligible for appointment to any office or position during his term of office.

(2) No candidate who lost in an election shall be eligible for appointment or reappointment to any office in the government, or in any government-owned or controlled corporation, within one year following such election.

Sec. 5. No officer or employee in the Civil Service, including members of the armed forces, shall engage directly or indirectly in any partisan political activity or take part in any election except to vote.

Sec. 6. The National Assembly shall provide for the standardization of compensation of government officials and employees, including those in government-owned or controlled corporations, taking into account the nature of the responsibilities pertaining to, and the qualifications required for, the positions concerned.

C. The Commission on Elections

Section 1. (1) There shall be an independent Commission on Elections composed of a Chairman and eight Commissioners who shall be natural-born citizens of the Philippines and, at the time of their appointment, at least thirty-five years of age and holders of a college degree. However, a majority thereof, including the Chairman, shall be members of the Philippine Bar who have been engaged in the practice of law for at least ten years.

(2) The Chairman and the Commissioners shall be appointed by the Prime Minister for a term of seven years without reappointment. Of the Commissioners first appointed, three shall hold office for seven years, three for five years, and the last three for three years. Appointment to any vacancy shall be only for the unexpired portion of the term of the predecessor.

Sec. 2. The Commission on Elections shall have the following powers and functions:

(1) Enforce and administer all laws relative to the conduct of elections.

(2) Be the sole judge of all contests relating to the elections, returns, and qualifications of all Members of the National Assembly and elective provincial and city officials.

(3) Decide, save those involving the right to vote, administrative questions affecting elections, including the determination of the number and location of polling places, the appointment of election officials and inspectors, and the registration of voters.

(4) Deputize, with the consent or at the instance of the Prime Minister, law enforcement agencies and instrumentalities of the Government, including the armed forces of the Philippines, for the purpose of ensuring free, orderly, and honest elections.

(5) Register and accredit political parties subject to the provisions of Section eight hereof.

(6) Recommend to the National Assembly effective measures to minimize election expenses and prohibit all forms of election frauds and malpractices, political opportunism, guest or nuisance candidacy, or other similar acts.

(7) Submit to the President, the Prime Minister, and the National Assembly a report on the conduct and manner of each election.

(8) Perform such other functions as may be provided by law.

Sec. 3. The Commission on Elections may sit *en banc* or in three divisions. All election cases may be heard and decided by divsions, except contests involving Members of the National Assembly, which shall be heard and decided *en banc*. Unless otherwise provided by law, all election cases shall be decided within ninety days from the date of their submission for decision.

Sec. 4. The Commission may recommend to the Prime Minister the removal of, or any other disciplinary action against, any officer or employee it has deputized, for violation or disregard of, or disobedience to, its decision, order, or directive.

Sec. 5. The enjoyment or utilization of all franchises or permits for the operation of transportation and other public utilities, media of communication or information, all grants, special privileges, or concessions granted by the Government, or any subdivision, agency, or instrumentality thereof, including any government-owned or controlled corporation, may be supervised or regulated by the Commission during the election period for the purpose of ensuring free, orderly, and honest elections.

Sec. 6. Unless otherwise fixed by the Commission in special cases, the election period shall commence ninety days before the day of election and shall end thirty days thereafter.

Sec. 7. No pardon, parole, or suspension of sentence for violation of the law or rules and regulations concerning elections shall be granted without the recommendation of the Commission.

Sec. 8. A political party shall be entitled to accreditation by the Commission if, in the immediately preceding election, such party has obtained at least the third highest number of votes cast in the constituency to which it seeks accreditation. No religious sect shall be registered as a political party, and no political party which seeks to achieve its goals through violence or subversion shall be entitled to accreditation.

Sec. 9. (1) *Bona fide* candidates for any public office shall be free from any form of harassment and discrimination.

(2) No party or candidate shall have membership in the registration board, board of election inspectors, board of canvassers, or other similar bodies.

Sec. 10. No elective public officer may change his political party affiliation during his term of office, and no candidate for any elective public office may change his political party affiliation within six months immediately preceding or following an election.

Sec. 11. Any decision, order, or ruling of the Commission may be brought to the Supreme Court on *certiorari* by the aggrieved party within thirty days from his receipt of a copy thereof.

D. The Commission on Audit

Section 1. (1) There shall be an independent Commission on Audit composed of a Chairman and two Commissioners, who shall be natural-born citizens of the Philippines and, at the time of their appointment, at least forty years of age and certified public accountants or members of the Philippine Bar for at least ten years.

(2) The Chairman and the Commissioners shall be appointed by the Prime Minister for a term of seven years without reappointment. Of the Commissioners first appointed, one shall hold office for seven years, another for five years, and the third for three years. Appointment to any vacancy shall be only for the unexpired portion of the term of the predecessor.

Sec. 2. The Commission on Audit shall have the following powers and functions:

(1) Examine, audit, and settle, in accordance with law and regulations, all accounts pertaining to the revenues and receipts of, and expenditures or uses

of funds and property, owned or held in trust by, or pertaining to, the Government, or any of its subdivisions, agencies, or instrumentalities, including government-owned or controlled corporations; keep the general accounts of the Government and, for such period as may be provided by law, preserve the vouchers pertaining thereto; and promulgate accounting and auditing rules and regulations including those for the prevention of irregular, unnecessary, excessive, or extravagant expenditures or uses of funds and property.

(2) Decide any case brought before it within sixty days from the date of its submission for resolution. Unless otherwise provided by law, any decision, order, or ruling of the Commission may be brought to the Supreme Court on *certiorari* by the aggrieved party within thirty days from his receipt of a copy thereof.

(3) Submit to the President, the Prime Minister, and the National Assembly, within the time fixed by law, an annual financial report of the Government, its subdivisions, agencies, and instrumentalities, including government-owned or controlled corporations, and recommend measures necessary to improve their efficiency and effectiveness. It shall submit such other reports as may be required by law.

(4) Perform such other duties and functions as may be prescribed by law.

Article XIII. Accountability of Public Officers

Section 1. Public office is a public trust. Public officers and employees shall serve with the highest degree of responsibility, integrity, loyalty, and efficiency, and shall remain accountable to the people.

Sec. 2. The President, the Members of the Supreme Court, and the Members of the Constitutional Commissions shall be removed from office on impeachment for, and conviction of, culpable violation of the Constitution, treason, bribery, other high crimes, or graft and corruption.

Sec. 3. The National Assembly shall have the exclusive power to initiate, try, and decide all cases of impeachment. Upon the filing of a verified complaint, the National Assembly may initiate impeachment by a vote of at least one-fifth of all its Members. No official shall be convicted without the concurrence of at least two-thirds of all the Members thereof. When the National Assembly sits in impeachment cases, its Members shall be on oath or affirmation.

Sec. 4. Judgments in cases of impeachment shall be limited to removal from office and disqualification to hold any office of honor, trust, or profit under the Republic of the Philippines, but the party convicted shall nevertheless be liable and subject to prosecution, trial, and punishment, in accordance with law.

Sec. 5. The National Assembly shall create a special court, to be known as *Sandiganbayan*, which shall have jurisdiction over criminal and civil cases involving graft and corrupt practices and such other offenses committed by public officers and employees, including those in government-owned or controlled corporations, in relation to their office as may be determined by law.

Sec. 6. The National Assembly shall create an office of the Ombudsman, to be known as *Tanodbayan*, which shall receive and investigate complaints relative to public office, including those in government-owned or controlled corporations, make appropriate recommendations, and in case of failure of justice as defined by law, file and prosecute the corresponding criminal, civil, or administrative case before the proper court or body.

Article XIV. The National Economy and the Patrimony of the Nation

Section 1. The National Assembly shall establish a National Economic and Development Authority, to be headed by the Prime Minister, which shall recommend to the National Assembly, after consultation with the private sector, local government units, and other appropriate public agencies, continuing, coordinated, and fully integrated social and economic plans and programs.

Sec. 2. The State shall regulate or prohibit private monopolies when the public interest so requires. No combinations in restraint of trade or unfair competition shall be allowed.

Sec. 3. The National Assembly shall, upon recommendation of the National Economic and Development Authority, reserve to citizens of the Philippines or to corporations or associations wholly owned by such citizens, certain traditional areas of investments when the national interest so dictates.

Sec. 4. The National Assembly shall not, except by general law, provide for the formation, organization, or regulation of private corporations, unless such corporations are owned or controlled by the Government or any subdivision or instrumentality thereof.

Sec. 5. No franchise, certificate, or any other form of authorization for the operation of a public utility shall be granted except to citizens of the Philippines or to corporations or associations organized under the laws of the Philippines at least sixty *per centum* of the capital of which is owned by such citizens, nor shall such franchise, certificate, or authorization be exclusive in character or for a longer period than fifty years. Neither shall any such franchise or right be granted except under the condition that it shall be subject to amendment, alteration, or repeal by the National Assembly when the public interest so requires. The State shall encourage equity participation in public utilities by the general public. The participation of foreign investors in the governing body of any public utility enterprise shall be limited to their proportionate share in the capital thereof.

Sec. 6. The State may, in the interest of national welfare or defense, establish and operate industries and means of transportation and communication, and, upon payment of just compensation, transfer to public ownership utilities and other private enterprises to be operated by the Government.

Sec. 7. In times of national emergency when the public interest so requires, the State may temporarily take over or direct the operation of any privately owned public utility or business affected with the public interest.

Sec. 8. All lands of the public domain, waters, minerals, coal, petroleum and other mineral oils, all forces of potential energy, fisheries, wildlife, and other natural resources of the Philippines belong to the State. With the exception of agricultural, industrial or commercial, residential, and resettlement lands of the public domain, natural resources shall not be alienated, and no license, concession, or lease for the exploration, development, exploitation, or utilization of any of the natural resources shall be granted for a period exceeding twenty-five years, renewable for not more than twenty-five years, except as to water rights for irrigation, water supply, fisheries, or industrial uses other than the development of water power, in which cases, beneficial use may be the measure and the limit of the grant.

Sec. 9. The disposition, exploration, development, exploitation, or utilization of any of the natural resources of the Philippines shall be limited to citizens of the Philippines, or to corporations or associations at least sixty *per centum* of the capital of which is owned by such citizens. The National Assembly, in the national interest, may allow such citizens, corporations, or associations to enter into service contracts for financial, technical, management, or other forms of assistance with any foreign person or entity for the exploration, development, exploitation, or utilization of any of the natural resources. Existing valid and binding service contracts for financial, technical, management, or other forms of assistance are hereby recognized as such.

Sec. 10. Lands of the public domain are classified into agricultural, industrial or commercial, residential, resettlement, mineral, timber or forest and grazing lands, and such other classes as may be provided by law.

Sec. 11. The National Assembly, taking into account conservation, ecological, and developmental requirements of the natural resources, shall determine by law the size of lands of the public domain which may be developed, held or acquired by, or leased to, any qualified individual, corporation, or association, and the conditions therefor. No private corporation or association may hold alienable lands of the public domain except by lease not to exceed one thousand hectares in area; nor may any citizen hold such lands by lease in excess of five hundred hectares or acquire by purchase or homestead in excess of twenty-four hectares. No private corporation or association may hold by lease, concession, license, or permit, timber or forest lands and other timber or forest resources in excess of one hundred thousand hectares; however, such area may be increased by the National Assembly upon recommendation of the National Economic and Development Authority.

Sec. 12. The State shall formulate and implement an agrarian reform program aimed at emancipating the tenant from the bondage of the soil and achieving the goals enunciated in this Constitution.

Sec. 13. The National Assembly may authorize, upon payment of just compensation, the expropriation of private lands to be subdivided into small lots and conveyed at cost to deserving citizens.

Sec. 14. Save in cases of hereditary succession, no private land shall be transferred or conveyed except to individuals, corporations, or associations qualified to acquire or hold lands of the public domain.

Sec. 15. Any provision of paragraph one, Section fourteen, Article Eight and of this Article notwithstanding, the Prime Minister may enter into international treaties or agreements as the national welfare and interest may require.

Article XV. General Provisions

Section 1. The flag of the Philippines shall be red, white, and blue, with a sun and three stars, as consecrated and honored by the people and recognized by law.

Sec. 2. The *interim* National Assembly may by law adopt a new name for the country, a national anthem, and a national seal, which shall all be truly reflective and symbolic of the ideals, history, and traditions of the people. Thereafter, the national name, anthem, and seal so adopted shall not be subject to change except by constitutional amendment.

Sec. 3. (1) This Constitution shall be officially promulgated in English and in Filipino, and translated into each dialect spoken by over fifty thousand people, and into Spanish and Arabic. In case of conflict, the English text shall prevail.

(2) The National Assembly shall take steps towards the development and formal adoption of a common national language to be known as Filipino.

(3) Until otherwise provided by law, English and Filipino shall be the official languages.

Sec. 4. All public officers and employees and members of the armed forces shall take an oath to support and defend the Constitution.

Sec. 5. No elective or appointive public officer or employee shall receive additional or double compensation unless specifically authorized by law, nor accept, without the consent of the National Assembly, any present, emolument, office, or title of any kind from any foreign state.

Sec. 6. No salary or any form of emolument of any public officer or employee, including constitutional officers, shall be exempt from payment of income tax.

Sec. 7. (1) The ownership and management of mass media shall be limited to citizens of the Philippines or to corporations or associations wholly owned and managed by such citizens.

(2) The governing body of every entity engaged in commercial telecommunications shall in all cases be controlled by citizens of the Philippines.

Sec. 8. (1) All educational institutions shall be under the supervision of, and subject to regulation by, the State. The State shall establish and maintain a complete, adequate, and integrated system of education relevant to the goals of national development.

(2) All institutions of higher learning shall enjoy academic freedom.

(3) The study of the Constitution shall be part of the curricula in all schools.

(4) All educational institutions shall aim to inculcate love of country, teach the duties of citizenship, and develop moral character, personal discipline, and scientific, technological, and vocational efficiency.

(5) The State shall maintain a system of free public elementary education and, in areas where finances permit, establish and maintain a system of free public education at least up to the secondary level.

(6) The State shall provide citizenship and vocational training to adult citizens and out-of-school youth, and create and maintain scholarships for poor and deserving students.

(7) Educational institutions, other than those established by religious orders, mission boards, and charitable organizations, shall be owned solely by citizens of the Philippines, or corporations or associations sixty *per centum* of the capital of which is owned by such citizens. The control and administration of educational institutions shall be vested in citizens of the Philippines. No educational institution shall be established exclusively for aliens, and no group of aliens shall comprise more than one-third of the enrolment in any school. The provisions of this sub-section shall not apply to schools established for foreign diplomatic personnel and their dependents and, unless otherwise provided by law, for other foreign temporary residents.

(8) At the option expressed in writing by the parents or guardians, and without cost to them and the Government, religion shall be taught to their children or wards in public elementary and high schools as may be provided by law.

Sec. 9. (1) The State shall promote scientific research and invention. The advancement of science and technology shall have priority in the national development.

(2) Filipino culture shall be preserved and developed for national identity. Arts and letters shall be under the patronage of the State.

(3) The exclusive right to inventions, writings, and artistic creations shall be secured to inventors, authors, and artists for a limited period. Scholarships, grants-in-aid, or other forms of incentives shall be provided for specially gifted citizens.

Sec. 10. It shall be the responsibility of the State to achieve and maintain population levels most conducive to the national welfare.

Sec. 11. The State shall consider the customs, traditions, beliefs, and interests of national cultural communities in the formulation and implementation of state policies.

Sec. 12. The State shall establish and maintain an integrated national police force whose organization, administration, and operation shall be provided by law.

Sec. 13. (1) The armed forces of the Philippines shall include a citizen army composed of all able-bodied citizens of the Philippines who shall undergo military training as may be provided by law. It shall keep a regular force necessary for the security of the State.

(2) The citizen army shall have a corps of trained officers and men in active duty status as may be necessary to train, service, and keep it in reasonable preparedness at all times.

Sec. 14. The National Assembly shall establish a central monetary authority which shall provide policy direction in the areas of money, banking, and credit. It shall have supervisory authority over the operations of banks and exercise such regulatory authority as may be provided by law over the operations of finance companies and other institutions performing similar functions. Until the National Assembly shall otherwise provide, the Central Bank of the Philippines, operating under existing laws, shall function as the central monetary authority.

Sec. 15. The separation of church and state shall be inviolable.

Sec. 16. The State may not be sued without its consent.

Article XVI. Amendments

Section 1. (1) Any amendment to, or revision of, this Constitution may be proposed by the National Assembly upon a vote of three-fourths of all its Members, or by a constitutional convention.

(2) The National Assembly may, by a vote of two-thirds of all its Members, call a constitutional convention or, by a majority vote of all its Members, submit the question of calling such a convention to the electorate in an election.

Sec. 2. Any amendment to, or revision of, this Constitution shall be valid when ratified by a majority of the votes cast in a plebiscite which shall be held not later than three months after the approval of such amendment or revision.

Article XVII. Transitory Provisions

Section 1. There shall be an *interim* National Assembly which shall exist immediately upon the ratification of this Constitution and shall continue until the

Members of the regular National Assembly shall have been elected and shall have assumed office following an election called for the purpose by the *interim* National Assembly. Except as otherwise provided in this Constitution, the *interim* National Assembly shall have the same powers and its Members shall have the same functions, responsibilities, rights, privileges, and disqualifications as the regular National Assembly and the Members thereof.

Sec. 2. The Members of the *interim* National Assembly shall be the incumbent President and Vice-President of the Philippines, those who served as President of the nineteen hundred and seventy-one Constitutional Convention, those Members of the Senate and the House of Representatives who shall express in writing to the Commission on Elections within thirty days after the ratification of this Constitution their option to serve therein, and those Delegates to the nineteen hundred and seventy-one Constitutional Convention who have opted to serve therein by voting affirmatively for this Article. They may take their oath of office before any officer authorized to administer oath and qualify thereto, after the ratification of this Constitution.

Sec. 3. (1) The incumbent President of the Philippines shall initially convene the *interim* National Assembly and shall preside over its sessions until the *interim* Speaker shall have been elected. He shall continue to exercise his powers and prerogatives under the nineteen hundred and thirty-five Constitution and the powers vested in the President and the Prime Minister under this Constitution until he calls upon the *interim* National Assembly to elect the *interim* President and the *interim* Prime Minister, who shall then exercise their respective powers vested by this Constitution.

(2) All proclamations, orders, decrees, instructions, and acts promulgated, issued or done by the incumbent President shall be part of the law of the land, and shall remain valid, legal, binding, and effective even after lifting of martial law or the ratification of this Constitution, unless modified, revoked, or superseded by subsequent proclamations, orders, decrees, instructions, or other acts of the incumbent President, or unless expressly and explicitly modified or repealed by the regular National Assembly.

Sec. 4. The *interim* Prime Minister and his Cabinet shall exercise all the powers and functions, and discharge the responsibilities of the regular Prime Minister and his Cabinet, and shall be subject to the same disqualifications provided in this Constitution.

Sec. 5. The *interim* National Assembly shall give priority to measures for the orderly transition from the presidential to the parliamentary system, the reorganization of the Government, the eradication of graft and corruption, the effective maintenance of peace and order, the implementation of declared agrarian reforms, the standardization of compensation of government employees, and such other measures as shall bridge the gap between the rich and the poor.

Sec. 6. The *interim* National Assembly shall reapportion the Assembly seats in accordance with Section two, Article Eight, of this Constitution.

Sec. 7. All existing laws not inconsistent with this Constitution shall remain operative until amended, modified, or repealed by the National Assembly.

Sec. 8. All courts existing at the time of the ratification of this Constitution shall continue and exercise their jurisdiction, until otherwise provided by law in accordance with this Constitution, and all cases pending in said courts shall be heard, tried, and determined under the laws then in force. The provisions of the existing Rules of Court not inconsistent with this Constitution shall remain operative unless amended, modified, or repealed by the Supreme Court or the National Assembly.

Sec. 9. All officials and employees in the existing Government of the Republic of the Philippines shall continue in office until otherwise provided by law or decreed by the incumbent President of the Philippines, but all officials whose appointments are by this Constitution vested in the Prime Minister shall vacate their respective offices upon the appointment and qualification of their successors.

Sec. 10. The incumbent members of the Judiciary may continue in office until they reach the age of seventy years, unless sooner replaced in accordance with the preceding section hereof.

Sec. 11. The rights and privileges granted to citizens of the United States or to corporations or associations owned or controlled by such citizens under the Ordinance appended to the nineteen hundred and thirty-five Constitution shall automatically terminate on the third day of July, nineteen hundred and seventy-four. Titles to private lands acquired by such persons before such date shall be valid as against other private persons only.

Sec. 12. All treaties, executive agreements, and contracts entered into by the Government, or any subdivision, agency, or instrumentality thereof, including government-owned or controlled corporations, are hereby recognized as legal, valid, and binding. When the national interest so requires, the incumbent President of the Philippines or the *interim* Prime Minister may review all contracts, concessions, permits or other forms of privileges for the exploration, development, exploitation, or utilization of natural resources entered into, granted, issued, or acquired before the ratification of this Constitution.

Sec. 13. Any public officer or employee separated from the service as a result of the reorganization effected under this Constitution shall, if entitled under the laws then in force, receive the retirement and other benefits accruing thereunder.

Sec. 14. All records, equipment, buildings, facilities, and properties of any office or body abolished or reorganized under this Constitution shall be transferred to the office or body to which its powers, functions, and responsibilities substantially pertain.

Sec. 15. The *interim* National Assembly, upon special call by the *interim* Prime Minister, may, by a majority vote of all its Members, propose amendments to this Constitution. Such amendments shall take effect when ratified in accordance with Article Sixteen hereof.

Sec. 16. This Constitution shall take effect immediately upon its ratification by a majority of the votes cast in a plebiscite called for the purpose and, except as herein provided, shall supersede the Constitution of nineteen hundred and thirty-five and all amendments thereto.

*The foregoing Constitution was approved by the Filipino people
in a referendum held between January 10, 1973 and January 15, 1973
through the Barangays (Citizens Assemblies), the result of which
was announced under Proclamation Numbered One Thousand
One Hundred Two, dated January 17, 1973, by His Excellency,
President Ferdinand E. Marcos. By virtue whereof, the Constitution
comes into full force and effect as of noon of January 17, 1973.*

PROCLAMATION NO. 1081 PROCLAIMING A STATE OF MARTIAL LAW IN THE PHILIPPINES

WHEREAS, on the basis of carefully evaluated and verified information, it is definitely established that lawless elements who are moved by a common or similar ideological conviction, design, strategy and goal and enjoying the active moral and material support of a foreign power and being guided and directed by intensely devoted, well trained, determined and ruthless groups of men and seeking refuge under the protection of our constitutional liberties to promote and attain their ends, have entered into a conspiracy and have in fact joined and banded their resources and forces together for the prime purposes of, and in fact they have been and are actually staging, undertaking and waging an armed insurrection and rebellion against the Government of the Republic of the Philippines in order to forcibly seize political and state power in this country, overthrow the duly constituted government, and supplant our existing political, social, economic and legal order with an entirely new one whose form of government, whose system of laws, whose conception of God and religion, whose notion of individual rights and family relations, and whose political, social, economic, legal and moral precepts are based on the Marxist-Leninist-Maoist teachings and beliefs;

WHEREAS, these lawless elements, acting in concert through seemingly innocent and harmless, although actually destructive, front organizations which have been infiltrated or deliberately formed by them, have continuously and systematically strengthened and broadened their memberships through sustained and careful recruiting and enlistment of new adherents from among our peasantry, laborers, professionals, intellectuals, students, and mass media personnel, and through such sustained and careful recruitment and enlistment have succeeded in spreading and expanding their control and influence over almost every segment and level of our society throughout the land in their ceaseless effort to erode and weaken the political, social, economic, legal and moral foundations of our existing government, and to influence, manipulate and move peasant, labor, student and terroristic organizations under their influence or control to commit, as in fact they have committed and still are committing, acts of violence, depredations, sabotage and injuries against our duly constituted authorities, against the members of our law enforcement agencies, and worst of all, against the peaceful members of our society;

WHEREAS, in the fanatical pursuit of their conspiracy and widespread acts of violence, depredations, sabotage and injuries against our people, and in order to provide the essential instrument to direct and carry out their criminal design and unlawful activities, and to achieve their ultimate sinister objectives, these lawless elements have in fact organized, established and are now maintaining a Central Committee, composed of young and dedicated radical students and intellectuals, which is charged with guiding and directing the armed struggle and propaganda assaults against our duly constituted government, and this Central Committee is now imposing its will and asserting its sham authority on certain segments of our population, especially in the rural areas, through varied means of subterfuge, deceit, coercion, threats, intimidations, machinations, treachery, violence and other modes of terror, and has been and is illegally exacting financial and other forms of tributes from our people to raise funds and material resources to support its insurrectionary and propaganda activities against our duly constituted government and against our peace-loving people;

WHEREAS, in order to carry out, as in fact they have carried out, their premeditated plan to stage, undertake and wage a full scale armed insurrection and rebellion in this country, these lawless elements have organized, established and are now maintaining a well trained, well armed and highly indoctrinated and greatly expanded insurrectionary force, popularly known as the New People's Army, which has since vigorously pursued and still is vigorously pursuing a relentless and ruthless armed struggle against our duly constituted government and whose unmitigated forays, raids, ambuscades, assaults and reign of terror and acts of lawlessness in the rural areas and in our urban centers brought about the treacherous and cold-blooded assassination of innocent civilians, military personnel of the government and local public officials in many parts of the country, notably in the Cagayan Valley, in Central Luzon, in the Southern Tagalog Region, in the Bicol Area, in the Visayas and in Mindanao, and whose daring and wanton guerrilla activities have generated and sown fear and panic among our people, have created a climate of chaos and disorder, produced a state of political, social, psychological and economic instability in our land, and have inflicted great suffering and irreparable injury to persons and property in our society;

WHEREAS, these lawless elements, their cadres, fellow-travelers, friends, sympathizers and supporters have for many years up to the present time been mounting sustained, massive and destructive propaganda assaults against our duly constituted government, its instrumentalities, agencies and officials, and also against our social, political, economic and religious institutions, through the publications, broadcasts and disseminations of deliberately slanted and overly exaggerated news stories and news commentaries as well as false, vile, foul and scurrilous statements, utterances, writings and pictures through the press-radio-television media and through leaflets, college campus newspapers and some newspapers published and still being published by these lawless elements, notably the "Ang Bayan," "Pulang Bandila" and the "Ang Komunista," all of which are clearly well-conceived, intended and calculated to malign and discredit our duly constituted government, its instrumentalities, agencies and officials before our people, making it appear to the people that our government has become so weak and so impotent to perform and discharge its functions and responsibilities in our society and to our people, and thus undermine and destroy the faith and loyalty and allegiance of our people in and alienate their support for their duly constituted government, its instrumentalities, agencies and officials, and thereby gradually erode and weaken as in fact they have so eroded and weakened the will of our people to sustain and defend our government and our democratic way of life;

WHEREAS, these lawless elements having taken up arms against our duly constituted government and against our people, and having committed and are still committing acts of armed insurrection and rebellion consisting of armed raids, forays, sorties, ambushes, wanton acts of murders, spoilage, plunder, looting, arsons, destruction of public and private buildings, and attacks against innocent and defenseless civilian lives and property, all of which activities have seriously endangered and continue to endanger public order and safety and security of the nation, and acting with cunning and manifest precision and deliberation and without regard to the health, safety and well-being of the people, are now implementing their plan to cause widespread, massive and systematic destruction and paralyzation of vital public utilities and services, particularly water systems, sources of electrical power, communication and transportation facilities, to the great detriment, suffering, injury and prejudice of our people and the nation and to generate a deep psychological fear and panic among our people;

WHEREAS, the Supreme Court in the cases brought before it, docketed as G.R. Nos. L-33964, L-33965, L-33973, L-33982, L-34004, L-34013, L-34039, L-34265, and L-34339, as a consequence of the suspension of the privilege of the writ of *habeas corpus* by me as President of the Philippines in my Proclamation No. 889, dated August 21, 1971, as amended, has found that in truth and in fact there exists an actual insurrection and rebellion in the country by a sizeable group of men who have publicly risen in arms to overthrow the government. Here is what the Supreme Court said in its decision promulgated on December 11, 1971:

> "x x x our jurisprudence attests abundantly to the Communist
> activities in the Philippines, especially in Manila, from the late
> twenties to the early thirties, then aimed principally at incitement
> to sedition or rebellion, as the immediate objective. Upon the estab-
> lishment of the Commonwealth of the Philippines, the movement
> seemed to have waned notably; but, the outbreak of World War II
> in the Pacific and the miseries, the devastation and havoc, and the
> proliferation of unlicensed firearms concomitant with the military
> occupation of the Philippines and its subsequent liberation, brought

about, in the late forties, a resurgence of the Communist threat, with such vigor as to be able to organize and operate in Central Luzon an army—called HUKBALAHAP, during the occupation, and renamed Hukbong Mapagpalaya ng Bayan (HMB) after liberation—which clashed several times with the armed forces of the Republic. This prompted then President Quirino to issue Proclamation No. 210, dated October 22, 1950, suspending the privilege of the writ of *habeas corpus,* the validity of which was upheld in Montenegro vs. Castañeda. Days before the promulgation of said Proclamation, or on October 18, 1950, members of the Communist Politburo in the Philippines were apprehended in Manila. Subsequently accused and convicted of the crime of rebellion, they served their respective sentences.

"The fifties saw a comparative lull in Communist activities, insofar as peace and order were concerned. Still, on June 20, 1957, Republic Act No. 1700, otherwise known as the Anti-Subversion Act, was approved, upon the grounds stated in the very preamble of said statute—that

"x x x the Communist Party of the Philippines, although purportedly a political party, is in fact an organized conspiracy to overthrow the Government of the Republic of the Philippines, not only by force and violence but also by deceit, subversion and other illegal means, for the purpose of establishing in the Philippines a totalitarian regime subject to alien domination and control;
"x x x the continued existence and activities of the Communist Party of the Philippines constitutes a *clear, present* and *grave* danger to the security of the Philippines; and
"x x x in the fact of the organized, systematic and persistent subversion, national in scope but international in direction, posed by the Communist Party of the Philippines and its activities, there is urgent need for special legislation to cope with this continuing menace to the freedom and security of the country x x x."

In the language of the Report on Central Luzon, submitted on September 4, 1971 by the Senate Ad Hoc Committee of Seven—copy of which Report was filed in these cases by the petitioners herein—

"The years following 1963 saw the successive emergence in the country of several mass organizations, notably the Lapiang Manggagawa (now the Socialist Party of the Philippines) among the workers; the Malayang Samahan ng Mga Magsasaka (MASAKA among the peasantry; the Kabataang Makabayan (KM) among the youth/students; and the Movement for the Advancement of Nationalism (MAN) among the intellectuals/professionals, the PKP has exerted all-out effort to infiltrate, influence and utilize these organizations in promoting its radical brand of nationalism."

Meanwhile, the Communist leaders in the Philippines had been split into two (2) groups, one of which—composed mainly of young radicals, constituting the Maoist faction—reorganized the Communist Party of the Philippines early in 1969 and established a New People's Army. This faction adheres to the Maoist concept of the "Protracted People's War or War of National Liberation." Its "Programme for a People's Democratic Revolution" states *inter alia*:

> "The Communist Party of the Philippines is determined to implement its general programme for a people's democratic revolution. All Filipino communists are ready to sacrifice their lives for the worthy cause of achieving the new type of democracy, of building a new Philippines that is genuinely and completely independent, democratic, united, just and prosperous . . .

    x x x   x x x   x x x

> "The central task of any revolutionary movement is to seize political power. The *Communist Party of the Philippines assumes this task* at a time that both the international and national situations are favorable to taking the road of armed revolution . . ."

"In the year 1969, the NPA had, according to the records of the Department of National Defense-conducted raids, resorted to kidnappings and taken part in other violent incidents numbering over 230, in which it inflicted 404 casualties, and, in turn, suffered 243 losses. In 1970, its record of violent incidents was about the same, but the NPA casualties more than doubled.

"At any rate, two (2) facts are undeniable: (a) all Communists, whether they belong to the traditional group or to the Maoist faction, believe that force and violence are indispensable to the attainment of their main and ultimate objective, and act in accordance with such belief, although they disagree on the means to be used at a given time and in a particular place; and (b) there is a New People's Army, *other,* of course, than the armed forces of the Republic and antagonistic thereto. Such New People's Army is *per se,* proof of the existence of a rebellion, especially considering that its establishment was *announced publicly* by the reorganized CPP. Such announcement is in the nature of a public challenge to the duly constituted authorities and may be likened to a declaration of war, sufficient to establish a war status or a condition of belligerency, even before the actual commencement of hostilities.

"We entertain, therefore, no doubts about the existence of a sizeable group of men who have publicly risen in arms to overthrow the government and have thus been and still are engaged in rebellion against the Government of the Philippines."

WHEREAS, these lawless elements have to a considerable extent succeeded in impeding our duly constituted authorities from performing their functions and discharging their duties and responsibilities in accordance with our laws and our Constitution to the great damage, prejudice and detriment of the people and the nation;

WHEREAS, it is evident that there is throughout the land a state of anarchy and lawlessness, chaos and disorder, turmoil and destruction of a magnitude equivalent to an actual war between the forces of our duly constituted government and the New People's Army and their satellite organizations because of the unmitigated forays, raids, ambuscades, assaults, violence, murders, assassinations, acts of terror, deceits, coercions, threats, intimidations, treachery, machinations, arsons, plunders and depredations committed and being committed by the aforesaid lawless elements who have pledged to the whole nation that they will not stop their dastardly effort and scheme until and unless they have fully attained their primary and ultimate purpose of forcibly seizing political and state power in this country by overthrowing our present duly constituted government, by destroying our democratic way of life and our established secular and religious institutions and beliefs, and by supplanting our existing political, social, economic, legal and moral order with an entirely new one whose form of government, whose notion of individual rights and family relations, and whose political, social, economic and moral precepts are based on the Marxist-Leninist-Maoist teachings and beliefs;

WHEREAS, the Supreme Court in its said decision concluded that the unlawful activities of the aforesaid lawless elements actually pose a clear, present and grave danger to public safety and the security of the nation and in support of that conclusion found that:

> "x x x the Executive had information and reports—subsequently confirmed, in many respects, by the above-mentioned Report of the Senate Ad Hoc Committee of Seven—to the effect that the Communist Party of the Philippines does not merely adhere to Lenin's idea of a swift armed uprising; that it has, also, adopted Ho Chi Minh's terrorist tactics and resorted to the assassination of uncooperative local officials; that, in line with this policy, the insurgents have killed 5 mayors, 20 barrio captains and 3 chiefs of police; that there were fourteen (14) meaningful bombing incidents in the Greater Manila Area in 1970; that the Constitutional Convention Hall was bombed on June 12, 1971; that soon after the Plaza Miranda incident, the NAWASA main pipe at the Quezon City-San Juan boundary was bombed; that this was followed closely by the bombing of the Manila City Hall, the COMELEC Building, the Congress Building and the MERALCO sub-station at Cubao, Quezon City; and that the respective residences of Senator Jose J. Roy and Congressman Eduardo Cojuangco were, likewise, bombed, as were the MERALCO main office premises, along Ortigas Avenue, and the Doctor's Pharmaceuticals, Inc. Building in Caloocan City.
>
> "x x x the reorganized Communist Party of the Philippines has, moreover, adopted Mao's concept of protracted people's war, aimed at the paralyzation of the will to resist of the government, of the political, economic and intellectual leadership, and of the people themselves; that conformably to such concept, the Party has placed special emphasis upon a most extensive and intensive program of subversion by the establishment of front organizations in urban centers, the organization of armed city partisans and the infiltration in student groups, labor unions, and farmer and professional groups; that the CPP has managed to infiltrate or establish and control nine (9) major labor organizations; that it has exploited the youth movement and succeeded in making Communist

fronts of eleven (11) major student or youth organizations; that
there are, accordingly, about thirty (30) mass organizations actively
advancing the CPP interests, among which are the Malayang
Samahan ng Magsasaka (MASAKA), the Kabataang Makabayan
(KM), the Movement for the Advancement of Nationalism (MAN),
the Samahang Demokratiko ng Kabataan (SDK), the Samahang
Molave (SM), and the Malayang Pagkakaisa ng Kabataang
Pilipino (MPKP); that, as of August, 1971, the KM had two hundred
forty-five (245) operational chapters throughout the Philippines, of
which seventy-three (73) were in the Greater Manila Area, sixty
(60) in Northern Luzon, forty-nine (49) in Central Luzon, forty-two
(42) in the Visayas and twenty-one (21) in Mindanao and Sulu;
that in 1970, the Party had recorded two hundred fifty-eight (258)
major demonstrations, of which about thirty-three (33) ended in
violence, resulting in fifteen (15) killed and over five hundred
(500) injured; that most of these actions were organized, coordinated
or led by the aforementioned front organizations; that the
violent demonstrations were generally instigated by a small, but
well-trained group of armed agitators; that the number of demonstrations heretofore staged in 1971 has already exceeded those of
1970; and that twenty-four (24) of these demonstrations were
violent and resulted in the death of fifteen (15) persons and the
injury of many more.

"Subsequent events x x x have also proven x x x the threat
to public safety posed by the New People's Army. Indeed, it appears
that, since August 21, 1971, it had in Northern Luzon six (6)
encounters and staged one (1) raid, in consequences of which seven
(7) soldiers lost their lives and two (2) others were wounded,
whereas the insurgents suffered five (5) casualties; that on August
26, 1971, a well-armed group of NPA, trained by defector Lt. Victor
Corpus, attacked the very command post of TF LAWIN in Isabela,
destroying two (2) helicopters and one (1) plane, and wounding
one (1) soldier; that the NPA had in Central Luzon a total of four
(4) encounters, with two (2) killed and three (3) wounded on
the side of the Government, one (1) BSDU killed and three (3)
KM-SDK leaders, an unidentified dissident, and Commander Panchito,
leader of the dissident group were killed; that on August 26,
1971, there was an encounter in the barrio of San Pedro, Iriga City,
Camarines Sur, between the PC and the NPA, in which a PC and
two (2) KM members were killed, that the current disturbances in
Cotabato and the Lanao provinces have been rendered more complex
by the involvement of the CPP/NPA, for, in mid-1971, a KM
group, headed by Jovencio Esparagoza, contacted the Higa-onan
tribes, in their settlement in Magsaysay, Misamis Oriental, and
offered them books, pamphlets and brochures of Mao Tse Tung, as
well as conducted teach-ins in the reservation; that Esparagoza
was reportedly killed on September 22, 1971 in an operation of the
PC in said reservation; and that there are now two (2) NPA cadres
in Mindanao.

"It should, also, be noted that adherents of the CPP and its front organizations are, according to intelligence findings, definitely capable of preparing powerful explosives out of locally available materials; that the bomb used in the Constitutional Convention Hall was a 'Claymore' mine, a powerful explosive device used by the U.S. Army, believed to have been one of many pilfered from the Subic Naval Base a few days before; that the President had received intelligence information to the effect that there was a July–August Plan involving a wave of assassinations, kidnappings, terrorism and mass destruction of property and that an extraordinary occurrence would signal the beginning of said event; that the rather serious condition of peace and order in Mindanao, particularly in Cotabato and Lanao, demanded the presence therein of forces sufficient to cope with the situation; that a sizeable part of our armed forces discharges other functions; and that the expansion of the CPP activities from Central Luzon to other parts of the country, particularly Manila and its suburbs, the Cagayan Valley, Ifugao, Zambales, Laguna Quezon and the Bicol Region, required that the rest of our armed forces be spread thin over a wide area."

WHEREAS, in the unwavering prosecution of their revolutionary war against the Filipino people and their duly constituted government, the aforesaid lawless elements have, in the months of May, June and July, 1972, succeeded in bringing and introducing into the country at Digoyo Point, Palanan, Isabela and at other undetermined points along the Pacific coastline of Luzon, a substantial quantity of war material consisting of M-14 rifles estimated to be some 3,500 pieces, several dozens of 40 mm rocket launchers which are said to be Chicom copies of a Russian prototype rocket launcher, large quantities of 80 mm rockets and ammunitions, and other combat paraphernalia, of which war material some had been discovered and captured by government military forces, and the bringing and introduction of such quantity and type of war material into the country is a mute but eloquent proof of the sinister plan of the aforesaid lawless elements to hasten the escalation of their present revolutionary war against the Filipino people and their legitimate government;

WHEREAS, in the execution of their overall revolutionary plan, the aforesaid lawless elements have prepared and released to their various field commanders and Party workers a document captioned "REGIONAL PROGRAM OF ACTION 1972," a copy of which was captured by elements of the 116th and 119th Philippine Constabulary Companies on June 18, 1972 at Barrio Taringsing, Cordon, Isabela, the text of which reads as follows:

"REGIONAL PROGRAM OF ACTION 1972

"The following Regional Program of Action for 1972 is prepared to be carried out as part of the overall plan of the party to foment discontent and precipitate the tide of nationwide mass revolution. The fascist Marcos and his reactionary members of Congress are expected to prepare themselves for the 1973 hence:

"January-June:

"1. Intensify recruitment of new party members especially from the workers-farmers class. Cadres are being trained in order to organize the different regional bureaus. These bureaus most concentrate on mass action and organization to promote advancement of the mass revolutionary movement. Reference is made to the 'Borador ng Programa sa Pagkilos at Ulat ng Panlipunang Pagsisiyasat' as approved by the Central Committee.

"2. Recruit and train armed city partisans and urban guerrillas and organize them into units under Party cadres and activists of mass organizations. These units must undergo specialized training on explosives and demolition and other forms of sabotage.

"3. Intensify recruitment and training of new members for the New People's Army in preparation for limited offensive in selected areas in the regions.

"4. Support a more aggressive program of agitation and propaganda against reactionary armed forces and against the Con Con.

"July–August:

"During this period the party expects the puppet Marcos government to allow increase in bus rates thus aggravating further the plight of students, workers and the farmers.

"1. All Regional Party Committees must plan for a general strike movement. The Regional Operational Commands must plan for armed support if the fascist armed forces of Marcos will try to intimidate the oppressed Filipino masses.

"2. Conduct sabotage against schools, colleges and universities hiking tuition fees.

"3. Conduct sabotage and agitation against puppet judges and courts hearing cases against top party leaders.

"4. Create regional chaos and disorder to dramatize the inability of the fascist Marcos government to keep and maintain peace and order thru:

"a) Robbery and hold-up of banks controlled by American imperialists and those belonging to the enemies of the people.
"b) Attack military camps, US bases and towns.
"c) More violent strikes and demonstrations.

"September–October:

"Increase intensity of violence, disorder and confusion:

"1. Intensify sabotage and bombing of government buildings and embassies and other utilities:

"a) Congress
"b) Supreme Court
"c) Con Con
"d) City Hall
"e) US Embassy
"f) Facilities of US Bases
"g) Provincial Capitols
"h) Power Plants
"i) PLDT
"j) Radio Stations

"2. Sporadic attacks on camps, towns and cities.

"3. Assassinate high government officials of Congress, Judiciary, Con Con and private individuals sympathetic to puppet Marcos.

"4. Establish provisional revolutionary government in towns and cities with the support of the masses.

"5. With the systematic support of our allies, establish provisional provincial revolutionary governments.

"CENTRAL COMMITTEE
COMMUNIST PARTY OF THE
PHILIPPINES"

WHEREAS, in line with their "REGIONAL PROGRAM OF ACTION 1972," the aforesaid lawless elements have of late been conducting intensified acts of violence and terrorisms during the current year in the Greater Manila Area such as the bombing of the Arca building at Taft Avenue, Pasay City, on March 15; of the Pilipinas Orient Airways board room at Domestic Road, Pasay City on April 23; of the Vietnamese Embassy on May 30; of the Court of Industrial Relations on June 23; of the Philippine Trust Company branch office in Cubao, Quezon City on June 24; of the Philamlife building at United Nations Avenue, Manila, on July 3; of the Tabacalera Cigar & Cigarette Factory Compound at Marquez de Comillas, Manila on July 27; of the PLDT exchange office at East Avenue, Quezon City, and of the Philippine Sugar Institute building at North Avenue, Diliman, Quezon City, both on August 15; of the Department of Social Welfare building at San Rafael Street, Sampaloc, Manila, on August 17; of a water main on Aurora Boulevard and Madison Avenue, Quezon City on August 19; of the Philamlife building again on August 30; this time causing severe destruction on the Far East Bank and Trust Company building nearby; of the armored car and building of the Philippine banking Corporation as well as the buildings of the Investment Development Inc. and the Daily Star Publications when another explosion took place on Railroad Street, Port Area, Manila, also on August 30; of Joe's Department Store on Carriedo Street, Quiapo, on September 5, causing death to one woman and injuries to some 38 individuals; and of the City Hall of Manila on September 8; of the watermains in San Juan, Rizal on September 12; of the San Miguel building in Makati, Rizal on September 14; and of the Quezon City Hall on September 18, 1972, as well as the attempted bombing of the Congress Building on July 18 when an unexploded bomb was found in the Senate Publication Division and the attempted bombing of the Department of Foreign Affairs on August 30;

WHEREAS, in line with the same "REGIONAL PROGRAM OF ACTION 1972," the aforesaid lawless elements have also fielded in the Greater Manila Area several of their "Sparrow Units" or "Simbad Units" to undertake liquidation missions against ranking government officials, military personnel and prominent citizens and to further heighten the destructions and depredations already inflicted by them upon our innocent people, all of which are being deliberately done to sow terror, fear and chaos amongst our population and to make the government look so helpless and incapable of protecting the lives and property of our people;

WHEREAS, in addition to the above-described social disorder, there is also the equally serious disorder in Mindanao and Sulu resulting from the unsettled conflict between certain elements of the Christian and Muslim population of Mindanao and Sulu, between the Christian "Ilagas" and the Muslim "Barracudas," and between our government troops, and certain lawless organizations such as the Mindanao Independence Movement;

WHEREAS, the Mindanao Independence Movement with the active material and financial assistance of foreign political and economic interests, is engaged in an open and unconcealed attempt to establish by violence and force a separate and independent political state out of the islands of Mindanao and Sulu which are historically, politically and by law parts of the territories and within the jurisdiction and sovereignty of the Republic of the Philippines;

WHEREAS, because of the aforesaid disorder resulting from armed clashes, killings, massacres, arsons, rapes, pillages, destruction of whole villages and towns and the inevitable cessation of agricultural and industrial operations, all of which have been brought about by the violence inflicted by the Christians, the Muslims, the "Ilagas," the "Barracudas," and the Mindanao Independence Movement against each other and against our government troops, a great many parts of the islands of Mindanao and Sulu are virtually now in a state of actual war;

WHEREAS, the violent disorder in Mindanao and Sulu has to date resulted in the killing of over 1,000 civilians and about 2,000 armed Muslims and Christians, not to mention the more than five hundred thousand of injured, displaced and homeless persons as well as the great number of casualties among our government troops, and the paralyzation of the economy of Mindanao and Sulu;

WHEREAS, because of the foregoing acts of armed insurrection, wanton destruction of human lives and property, unabated and unrestrained propaganda attacks against the government and its institutions, instrumentalities, agencies and officials, and the rapidly expanding ranks of the aforesaid lawless elements, and because of the spreading lawlessness and anarchy thoughout the land, all of which have prevented the government to exercise its authority, extend to its citizenry the protection of its laws and in general exercise its sovereignty over all of its territories, caused serious demoralization among our people and have made the public apprehensive and fearful, and finally because public order and safety and the security of this nation demand that immediate, swift, decisive and effective action be taken to protect and insure the peace, order and security of the country and its population and to maintain the authority of the government;

WHEREAS, in cases of invasion, insurrection or rebellion or imminent danger thereof, I, as President of the Philippines, have under the Constitution, three courses of action open to me, namely: (a) call out the armed forces to suppress the present lawless violence; (b) suspend the privilege of the writ of habeas corpus to make the arrest and apprehension of these lawless elements easier and more effective; or (c) place the Philippines or any part thereof under martial law;

WHEREAS, I have already utilized the first two courses of action, first, by calling upon the armed forces to suppress the aforesaid lawless violence, committing to that specific job almost 50% of the entire armed forces of the country and creating several task forces for that purpose such as Task Force Saranay, Task Force Palanan, Task Force Isarog, Task Force Pagkakaisa and Task Force Lancaf, and second, by suspending the privilege of the writ of habeas corpus on August 21, 1971 up to January 11, 1972, but inspite of all that, both courses of action were found inadequate and ineffective to contain, much less solve, the present rebellion and lawlessness in the country as shown by the fact that:

1. The radical left has increased the number and area of operation of its front organizations and has intensified the recruitment and training of new adherents in the urban rural areas especially from among the youth;

2. The Kabataang Makabayan (KM), the most militant and outspoken front organization of the radical left, has increased the number of its chapters from 200 as of the end of 1970 to 317 as of July 31, 1972 and its membership from 10,000 as of the end of 1970 to 15,000 as of the end of July, 1972, showing very clearly the rapid growth of the communist movement in this country;

3. The Samahang Demokratiko Ng Kabataang (SDK), another militant and outspoken front organization of the radical left, has also increased the number of its chapters from an insignificant number at the end of 1970 to 159 as of the end of July, 1972 and has now a membership of some 1,495 highly indoctrinated, intensely committed and almost fanatically devoted individuals;

4. The New People's Army, the most active and the most violent and ruthless military arm of the radical left, has increased its total strength from an estimated 6,500 (composed of 560 regulars, 1,500 combat support and 4,400 service support) as of January 1, 1972 to about 7,900 (composed of 1,028 regulars, 1,800 combat support and 5,025 service support) as of July 31, 1972, showing a marked increase in its regular troops of over 100% in such a short period of six months;

5. The establishment of sanctuaries for the insurgents in Isabela, in Zambales, in Camarines Sur, and in some parts of Mindanao, a development heretofore unknown in our campaign against subversion and insurgency in this country;

6. The disappearance and dropping out of school of some 3,000 high school and college students and who are reported to have joined with the insurgents for training in the handling of firearms and explosives;

7. The bringing and introduction into the country of substantial war material consisting of military hardware and supplies through the MV Karagatan at Digoyo Point, Palanan, Isabela, and the fact that many of these military hardware and supplies are now in the hands of the insurgents and are being used against our government troops;

8. The infiltration and control of the media by persons who are sympathetic to the insurgents and the consequent intensification of their propaganda assault against the government and the military establishment of the government;

9. The formation of the grass root level of "political power organ," heretofore unknown in the history of the Communist movement in this country, composed of Barrio Organizing Committees (BOCs) to mobilize the barrio people for active involvement in the revolution; the Barrio Revolutionary Committees (BRCs) to act as "local government" in barrios considered as CPP/NPA bailiwicks; the Workers Organizing Committees (WOCs) to organize workers from all sectors; the School Organizing Committees (SOCs) to conduct agitation and propaganda activities and help in the expansion of front groups among the studentry; and the Community Organizing Committees (COCs) which operate in the urban areas in the same manner as the BOCs.

WHEREAS, the rebellion and armed action undertaken by these lawless elements of the communist and other armed aggrupations organized to overthrow the Republic of the Philippines by armed violence and force have assumed the magnitude of an actual state of war against our people and the Republic of the Philippines;

NOW, THEREFORE, I, FERDINAND E. MARCOS, President of the Philippines, by virtue of the powers vested upon me by Article VII, Section 10, Paragraph (2) of the Constitution, do hereby place the entire Philippines as defined in Article I, Section 1 of the Constitution under martial law and, in my capacity as their commander-in-chief, do hereby command the Armed Forces of the Philippines, to maintain law and order throughout the Philippines, prevent or suppress all forms of lawless violence as well as any act of insurrection or rebellion and to enforce obedience to all the laws and decrees, orders and regulations promulgated by me personally or upon my direction.

In addition, I do hereby order that all persons presently detained, as well as all others who may thereafter be similarly detained for the crimes of insurrection or rebellion, and all other crimes and offenses committed in furtherance or on the occasion thereof, incident thereto, or in connection therewith, for crimes against national security and the law of nations, crimes against public order, crimes involving usurpation of authority, rank, title and improper use of names, uniforms and insignia, crimes committed by public officers, and for such other crimes as will be enumerated in Orders that I shall subsequently promulgated upon my direction shall be kept under detention until otherwise ordered released by me or by my duly designated representative.

IN WITNESS WHEREOF, I have hereunto set my hand and caused the seal of the Republic of the Philippines to be affixed.

Done in the City of Manila, this 21st day of September, in the year of Our Lord, nineteen hundred and seventy-two.

FERDINAND E. MARCOS
President
Republic of the Philippines

By the President:

ROBERTO V. REYES
Acting Executive Secretary

REFERENCES

Adams, John Quincy. *The Great Quotations*. Comp. by George Seldes. Secaucus: Lyle Stuart, Inc., 1966.

Agar, Herbert. *The Perils of Democracy*. Chester Springs: Dufour Editions, Inc., 1966.

Ambrose, St. *The Great Quotations*. Comp. by George Seldes. Secaucus: Lyle Stuart, Inc., 1966.

Aquinas, St. Thomas. *The Basic Works of St. Thomas Aquinas*. Ed. by Anton Pegis. New York: Random House, Inc., 1945.

Arendt, Hannah. *On Revolution*. New York: Viking Press, Inc., 1965.

Aristotle. *The Basic Works of Aristotle*. Ed. by Richard P. McKeon. New York: Random House, Inc., 1941.

Ayub-Khan, Mohammed. Paul E. Sigmund, Jr., *The Ideologies of Developing Nations*. New York: Praeger Publishers, 1972.

Bakunin, Mikhail. *The Political Philosophy of Bakunin*. By G. P. Maximoff. New York: Free Press, 1953.

Brinton, Crane. *Anatomy of Revolution*. New York: Random House, 1938.

Burke, Edmund. *Reflections on the Revolution in France*. Ed. by Thomas E. Mahoney. Indianapolis: Bobbs-Merrill Company, Inc., 1955.

Calderon, Felipe. Writings collected in the National Archives of the Philippines.

Cardozo, Benjamin N. *The Nature of the Judicial Process*. New Haven: Yale University Press, 1921.

257

Carlyle, Thomas. *The Great Quotations*. Comp. by George Seldes. Secaucus: Lyle Stuart, Inc., 1966.

Cassirer, Ernst. *Myth of the State*. New Haven: Yale University Press, 1946.

Chrysostom, St. *The Great Quotations*. Comp. by George Seldes. Secaucus: Lyle Stuart, Inc., 1966.

Churchill, Winston. *The Great Quotations*. Comp. by George Seldes. Secaucus: Lyle Stuart, Inc., 1966.

Clement of Alexandria. *The Great Quotations*. Comp. by George Seldes. Secaucus: Lyle Stuart, Inc., 1966.

Concepcion, Roberto. Writings collected in the National Archives of the Philippines.

Croce, Benedetto. *History as the Story of Liberty*. Chicago: Henry Regnery, Company, 1970.

Dahl, Robert A. *After the Revolution: Authority in a Good Society*. New Haven: Yale University Press, 1970.

D'Holbach, Paul. *The Great Quotations*. Comp. by George Seldes. Secaucus: Lyle Stuart, Inc., 1966.

Duverger, Maurice. *The Idea of Politics*. London: Methuen, 1967.

Ellul, Jacques. *The Political Illusion*. New York: Vintage, 1972.

Hamilton, Alexander. *The Alexander Hamilton Reader*. Ed. by Margaret E. Hall. New York: Oceana Publications, Inc., 1957.

Hensman, C. R. *Rich Against Poor: The Reality of Aid*. Cambridge: Schenkman Publishing Company, Inc., 1972.

Hoffer, Eric. *The True Believer*. New York: Harper & Row, 1951.

Huntington, Samuel P. *Political Order in Changing Societies*. New Haven: Yale University Press, 1968.

Jefferson, Thomas. Letter to Col. Edward Carrington, January 16, 1787 in *The Works of Thomas Jefferson*. Ed. by Paul L. Ford. New York: Da Capo Press, Inc., 1899.

Kant, Immanuel. *The Critique of Practical Reason*. Trans. Lewis W. Beck. Indianapolis: Bobbs-Merrill, Company, Inc., 1956.

Kefauver, Estes. *The Great Quotations*. Comp. by George Seldes. Secaucus: Lyle Stuart, Inc., 1966.

Lenin, Vladimir I. *Selected Works*. New York: International Publishers Company, Inc., 1967.

Leo XIII. *Rerum Novarum*.

Lincoln, Abraham. *Abraham Lincoln: Life and Writings*. New York: Random House, Inc., 1942.

Lippmann, Walter. *The Public Philosophy*. Boston: Little, Brown & Company, 1955.

Locke, John. *Works*. New York: Adler, 1963.

Mabini, Apolinario. Letters collected in the National Archives of Philippines.

Mao Tse-tung. *Selected Works*. Peking. Foreign Languages Press, 1970.

Marcuse, Herbert. *An Essay on Liberation.* Boston: Beacon House, Inc., 1969.

Marx, Karl. *Selected Works of Marx and Engels.* New York: International Publishers Company, Inc., 1967.

Mill, John Stuart. *Utilitarianism, Liberty and Representative Government.* New York: E. P. Dutton & Co., Inc., 1951.

Myrdal, Gunnar. *Economic Theory and Underdeveloped Regions.* London: Methuen, 1969.

Nehru, Jawaharlal. *The Ideologies of Developing Nations* by Paul E. Sigmund, Jr. New York: Praeger Publishers, 1972.

Paul VI. *Populorum Progresso.*

Paz, Octavio. *The Labyrinth of Solitude: Life and Thought in Mexico.* London: Allen Lane, 1967.

Plato. *The Dialogues of Plato.* Ed. by William C. Greene. New York: Liveright Publishing Corporation, 1927.

Proudhon, P. J. *The Great Quotations.* Comp. by George Seldes. Secaucus: Lyle Stuart, Inc., 1966.

Pye, Lucian W. *Politics, Personality, and Nation Building.* New Haven: Yale University Press, 1962.

Rand Corporation. *A Crisis of Ambiguity,* 1971.

Rizal, Jose P. *El Filibusterismo.* Quezon City: R. Martinez, 1957.

————. *La Solidaridad.* Ed. by Guadalupe Fores Guanzon. Quezon City: University of the Philippines Press, 1967.

————. *Noli Me Tangere.* Quezon City: Capitol Publishing House, 1956.

Robespierre, Maximilien M. Speech before the Convention, February 5, 1794. *The Great Quotations.* Comp. by George Seldes. Secaucus: Lyle Stuart, Inc., 1966.

Roosevelt, Franklin D. *The Great Quotations.* Comp. by George Seldes. Secaucus: Lyle Stuart, Inc., 1966.

Roosevelt, Theodore. *The Great Quotations.* Comp. by George Seldes. Secaucus: Lyle Stuart, Inc., 1966.

Shaw, George Bernard. *The Intelligent Woman's Guide to Socialism, Capitalism, Sovietism and Fascism.* London: Pelican, 1965.

Smith, Adam. *Adam Smith Today: An Inquiry into the Causes for the Wealth of Nations.* New York: Kennikat Press, Inc., 1969.

Valeo, Frank. Report submitted by Senator Mike Mansfield to the United States Senate, 1972.

Webster, Daniel. *Letters.* New York: Haskell House, 1969.

INDEX